Earth Harmony
Places of Power, Holiness and Healing

2nd Edition

Nigel Pennick

Earth Harmony
Places of Power, Holiness and Healing

2nd Edition

©1997 Nigel Pennick

ISBN 1 898307 97 0

Cover design by Paul Mason
Cover illustration by Nigel Pennick

Published by:

Capall Bann Publishing
Freshfields
Chieveley
Berks
RG20 8TF

Contents

Foreword

This book is a completely rewritten version of my original *Earth Harmony*, which was published by Century in London in 1987. Since then, my researches and practice have continued, and some other circumstances have changed in the decade since I wrote the original text. This has necessitated my updating and deepening of certain aspects of the work, most especially the principles underlying the Anima Loci concept. However, the principles of practice described in the original text remain as they were, for they continue to represent a venerable living tradition, and my original intention was to provide a user's guide to the art of location that is called Earth Harmony. To enhance the expanded and revised text, I have prepared new illustrations and diagrams that complement and add to the previous work, making it the most comprehensive guide to the practice of traditional European location yet produced.

Nigel Campbell Pennick, Bar Hill, August 27, 1996 ce.

Introduction

"We want to crystallise the infinity of the cosmos and give expression to it in form" - Hendrikus Theodorus Wijdeveld.

The aim of Earth Harmony is the reintegration of inevitably intrusive human activities with the natural environment and the flow of events. All over the world, traditions abound in which Earth Harmony has been observed in the layout of places of assembly, government, habitation, worship and sepulture. The best known of these is the Chinese Feng-Shui, whose complex yet consistent array of methods has been the subject of considerable study in the West. Less well known here, but still another living school of Earth Harmony, is the Hindu system of Vastuvidya, which is concerned with the location and design of sacred places and buildings, and with the appropriate harmonisation of houses into the physical and psychical environments. A third well-developed system was the Burmese system of Yattara. Fourthly, on the Indian Ocean island of Madagascar are the practitioners of Vintana, which melds traditions derived from Malay, Chinese and Arabic sources with indigenous African practices. In Madagascar, this branch of geomancy is used in the determination of auspicious sites for houses and tombs, and their internal layout. Last, but not least in this list, and most relevant to European culture, is the European system of Location, which has roots far back more than 6000 years ago in the archaic megalithic era of northern Europe, ancient Egypt, Greece and the Etruscan Discipline.

The appropriate harmony that we can recognise in traditional landscapes comes from a precise blending of natural and human-made forms and patterns. This harmonious craft brings the place and the person into perfect tune with one another, with the consequent reduction of bad influences and the enhancement of the beneficial character of a site. This is achieved by harmonising human lives with the underlying structure of the universe - the cosmic order - by bringing opposing or complementary principles into a dynamic balance with one another. To create true harmony, every building and every feature of the landscape, natural and artificial, has to occupy the position appropriate to its nature and human requirements. To be at the right place facing the right direction performing the appropriate action at the proper time is to be both ceremonially correct and practically efficient. It is no less than harmonisation with the whole universe.

In pre-industrial Europe, local and national systems of Earth Harmony existed everywhere, part of everyday life. In ancient Greece and Rome, sophisticated methods of location were used alongside inspired intuition to find the best places for temples and houses, and the ancient Etruscan Augurs used a highly-sophisticated system of reading the landscape. Officials such as the Locator Civitatis were employed by Emperors, Kings and prelates to locate, design and recruit inhabitants for new cities in medieval Europe. Knowledge of the four elements, the eight winds and their directions and their relationship to timekeeping and village layout has been maintained in unbroken continuity until the present day.

The fundamental principles which underlay all of these practices are based upon the most primal aspects of life on Earth and the structure and cycles of the cosmos. This book is a continuation of this venerable tradition, which has survived into the present day as folk custom and usage. Today, at last, it can be understood in educated circles as something of intrinsic value rather than mere 'superstition'. This book reclaims the former worth of our heritage, providing practical assistance for those who wish to practice this craft in the present day.

The wheel of the day, which, related to the directions, is the basis of traditional European earth wisdom, and is manifested most directly in sundials.

Chapter 1
Harmony With the Earth

Civilisation and Tradition

Contemporary civilisation is unlike any that has existed on earth before. It has evolved from earlier ways of doing things, and in so doing has deviated further and further from that balance which earth harmony represents. The predominant modern way of dealing with the world is based on a perceived dominance over nature, and a preoccupation with purely material things. This world view sees existence as a series of static tableaux which are capable of being dismantled and analysed - 'deconstructed' - then reassembled in an artificial way. But this way of thinking and acting overrides the natural dynamic interactions of things. Natural variability and subtle influences are overridden by standardisation or ignored by statistical interpretations. Thus, science attempts not just to control nature, but to create a substitute for it. This implicit rejection of things natural and of human methods of harmonisation with nature is the fundamental basis of the predominant culture of our times, yet it is an unfulfilling, one-sided, and, ultimately, dangerous tendency. Technology has given people the means to override nature in a seemingly dominant mastery, subduing the Earth rather than living in partnership with it, yet the spectacular failures of modern technology and impending ecological crises are an indication that this mastery is illusory.

To-day, we are living in a pluralistic culture, however, and the mechanistic materialist view of the world, despite its brilliant achievements in science and technology, is but one part of that culture. Academic studies and improved communications have enabled us to come into contact with diverse traditions, practices and techniques from many cultures, and given us means of evaluating them. Everyday geomantic practices of peoples from different parts of the world have been examined with a comparative overview, and the underlying common principles are now understood. Everything living is in a state of constant evolution, and from an understanding of the basic principles, reclaimed, revived and practised, it is possible to develop new living concepts and techniques. Earth Harmony is based upon these same global principles, reclaiming their primal power and value for everyone to use.

Only Harmony is Stable

There can be no long-term survival in those things which ignore the laws of nature. The complex relationships between the earth, humanity and the cosmos are subject to the laws of nature, which must be in equilibrium in order to continue without catastrophic failure. The traditional view of the world, which has existed for the greater part of human history, is based upon this understanding of the necessity to work with rather than against nature. This profound familiarity with nature, and a willingness to go in accordance with the cosmic laws rather than attempting the ultimately futile act of commanding and controlling them, is the keynote of earth harmony. Through earth harmony, every aspect of life, human relationships, the built environment, the arts, crafts and sciences can be interwoven so closely that they become complementary parts of a holistic unity. Many human cultural traditions display this awareness in a way which shows its universal nature, regardless of era, race or creed. This ethos lies at the roots of various venerable traditions including that of ancient Northern Europe, Chinese Taoism, Japanese Shinto, the world-view of Native Americans, and certain African and south Asian cultures.

This harmonisation between human and natural does not discriminate between mind, body and spirit, past present and future, for this essence is unity. It is the embodiment of the individual in the whole, a total harmonious immersion in the universal reality. Here, there can be no division between the human body and the Earth: it is the point at which the universal and the particular are integrated in the One. It is a recognition of the essential harmony of the cosmos and the human being's identity with it. According to the traditional ways of earth harmony, life is to be lived in concordance with the natural order of things, the cyclic law of alternation. the vibrant patterns of spontaneous order. The predominant contemporary cultural view is in opposition to this. It is a dialectical, dualistic, quantitative, mechanistic, statistical, interruption of the natural order of the world, and attempts to substitute abstract and conceptual order, because it teaches that all order is arbitrary. The modern way breaks the natural order implicit in life, setting up an artificial system as a regulatory mechanism, but because it has no relationship to the natural order, it is unstable and forever in conflict. It attempts to control nature by overcoming it, constraining natural existence into artificial systems. This is most obvious in the modern city where all of the natural cycles of life, daily and seasonal changes and, local characteristics are 'ironed out' by regulations and technology. Society is in danger of forgetting that place has much

6

significance to us. Technological advances over the last two centuries have given human beings the power to travel vast distances, even beyond the confines of our planet, in a short space of time. At the same time, transportation systems have altered the face of the landscape, and transformed the character of cities. The dowser and consciousness researcher John Steele has called this present loss of awareness 'geomantic amnesia', a condition where place is no longer recognised as having any effect upon individuals' state of mind or well-being.

As part of humankind, each human being is more than just an independent reality, but as a part of nature, is a component of the totality that is the universe. This state of totality contains within it the information for everything, just like a hologram possesses within every part of it an encoding of the entire picture. The implications of this universal structural order is that just as with a hologram, the picture can be reconstructed when the appropriate light is passed through it, so when the correct actions are performed, a similar harmonisation can be achieved with our own lives and consciousness. This universal structural order has been recognised by people in past times in the form of perfect models or archetypes, which, though never fully expressed in the material world, have served as images of perfection towards which people have worked. Although it is not possible to gain such a state of total perfection on Earth, a recognition of this underlying order can be used as a standard by which to gauge our actions.

Human Individuality and Place

Many people are trapped in the notion of the total separate existence of the individual, and have a world view that is limited by this personal perception. They consider their own personal consciousness to be the world, and that any other realities outside themselves are reflected in their own experience. This concept is implicit in the idea of the portable person, with a fixed reality independent of time or place. Seeing ourselves as separate individuals leads naturally to the idea that we are separate from the place in which we find ourselves. The idea that "I" in Cambridge am the same as "I" in Iraklion is a commonly held fallacy based upon this concept of the individual's separation from the world. But we are not separate from either our immediate surroundings, or from the world as a whole.As human beings, we all share the same common features of bodily structure, physical, psychological and spiritual.requirements. We all exist within the same ranges of temperature, oxygen requirement, food needs etc., and so these common necessities condition our perception of the world around us.

Because of this, we react in more or less the same way to a variety of stimuli, especially an absence of things we need, or the presence of things we perceive as harmful. We are continuous with the local environment. We breathe its air: we eat its food; we feel its warmth or coldness; we are subject to its magnetic, gravitational and electric fields; we hear its sounds and smell its smells. We are affected psychologically and psychically by everything around us at all times.

The erroneous belief that we are separate, impartial observers of the world is implicit in both law and science. There, it is held to be self-evident that we can sit outside reality and observe it, draw conclusions and make judgements. Classical science, especially, is based upon this idea of objective reality, that the observer has no part in the event under observation. In physics, the realisation that this may not be the case has been understood gradually. The idea that the outcome of an experiment depends upon the observer at first seems heretical to those educated in scientific modes of thought. If we substitute the word 'participator' for 'observer', then we describe better the participation of our consciousness in the creation of what we perceive to be reality. As participators, we do not separate ourselves from the events and things we strive to observe. We can view consciousness, energy and matter as different points in the same continuum, and if we view things in this way, we can better harmonise our actions with the world.

World Viewing

The way we view the world is determined by the structure of our bodies, our physical existence in space and time. Our bodies have a fourfold form: in front, behind, left and right. Wherever we are, we perceive the world in terms of our body's position and of our bodily directions. Traditional perceptions of the Earth speak of the five directions - north, east, south, west, and here, the definition of human space. Our bodily structure defines the four directions and here, but also we have orientation, that is a front and back. It is this orientation that gives us our perspective on the world, and our perception of space and time.

As an example, if we were to be taken to a flat, featureless landscape with no indication of where we were, observation of the apparent course of the sun would give us our bearings in space and time. At the rising of the sun, we would perceive the eastward direction, and if we observed the position of sunset, we could then determine south as the midpoint between these. If the sun was in the due south at midday, then we would know we were north of the equator. By facing south we could observe the sun's yearly cycle, from its northernmost rising at the summer solstice to its most southerly at midwinter.

The apparent motion of the sun when viewed from any fixed place varies with season and time of day. At any time of the year, the highest point of the sun is always midday, and at midsummer - the solstice - the midday sun is at the highest point it will ever reach at that latitude. This angle depends on the geographical location of the observer, and is larger the nearer one approaches the equator. Conversely, the sun's lowest elevation at midday comes at midwinter - the winter solstice. In the northern hemisphere, the midday sun stands at due south.

The directions of sunrise and sunset are dependent on the time of year. At the midsummer solstice, the longest day, the sun is not only at its highest elevation in the sky, but also above the horizon for the longest period. In the northern hemisphere, this means that it rises and sets at its most northern points on the horizon. At midwinter, the shortest day, it rises and sets at its most southerly. Between these points are the equinoxes, the times when the length of day and night are equal. At these times, the sun rises due east and sets due west, and stands at its middle height at midday. The equinoxes equally divide both the day and the year into their complementary opposites of light and dark. The further north one goes, the further north the sun rises at midsummer, until when one is north of the Arctic Circle, we have the phenomenon of the 'Midnight Sun', when the sun does not set at all, but runs along the northern horizon and is 'Sun Due North' at midnight. On a completely flat horizon, midsummer sunrise is diametrically opposite midwinter sunset and midwinter sunrise is opposite midsummer sunset. The sunrises and sunsets of opposite parts of the year can be viewed on the horizon at precise positions determined by the latitude of the viewing place. Thus a viewer from a fixed place of observation can see that the horizon is divided into segments by the important turning- and crossing-points of the sun during its apparent course through the annual cycle.

The sun's main positions are marked by its rising at midsummer towards the northeast, through due east at the spring and autumnal equinoxes, the southeast rising point at midwinter, the mid-day crossing point at due south, the midwinter sunset to southwest, equinox sunset at due west and finally midsummer sunset. In addition to these seven main positions is sun in the due north, the point of midnight between sunset and sunrise, visible here only at midsummer north of the arctic circle, as the 'Midnight Sun'.

Each of these horizon points relates to a time of day, most obviously the 6 am rising of the sun at the equinox, which is due east, midday as due south and due west as 6 pm. From this it is obvious that any direction has a correspondence in a time of day, and also to a time of year: due north to midwinter, east to spring equinox, south to midsummer and west to autumn equinox. Between these four directional time markers, the subsidiary directions relate to the traditional sacred festivals of the year. In traditional societies as far apart as Peru to Scandinavia, these points on the horizon were marked by standing stones, cairns or towers, or the viewing-point was designed to use natural markers such as mountain peaks. Sunrise or sunset over these points mark transitions from one season to another, and the festivals of the religious or agricultural year. These transition-points are also symbols of the transitions we all pass through in our lives.

The division of the horizon uses the principle of halving. Halfway between north and east are northeast, south and east, southeast, and so on. Continued halving leads to 8, 16 and 32-fold divisions. In Norway, in addition to the four main direction names, there were four others: northeast was called Landnorth; southeast, Landsouth; northwest, Outnorth; and southwest, Outsouth. From the halving principle, it follows that each true direction lies at the centre of a region of the sky with the same name. In the Northern European tradition, these 8 regions are called aett, and the true, astronomical direction is an aetting. For example, the northern aett is the sector between North-North-West and North-North-East, and at its centre, the aetting is true North. Traditional time-reckoning defines night as the time taken for the sun to, cross this aett.

The directions underlie everything in traditional life - time, the division of space, homestead and family, landscape, writing systems and religious practices, all had an eightfold nature. Ancient peoples developed a method of time telling based upon the use of markers visible on the horizon. These markers, viewed of course from a special point, usually the house stone outside the door, or a stone in the middle of the village,can be seen still in some places. Sometimes they are standing stones, or natural gaps in the hills or mountains which defined the day by marking the passage of the sun. In Iceland, the passage of the sun through the northern aett was the legal definition of night-time: the sun in the due north was thus midnight, visible at midsummer north of the Arctic Circle as the midnight sun. Further south, the sun is still in that position even though we cannot see it. In the northeastern aett, the sun is in Uht, the greying of day. When the sun reaches the eastern aett, morning begins. Traditionally, the sun in the East-North-East is daybreak, and in the summer half of the year, the time to get up, Rismal. When the sun is due east is midmorning. This morning period ends with the traditional time of breakfast, the daytime meal. At this time, the sun is in the East-South-East, the Dagmal point, which is one of the important horizon markers. On old sundials, this major point is marked by a Dag-rune or a swastika.

The next period is Daytime, followed by High Day, at the middle of which is the aetting Mid-day, Noon, when the sun is due south. At the end of that period, the sun passes into Undorne, at the end of which is the beginning of the Evening period, West-South-West, Eyktarstadr, which in the summer half of the year was the time to stop work. This point is directly opposite Rismal, dividing the horizon and the day into its two complementary halves. After Eyktarstadr, evening begins, with the sun due west being midevening. On the day in autumn when the sun sets over this Eyktastadr, the winter half of the year begins. In the winter half, when it is dark a lot in the north, the telling of time by the stars relates to the same points. This method can be seen in stone circles in Britain, where the shape of the tops of the standing stones is the same as the shape of the horizon, when viewed from the correct part of the circle. This enabled a correct viewpoint of th horizon to be established.

The eightfold division of time, shown in the landscape, relates to sunrise and sunsets during the year, linking the home, landscape, year and festivals in one holistic continuum. The further north one goes, the more recognisable this is, for the positions of sunrise and sunset at midsummer and midwinter become further and further apart, until north of the arctic circle, we get darkness at midwinter and 24 hour daylight at midsummer. The positions of sunrises and sunsets are marked in ancient landscapes by standing stones, earth mounds, piles of stones, sacred mountain peaks and other markers. Sunrise or set over certain of these points, viewed from a certain central place, marked transitions from one season to another, or the key festivals of the eightfold year. The eightfold division of the year interposes the main festivals between the solar extremes and equalities, an eightfold solar system that interacts with the 13 fold lunar system.

Solar and Fire Festivals

There are two groups of festivals in the eightfold year: the Solar Festivals and the so-called Fire Festivals. The Solar Festivals are the two equinoxes and the two solstices. The four Fire Festivals are variously named. Each has at least one traditional name and three of them have Christian festivals associated with them. According to ancient custom, some of the observances of the Fire festivals commence at sunset on the preceding evening, and this practice, still observed in Jewish law, survives in Christmas Eve and New year's Eve. The Fire Festivals are Samhain (summer's end), otherwise known as Hallowe'en or All Saints', which is October 31 evening/November 1st; Imbolc, otherwise Brigantia, which is the Christian festival of Candlemas, February 1st; Beltane, May Day; and Lughnasadh or Lammas, August 1. These festivals are earthly rather than celestial in orientation, and are connected with the seasons of growth, seedtime and fallow.

Samhain

In the Celtic tradition, the year began at Samhain, the modern Hallowe'en. This is the beginning of the winter part of the year, when the declining light is very noticeable. Samhain was the Celtic festival of the dead, involving ceremonial bonfires of purification. By burning an effigy of the sorrows and terrors of the past year, it removed the old and ushered in the new. In England, the festival became Guy Fawkes' night, where the effigy of an evil man replaced the effigies of the spirits of evil of old. As the end of the old year and the commencement of the new, this is an "eerie" time when the worlds of the living and the dead meet at the boundary-point, the "no man's land" of time. Here, the division between the worlds is thin, and Hallowe'en is associated with demonic spirits, witches and ghosts. When Christianised, the festival became All Saints' and All Souls' Days, when the souls of the departed were remembered and celebrated. The old tradition of guising, blackening faces, wearing masks and abnormal costumes, is still practised at Hallowe'en. In parts of Germany today, various festivals involve the use of elaborately carved and painted masks of traditional design which are worn during ceremonies to create anonymity and to frighten away demonic forces. It is likely that the carved masks around Romanesque and later churches, used as protection, are the stone replicas of real masks that hung around the wooden temples of Pagan times.

Samhain is also a time when divination may be performed, using apples, candles or nuts, to foretell the fortunes of the individual in the coming year. Another method is to pour molten lead or wax into water and from the shapes it assumed to read fortunes. In ancient times, this day was a time of amnesty and free passage, a sort of universal sanctuary when the whole Earth was a sacred temple. The direction of Samhain in the year circle is northwesterly, equivalent to about 10 pm in the day, and marks the entry to the winter quarter of the year.

Yuletíde, the Winter Solstice

The winter solstice marks the death and rebirth of the sun, its shortest appearance above the horizon, its most southerly rising and setting points and its lowest elevation at midday. In ancient Rome, it was the festival of Sol Invictus, the Undefeated Sun, and all over Europe, Yule has been traditionally a time of celebration, that the light has reached its lowest ebb and is beginning to come back. As recognition of this, an oak log was ritually burned, being kindled from the charcoal of the previous year's log. The ashes and charcoal of the Yule log were used for purification rites.

The ashes of the Yule log were scattered in fields to promote fertility,or into wells for purification. The Christmas tree is the most potent symbol of this tradition today, representing the continuity of life through winter, the night, and death. As with Samhain, the solstitial festivities have become connected with several days around the festival, especially New Year's Day, when people 'see in' the New Year through midnight, the time-direction of the winter solstice, symbolising the transition from the old to the new that Yule has represented for thousands of years.

Imbolc/Brígantía/Candlemas

This festival, celebrated on February 1st., symbolises the first stirring of the seeds in the ground, and the first tentative indications of the forthcoming springtime. Thus it symbolises the spiritual commencement of process, the mystery of the potential plant, flower and fruit implicit in the germinating seed. In Ireland, straw images of Bride were made on Brigantia Eve, and food offerings for her were left outside. At the shrine of St Bride (452-525 c.e.) at Kildare, Ireland, a perpetual flame was tended by nineteen nuns. Her day is associated with the Christian festival of the Purification of the Virgin, Candlemas, celebrated by lighting torches or candles at midnight, symbolising awakening. At Imbolc, we enter the spring quarter of the year, and the growing light symbolised by Pagan torch and Christian candle alike.. The time-direction of Imbolc is north-easterly, 3 am.

The Vernal Equinox

On or around March 21, this is traditionally known as the first day of spring, and ushers in the light half of the year. A major turning-point, its time direction is due east, 6 am.

Beltane/May Day

May Day is traditionally the entry into the summer quarter of the year. A major rite was the kindling of the Beltane fires. On May Eve, all fires in the neighbourhood were extinguished, so that the element of fire would be absent through that night. At sunrise on May Day, a new fire was generated by ritually kindling it by means of a wooden spindle turned in a wooden socket. The Beltane or Need-Fire so generated was composed of the wood of nine different types of sacred tree. It was ceremonially lit on the middle square of a square of 9 turves, the eight around it having been removed. To jump through the flames was to be purified. Gorse and broom were set fire to and animals are driven through the purifying smoke. Each household would take fire from the Beltane Fire and re-light their hearth from it.

In Germany, May Eve is Walpurgisnacht, when the witches ride, the equivalent of the British and American festival of Hallowe'en. May Day is exactly opposite Samhain in the year circle. It is traditional to decorate houses with blossom and branches around the doors to bring good fortune in the summer months, and to set up May Bushes, May Trees or Maypoles.. The Maypole around which people dance around the local version of the world pillar or cosmic axis, and echoes the means by which the Beltane Fire was lit. The time-direction of May Day is equivalent to 9 am., and south-east.

Midsummer's Day

Midsummer's Day is the longest day, at the centre of the summer quarter of the year. Here, the sun rises and sets at its most northerly points, is above th horizon for the longest period, and attains its highest elevation in the sky. Midsummer sunrise is the direction of the major orientation of many stone circles, the most famous of which is Stonehenge. Viewed from the centre of the circle, the sun rises at the solstice on the alignment of the straight track known as The Avenue and over the outlying menhir called the Heelstone.

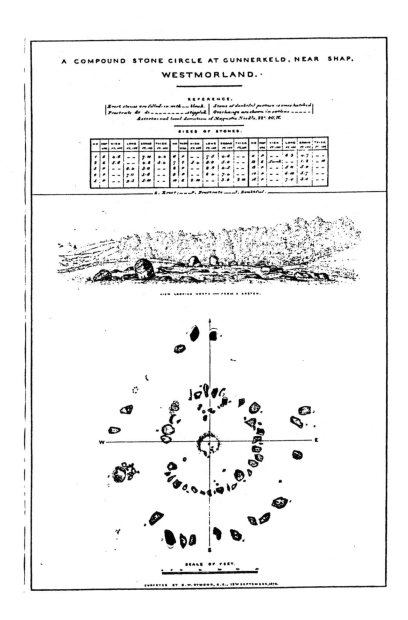

The stone circle at Gunnerkeld in Cumbria. Drawing by the notable megalith researcher C.W.Dymond, 1872.

Midsummer is celebrated as a festival of the culmination of the light, and for many years members of various factions of Druidism performed their rites at Stonehenge on this day. The time-direction of midsummer is midday and due south.

Lughnasaдh/Lammas

Lammas Day, August 1st, is the festival of the first loaf, the name coming from Loaf-Mass, when it was customary to cut the first corn, bake the bread and present it as an offering in church. The modern ceremonies of Harvest Festival are derived from the Lammas observance. Lammas symbolises the fruition of the yearly cycle in the slaughter of 'John Barleycorn', marking the end of maturity and the onset of decline towards death in winter. Lammas was a time of the great customary fairs, when merrymaking and sports would be combined with the business of hiring workers for the winter. Like May Day, whose name Beltane comes from the old Celtic god Belenos, the pre-Christian name Lughnasadh comes from the Celtic god of light and wisdom, Lugh. Its time-direction is 3 pm and south-west.

Autumnal Equinox

The eighth festival of the year is the autumnal equinox, when the light half of the year gives way to the dark. It is the evening of the year, and its time-direction is 6 pm and due west.

Circular Motion and the Earth

The relationship of the festivals with the seasons, symbolised on ancient rock carvings by the sky wheel, is seen in the circular motion of sacred dance, all movements requiring good luck being carried out deiseil - sunwise, turning to the right. Boats were turned about sunwise, rope was coiled that way, the sacred fire wheel rotated deiseil. and to-day the 'superstitious' stir their tea clockwise.

This eightfold division of time, physically marked in the landscape, relates the form of the human body to the celestial phenomena of day and year as a holistic continuum. Many world myths describe the Earth's foundation as or on the body of a human, demon or giant. Symbolically, this gives the human bodily form as the measure of the world, both symbolically and physically. "Man is the measure of all things", was an important maxim of ancient Greek philosophy. The concept of Man the Microcosm, that the human body contains the essential aspects of the entire universe, is at the basis the

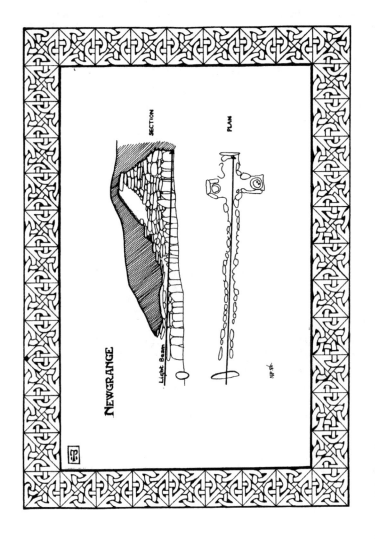

The megalith chamber at Newgrange in Ireland is expertly orientated so that the sun at Midwinter shines through the passage, illuminating the stones at the far end.

European Hermetic tradition and many other developed traditional beliefs throughout the world.

At the centre of the slain giant, or Man the Microcosm, is the navel of the world, the centre of the vital spirit of both human and earth energies. And sacred measure is of course derived from the human body and the physical dimensions of the Earth. At the core of this, however, is not the structure of the human body, but the consciousness, which enables humans to investigate, understand and interact in an effective way with their environment. The festivals of the year are just one way in which humans interact with the ever-changing cycle of the seasons, for the obvious influences such as day length and average temperatures are only a small part of the influences, mainly unseen, which act upon us all. There is the waxing and waning of the Moon, which most obviously controls the tides of the sea, but less perceptibly affects the weather, underground water flows, human emotions and female cycles.

In any solar year, there are 13 lunar cycles which interact with the solar year cycle, a greater cycle which takes 19 years to come back to the same place. The sun itself is subject to internal cycles of sunspot intensity which has a cycle of 11 years, producing variations in various kinds of solar radiation over this period. Less obvious influences are dealt with by astrologers, who relate the position of the planets to certain qualities of time. It is perhaps this aspect of multiple influences which is best known to the average person, though the mechanisms which underlay astrology are open to investigation. The web of correspondences between human beings, the cosmic cycles and particular places are important, and by investigating and using the laws embodied in these correspondences, we can use this knowledge for enhancing our own well-being.

Orientation

The word orientation is derived from the classical Latin word oriri, meaning to rise. In its original meaning with regard to direction, it means the rising of the sun. The medieval Latin word orientare was more specific, meaning the placement or alignment of something towards the east. This meaning became extended to mean alignment towards something, and now the word orientation is used in this context.

Orientation implies a recognition of direction, which in turn needs an awareness of place. All over the world, orientation has been an integral part of architecture, from the smallest dwellings of the peasantry to the grandest palaces of kings and the temples of the gods. Our word orientation is used for this practice because churches were aligned with the altar at the eastern end. Because the rules regarding the alignment of secular buildings were far more complex, and not apparent to the uninitiated, only the eastward alignment of churches was recognised. Orientation, the technical term for this practice, was extended to any deliberate alignment of a building.

Like the stone circles and Pagan temples which preceded many of them, churches were aligned towards celestial phenomena. In his Ten Books on Architecture, the influential Roman architect Vitruvius gave the rules for the harmonious location and alignment of cities and temples:

"The quarter towards which temples of the immortal gods ought to face is to be determined on the principle that, if there is no reason to hinder and the choice is free, the temple and the image placed in the sanctuary should face the western quarter of the sky. This will enable those who approach the altar with offerings or sacrifices to face the direction of sunrise in looking towards the image of the temple, and thus those who are undertaking vows will look towards the quarter from whence the sun comes forth".

In the Christian tradition, which followed on from Pagan Roman practice, most churches are orientated towards the sunrise on the day dedicated to the patron saint of the church. A church of St Felix, for instance, should orientate towards sunrise on January 14; St George, April 23; St Pancras, May 12; St Radegund, August 13; St Martin, November 11, and so on. This alignment towards saints' day sunrise was determined with a ceremony conducted after a night of devotional exercises. The rising sun was observed on site by the builders, who ranged a line between the altar site and the position of the sun visible on the horizon. This line became the axis of the church, so that on each saint's day, sunrise would shine directly along the axis of the church.

Sometimes, orientation refers to the alignment of something towards an earthly place of power. The orientation of synagogues towards Jerusalem and mosques towards Mecca are important instances of this practice in the Western Tradition. This awareness of place and time is identical with that of the ancient megalith builders, whose 'passage graves' align towards solar events. Newgrange, the greatest Irish 'passage grave', built around 3100 B.C.E., was so designed that at midwinter sunrise, a beam of light is directed upon a triple spiral carving at the far end of the chamber, over 60 feet inside. Many other similarly ancient sacred structures have this solar geometry built into them. The projection of a ray of sunlight at a precise time on a specific day of the year guaranteed the illumination of the sacred image at a time related to the orientation of the sacred structure. This flash of illumination reproduced precisely the solar conditions prevailing at the time of foundation, special and unique conditions for the performance of whatever rituals or observances were appropriate. The construction of a building that relates to celestial phenomena, whether it is a passage grave, a Pagan temple, a church, or a modern astronomical observatory, needs a precise awareness of those celestial phenomena. The loss of awareness of these important factors in the industrial era has meant that a whole dimension in architecture is absent from our lives. It is only since the advent of solar architecture, where energy-efficiency is the prime consideration, that orientation has become an issue again.

Ancient tradition prescribed orientation as a natural matter of course. An old Irish locational rhyme says "A southern aspect for warmth, A stream across the glebe, Choice, prosperous land which would be good for every plant." In seventeenth century England, orientation was an important factor in the geolocation of the country estates of the aristocracy. The factors surrounding the house and gardens at Chatsworth, in the English Peak District were expounded in a poem called *The Wonders of the Peake*, written by Charles Cotton in 1681. Here, he compares the splendid house and gardens with the wilderness outside, an achievement accomplished by careful location and orientation:

"This Palace, with wild prospects girded round,
Stands in the middle of a falling ground,
At a black Mountains foot, whose craggy brow
Secures from Eastern-Tempests all below,
Under whose shelter Trees and Flowers grow,
With early Blossom, maugre native snow;
Which elsewhere round a Tyranny maintains,
And binds crampt Nature long in Crystal-Chains.
The Fabrick's noble Front faces the Pest,
Turning her fair broad shoulders to the East,
On the South-side the stately Gardens lye,
Where the scorn'd Peak rivals proud Italy.

And on the North sev'ral inferior plots,
For servile use do scatter'd lye in spots".

When a demand arose for books on gardening, orientation was emphasised. Seventeenth century French treatises on Parterres (flower gardens) frequently recommended that a Parterre should have an eastward orientation, and be sheltered from the north winds by a wall. In an influential 1706 work on gardening titled *The Retir'd Gard'ner*, which was actually a translation and adaptation of a seventeenth century French treatise, George London (d.1714) and Henry Wise (1653-1738) give orientational advice:

"'Tis true, a Piece of Ground that lyes sloping, and looks towards the rising Sun, is most esteem'd, because the Water runs easier from it, and the Sun at his Rising coming to dart on the Flowers in a Parterre thus situated, so enlivens them, that by means of his Heat on the Morning Dew still remaining upon them, they become much more vigorous in their Growth, than if the Parterre was in another Situation.."

Just as plants thrive or fail according to orientation, so, according to traditional belief, do humans, so our older settlements, like medieval towns or country mansions, reflect this. The north-south axis is fundamental in the traditional layout of northern European and Asiatic human settlements. Farmhouses and royal halls were aligned east-west so that the high seat on the northern long wall faced the sun's high point in the south; the lower seat on the opposite wall faced the high point of the northern sky. This orientation was not only used internally, for the Northern Tradition records a precise form for building villages, which was used in the Norse settlements of Iceland and Greenland. The village was built from south to north, the second settler taking the land to the north of the first. The younger son of the settler had rights on the southernmost plot of land, and so on. Comparable village layouts defined by relationships exist today in various tribes in southern Africa. In Britain, we can find this south-north axis surviving today in the church alignments at Cambridge and York. At Cambridge, the Seven-Church Ley runs almost due north-south and is laid out using precise measure. At York, the Corridor of Sanctity has a similar form. The parts of these cities through which the lines run were both laid out by Pagan settlers from Denmark, and it is most likely that the churches on the lines were built on the sites of Pagan places of power.

The Eight Winds are related to earthly direction, the seasons, the festivals of the year and the four elements in European geomantic tradition.

The Centre of Balance and the Four Elements

Because justice was seen as a manifestation of the laws of God or the cosmic order, places of legal and government assembly were always orientated and laid out as an image of the cosmic order. In the north of Europe, the Moot Hill, where local government met in former times, was aligned in the 4 directions. Its ideal form existed at the Sjöborg at Sola, Norway, a moot point for the neighbourhood. This was a stone circle which had eight lines of stones radiating from the building at the centre to the eight aettings. At such a moot point, the King and law speaker stood in the north facing south, and plaintiffs came from the south to the north towards justice. In legal proceedings that were not a contest, participants came from east and west, for they were not in conflict with or appealing directly to the regal and godly law, whose residence was the north.

In the European martial arts, serious judicial combat was conducted from north to south. When the combats were ritualised and not 'in earnest', to the death, such as at displays of skill and tournaments, these were aligned east - west. The King or lord then sat at the side in the north. The symbolism here is that when the north faces the south, the complementary opposites face each other, but when east faces west, the balance is between the two.

Earth Harmony seeks to create a balance between conflicting or opposing factors which come to bear on a place and its interaction with humans: it is concerned with finding the middle way of balance and harmony rather than the imposition of a single dominant force overriding everything else. This attempt towards harmonisation can be described in terms of the Four Elements of the western tradition. These Four Elements are an analogical way of describing related factors operating in and behind the environment. These elements, Fire, Air, Water and Earth, delineate the various classes of factor having influence upon any place. The Four Elements are a means of categorisation which is based on the western Hermetic tradition, and, being eternal archetypes, lend themselves to a modern interpretation relevant to to-day's needs.

Fire

Fire relates to phenomena which can be measured with scientific instruments, and those more subtle energies generated by human activity. The first category includes magnetic, electrostatic and electric fields, cosmic

Local customs, such as the parading of the Straw Bear at Whittlesey in the Cambridgeshire Fens every January, encapsulates the intangible human spirit that manifests in certain places.

rays, natural and artificially-produced radiation. The latter includes noise, psychological and psychic disturbances.

Air

Air is more readily apparent: it is the overall quality of the air; the airflow in and around a place, the direction and average force of the prevailing wind; the mind; and the general 'atmosphere' surrounding a place. Every culture has traditions about the qualities of the winds, which are sometimes used as a way of describing the directions.

Water

Water includes the watercourses and standing water of the locality, both on the surface and underground. This includes seas, lakes, creeks, rivers, streams, ditches, drains, sewers and water supply pipes. Also it includes the natural rainfall and the runoff from the surface. The flow of traffic along a road may also be treated as a watercourse. In all cases, the direction of the flow is all important, or, in the case of the sea and estuaries, the tidal flux. In addition to the flow of water and the forms of watercourses, the quality of water is important. Here, folk tradition ascribes healing qualities to mineral springs, sanctified by deities and saints as 'holy wells'. Although less cared-about today, medicinal springs and holy wells are still important. The existence to-day of major breweries in Dublin and Burton-on-Trent stems form the water quality of former holy wells which still supply high-quality water for brewing.

Earth

Earth includes landforms and landscape structure, underlying geological formations, qualities and types of soil, building materials and their interaction with sites.

Character

Every place has its own unique character, and different people and things react to this character in various ways. This relationship between person and place, and the cause of it has been explained in many ways over the years and in different cultures. Certain places in the landscape have always been recognised as having "life breath", and the craft of Earth Harmony was and is to discover these sites and to determine their individual qualities. The western view of reality, which is based largely on a description of the world in terms of things that are measurable with technological instrumentation,

Wheel of the directions and human consciousness.

26

does not consider the question of such places. Like the emotions aroused by the arts, they can be only partially explained, if at all, by science. Although measurable energies have been detected by independent researchers, the indications are that the energies present at these places are complex, cyclic and intermittent. As any forces present are not obviously apparent, and their relationships are not readily explicable by simple equations, their reality is equivocal and not easily analysed. This clash of cultures is sometimes made more difficult by the language used traditionally to describe the qualities of a site in the landscape, which is symbolic and poetic.

Often, terms such as "movement" have a different meaning from that accepted in everyday talk. However, this is not so abnormal as may at first appear. In painting, for instance, movement, rhythm, tone, texture etc. have a different meaning from the same terms in music, and certainly different from their meaning in physics. Science has nothing to say about these qualities in the arts, or the nature what they are describing. In any area where human perception, consciousness and emotions interact with non-human factors, simple scientific descriptions in the physical sense are inadequate. In the description of the totality of subtle factors that can be understood intuitively at a site, intuitive language is all that can be used. Naturally, such intuitive language is coloured by cultural factors, hence the descriptions of demons and dragons etc., when dealing with the Earth.

Dualism vs. Balance

We live in a predominantly dualistic culture. The prevalent system operates on the belief that there are two polarities in conflict with one another, and that compromise - that is balance - between them is somehow a failure. The concept of a balanced relationship between opposites is overwhelmed by a concept of combat to the death, and the final ascendancy of one over the other, or even the complete elimination of its opposite. This dualistic thinking underlies politics, much of religion and the arms race, with consequences only too apparent in the world to-day. The idea that something which cannot be demonstrated by the current scientific or political paradigms to be positively good must automatically be bad is derived from this Manichaean world view. It leads to the wish to abolish things which cannot be shown to be 'good' , or even the tendency to see them as bad because they cannot be proven to be good. This viewpoint implicitly denies neutrality or other non-extreme qualities which depend upon an interaction with individuals, and therefore exist as dynamically altering qualities. The implication of the dualistic viewpoint is that anything in imbalance is so because of a single external opposite affecting it in some way. It suggests that the removal of this external influence will in itself restore balance. When we examine it without prejudice, it is clear that imbalance is not a single state: there can be imbalance in either of two directions, towards the direction of excess, or on the other hand, towards scarcity and lack. These qualities can be expressed as in the table below:

Imbalance	Balance	Imbalance
Negative		Positive
Excess of negative		Excess of positive
Shortage of positive		Shortage of negative
Degeneration		Rigidity, Fixity
Change for its own sake		Complacency, Inactivity
Dissolution		Obsession
Fragmentation		Centralisation
Impatience		Resignation
Anarchic revolution		Rigid authoritarian orthodoxy
Inaccuracy		Pedantry
Irregularity		Inflexible order
Blinding darkness		Blinding light
Restless motion		Inactivity
Unlimited action		Limited action
Bewildering diversity		Uniformity

From the above, it can be seen that an imbalance in either direction is undesirable, but that the results of these imbalances are in themselves opposite states. Everything which exists is in a state between absolutes, and in transition. There are no eternal, unchanging qualities in the world. "...For time transforms the nature of the entire world, and inevitably everything passes on from one stage to another. Nothing remains constant: all is in flux; all things are is altered by nature and forced to change. As one thing declines, decays and droops with age, another thrives and emerges from obscurity. In this way, then, time alters the nature of the entire world, and the earth passes on from one stage to another, so that what she once bore, she can bear no longer, while she can bear what she did not bear before.", wrote the Roman philosopher Lucretius in his work *De Rerum Naturae* (c. 60 BCE).

Each relationship between things, or people, is the result of a struggle or tension between the opposite forces which are resolved and unified within the

28

structure, which exists within time. By unifying seeming opposites, we can reintegrate the whole and attain that state which many faiths call 'holiness'. Holy means "that which has wholeness". Everything that exists is worthy of veneration, and the "holy" covers all that is venerable. A mountain, a spring, a rock, a tree, can possess venerable qualities and be "holy". In reality, there can be no separation of any part of existence. The human race is descended biologically from the identical primordial holiness as the mountain, spring, rock or tree. Because of this, persons of great spiritual presence, after their death, have become "holy", being venerated as possessing godlike qualities. There are examples from every religious tradition in the West: Imhotep, Pythagoras, Petosiris, Odin, Apollonius, Jesus, etc. The process of becoming holy, venerable, or "deified" is the process of the accomplishment of one's form. To accomplish one's form is the fulfilment of the essential part of one's inherent potential. A place is holy whenever it fulfils its inherent potential either through its natural form or by human harmonisation. The attainment of the ideal equilibrium, both internally and in one's relationship to the surrounding environment with all that means is to be at the right place at the right time facing the right direction, doing the right thing. It is the achievement of perfect harmony with all things.

The Regenturm housing complex at Plochingen, Baden-Wurttemberg

Chapter 2
The Hidden Landscape

"The more different things there are, the richer the world. It approaches paradise: many different things living next to each other" - Friedensreich Hundertwasser.

How we experience the landscape depends to some extent on our individual outlook. The artist, poet, soldier, geographer, geologist, civil engineer or geomant will perceive the character of different landscapes according to their particular discipline. Description of the landscape falls within the realm of geography, for it is here that a systematic attempt to analyse the landscape has been made. However, by using scientifically-based approximations, geography is largely a descriptive and documentary discipline with no remit to study anything else. It does not appraise itself to the effects which the landscape might produce on its inhabitants, or those who experience it. Because this approach is not open to scientific analysis, it is left alone by geographers, who have plenty of work to do in their own sphere, anyway.

Our experience of landscape may be analysed as consisting of two linked factors: a direct experience of the forces in the landscape, and our cultural reaction to them. Because we live in an environment where almost every part is modified artificially, we must necessarily perceive the landscape differently from our pre-industrial forebears. In less technologically advanced societies, and that includes our own past, everyday life depended upon the climate, the character of the land, and the materials available locally. The immediate locality was the only place which was important, for there were no means of transporting or transmitting materials and energy to another place. With the industrial revolution, all of this changed. For the first time, it was possible to transport materials and transmit energy for heating and lighting. But this new power over the environment reduced people's perception of the continuing importance of place. Because it was possible now to demolish hills or drain waterways, it was assumed also that these places had no innate character other than those imposed upon them by human activity. This assumption comes from the narrow view of things: that they can be taken out of their context, dismembered and analysed. Whilst much of science has made its discoveries in this way, it is clear that this gives only a partial view of the nature of reality. Their interaction with the world, their ecology in the widest sense, is not investigated when the narrow view is taken; indeed, it is only possible to study them when the interactions are removed and the 'object' placed in the 'controlled environment' of the laboratory.

The scientific method has its place, for without it we would not enjoy the undoubted benefits of modern technology. But we must remember that this method has a specific use in limited areas. The environment is a massively complex holistic interaction of factors continually changing with such rapidity that they cannot be pinned down absolutely by scientific analysis. But because we are confronted with a bewildering array of ever-changing factors does not mean that we should dismiss them as unknowable or uncontrollable. Using a systematic method, we can categorise a few of the factors, but their interactions defy analysis and our interaction with them goes into the intuitive area. Here, the experiences of wizards, locators, shamans and artists are of value, for they are dealing with the direct human experience of the material and non-material worlds. The scientific method, which is at the basis of most education, necessarily attempts to remove the human factor from experimental analysis.

The basic tenet of experimental science is that the results of an experiment should be reproducible, regardless of the laboratory where the experiment is performed, and regardless of the identity of the person performing it. This rigorously-defined method gains valuable information which is considered to be objective truth, existing in some superior realm beyond human beings. Unfortunately, but inevitably, this was extended into areas of individual experience, and the wrong assumption that what I experience must automatically be that which you experience arose. The experiences of wizards, geomants, shamans and artists have been dismissed as 'subjective' as opposed to the 'objective realities' of science, and thereby belittled. These sensations, real to those who experience them, cannot be categorised scientifically, unless they are insultingly categorised as forms of madness. However, many of these experiences are known to the majority of the population, albeit in less extreme and complete forms than in those who have cultivated the faculties needed to experience them. Even the greatest scientific discoveries have come through the intuitive faculty of the scientists who made them. Our experience of places cannot be categorised scientifically other than by a basic analysis of temperature, light, air pressure, etc. Beyond these physical characteristics, we are in the realm of psychology, intuition and the psychic. If we experience a place as menacing or disorientating, then this is a real experience which affects our feelings and behaviour. If we are told then that our experiences have no validity in scientific terms and that we ought to feel good there, this is not because we are wrong, but because the scientific analysis is lacking in something with regard to us. The attempted removal of the human element, with all that that implies, from the scientific method has led to cruel indifference in some areas and an ignoring of human needs in others. In the area of our interaction with the world, and the restoration of an harmonious balance between the heavens, human beings and the earth, the scientific method is only one element in our search for understanding. It is because of this that most purely scientific investigations of place phenomena have proved inconclusive.

The very strong sensations felt by many people at certain places can be explained in various ways, some of which are acceptable to modern scientific viewpoints, and others which are not. The feelings that some people experience at a site are subjective, that is there is no immediate external reference by which they can be checked. The only way this can be done is if the same experiences are felt by different people who have no knowledge of the experiences there of others. Because of the very personal nature of these experiences, their analysis has proved exceedingly difficult. In such a difficult area of investigation, it is only to be expected, then, that there are several schools of thought as to why people have certain experiences at certain places. Some people of the presently-fashionable 'deconstructionist' school even deny that anyone has any real experience at all. This is a viewpoint that defies investigation, for most of those who hold the view do so dogmatically, dismissing all evidence as 'subjective'. To deny the admissibility of all evidence is in itself a belief that there is none: in its way it is as unhelpful to the gaining of useful knowledge as would be the uncritical belief in every claim of the presence of elementals and fairies at those sites. Despite the protests of those who believe there is no experience, this analysis of human response to the spirit of the place or Anima Loci has been going on since the seventeenth century, and yet still no universally acceptable solution to the problem has been discovered.

One popular theory to account for these feelings is that of imprinting. At an early age, so the theory goes, we undergo quite arbitrarily certain experiences at certain types of place, after which those or similar places elicit memories of the feelings first experienced there. One of the first commentators to put forward this theory was Joseph Addison. In 1712, he wrote in the magazine The Spectator:

> *"We may observe, that any single Circumstance of what we have formerly seen often raises up a whole Scene of Imagery, and awakens numberless Ideas that before slept in the Imagination; such a particular Smell or Colour is able to fill the Mind, on a sudden, with the Picture of Fields or Gardens where we first met with it, and to bring up into View all the Variety of Images that once attended to it...."*

Associated with this idea of imprinting is that of an instinctive reaction to landscape. This idea arose in the wake of Lamarck and Darwin with their various theories of evolution. Here, the experience is explained in terms of our animal ancestors' need for survival in a hostile world. The prospect/refuge theory of landscape, describing our response to the country in terms of the capability of seeing without being seen, is derived from this. It explains the attractiveness of certain places as related to the evolutionary necessity of survival. This sociobiological view of our experience sees our reaction as somehow having been ingrained into human nature as a biological instinct. Here, consciousness plays no part - it is a programmed reaction to a potentially hostile environment. It is possible to view the entire aesthetic approach to landscape in these terms, although, as will become apparent later, it is clear that they do not explain everything.

Moving on from the purely biological interpretations, where the experience (if real at all) is seen as essentially internal, we must consider possible external influences. Aesthetic approaches to landscape - and even the word landscape itself - are derived from the observation of the landscape as a spectacle. Often, landscape is appreciated as a form of natural art, to be observed as one would a painting. But our view of landscape is conditioned by our present-day culture, especially the experience of tourism. For example, until the era of Romanticism in the nineteenth century, mountains were feared as 'terrible' in both the physical and psychic sense. No-one was allowed to set foot on Mont Pilatus, near Lucerne in Switzerland, as it was reputed to be cursed with the wraith of Pontius Pilate, so nobody did. In the eighteenth century, travellers crossing Mont Blanc had the curtains drawn across the windows of their coaches to avoid experiencing the terrifying view of the Alps. The sea, too, aroused feelings of fear, not only because of the uncertain dangers of sailing on it, but also from the awesome sense of unlimited power one can feel there. After the technological revolution, when the works of man had seemingly tamed and harnessed the power of nature, these terrifying places became interesting examples of that natural power, to be visited without fear as one might visit a zoo to see a tiger in a cage.

Looking at landscape from the touristic viewpoint, many analysts use the prospect/refuge theory. This theory is at the root of much 'landscape gardening', especially that of the eighteenth and nineteenth centuries. Prospect/refuge theory sees the landscape as a series of 'focal points', determined by the visual qualities experienced from these places. These points are almost arbitrary, excepting that they conform to the undulations of the landforms. Understanding the landscape only as a spectacle, even an instinctive one, however, prevents us from experiencing it directly. We are made into observers, viewing the landscape as we would a painting, theatre or video, and because we are not experiencing being present there, it is a second-hand experience. Even the word 'focal point', much beloved of planners, comes from the terminology of painters and photographers, and looking at reality as if it were a picture with perspective. Much of our view of the world is like this, from television to tourism, where the mere spectacle experienced by the tourist in a sightseeing bus is considered by many to be an experience of the character and nature of a country. These focal points are seen in different terms by those who recognise a more subtle structure of the landscape. An intimate knowledge of the character of a landscape involves more than just an artistic appreciation or even the skills of the guide or tracker, for there are many subtle elements which are not apparent to the untrained or unsensitive mind. To-day it is possible to take a broader view, with rediscovery of alignments, symbolism and ancient orientation and the reawakening of a consciousness long submerged in the mass modern culture.

.

Chapter 3
The Anima Loci

Landscape is the nurturer of all human life. Without a grounding in Mother Earth, human culture has no basis: life, soul and even conscious thought is impossible. This is the essence of the German concept of Heimat, which, interestingly, cannot be translated into English, but which involves everything to do with one's ancestral home landscape - something many people have to do without. Although it is essentially personal, at its deepest level, this recognition transcends cultural and religious boundaries. When we talk about the character of a location, we often use the expression 'spirit of place', so in attempting to understand better this character, we must examine what we mean by 'spirit'. The word spirit has two connected but distinct meanings: firstly, a feel, sense, or character; and secondly, a discarnate, supernatural, entity or being, probably with its own consciousness and personality. In describing the character of a place, the old Latin expression Genius Loci, 'spirit of place' has elements of both of these meanings unified in a place and perceived by the human consciousness as a totality.

However, 'Genius Loci' has the implicit meaning that it somehow is separate from the land itself, when actually it is the 'soul' of the place that animates it with regard to human perception. Thus, when the Anima Loci is present, the land is ensouled, and human beings can come into a personal relationship with it. In various cultures and at different times, people have understood the spirit of a place as a feeling or atmosphere, whilst others have experienced the presence of beings. The two are not so distinct as might at first appear. The imaginative act of personification of an object or a place, interpreting its character as personality, is common. From the named swords of ancient warriors, such as Excalibur to modern fighter aircraft like the Tornado, personality has been attached to seemingly inanimate objects. Flags, weapons, bells, guitars,railway locomotives and cars have all been given names and imbued with personality by their owners. Non-mobile property, like buildings, located in a specific setting, and influenced by relatively unchanging surroundings, possess their own character which may be interpreted as a personality or manifest itself as a spirit in the supernatural sense.

To those people who have only experienced conventional education and the mass media, the concept that there is anything about a place which can be called a 'spirit' is a notion which they have never encountered. However, there are so many instances, ancient and modern, of this, that it is unreasonable not to recognise it. Although it often fails to accomplish its aims, the phenomenon of tourism, which began in ancient Roman times, is a tacit recognition of the wish to encounter the spirit of a place. Certain places, considered special because of their architecture, 'scenery', or association with a famous person real or fictional, are magnets to visitors who come to be in the presence of the spirit or character there.

Önd

Throughout the world, traditional cultures have named the subtle 'cosmic breath' which pervades and animates all existence. Many terms have been used to describe the underlying cause of the perceived qualities at a site. There are as many names for this energy as there are traditions on Earth. According to age-old European tradition, this power has been described as the Pneuma, Önd, The Eight Winds, Nwyvre, the Vital Spirit and exhalations of the spirit of place. Alchemists described it as the Anima Mundi, the Quintessence or the Universal Plastic Medium, whilst in the East Anglian 'nameless art', it is Spirament. To rhabdomants and dowsers it has been Earth Rays, Radiesthetic Fields, Telluric Lines, Geobiological Fields and Earth Energies. Theosophically-inclined occultists have seen it manifest as Etheric Currents or Vril, whilst Christian mystics envisaged it in terms of Lines of Spiritual Power. Alternative scientists of the nineteenth and twentieth centuries have described it as Odyle, Orgone, Field Anomalies or Field Intensity Variations. In the East, the qualities are seen as coming from the flow and accumulation of a "life breath" called Ch'i, Prana or Ki. Like electricity or gravity, in itself, it is neither good nor bad. Energy can be a source of life or death, creation or destruction. It is through its perceived effects on human beings that we call it good or bad, for without our consciousness it cannot be recognised.

In the Northern European Tradition, which is the system best applied in northern Europe, the power called Önd is the driving force. Önd is the fundamental living energy of the cosmos which connects and relates all things. This primal energy exists in everyone, and in all parts of the cosmos in some form or another. Every individual's portion of this primal energy, being beyond the physical, is a direct connection with the totality of everything. Awareness is a manifestation of Önd, an energy which can be directed to any part of the body, or beyond it. Essentially, Önd is life, as long as Önd is present, life continues,but when Önd is gone, life ends. The management and control of Önd is therefore the mastery of life, health, harmony, and energy Önd is a unifying force, being the energy or primal force which has existed since the inception of the cosmos, being independent of time and space. In the human individual, who is the emanation of universal nature, all consciousness stems from Önd and returns to nature at death.

According to tradition, Önd is neutral in character. It is capable of picking up surrounding influences, behaving as a sort of medium for them. Thereby, Önd is coloured and patterned by the qualities of the places in which it occurs. In a natural condition, without human interference, the Önd at any place is patterned in conformity with the natural patterns and colours of the place: it is in perfect alignment with the Anima Loci in its ever-altering fluxes of character. When it is present in certain forms in the earth, it is Nwyvre, the 'dragon power', which behaves in a certain characteristic way. When human activity intervenes, that, too, affects the patterns and colours of Önd. Then, either the qualities of the Anima Loci are reinforced (sanctification), altered (on-lay), or destroyed (alfreka).

The power of Önd has been used, knowingly or unknowingly, in the west in both mainstream religion and occultism. At the end of the last century, A.P.Sinnett, a leading member of the London Lodge of the Theosophical Society investigated this power. In 1895, he wrote *"There are great etheric currents constantly sweeping over the surface of the earth from pole to pole in volume which makes their power as irresistible as the rising tide; and there are methods by which this stupendous force may be safely utilised, though unskilful attempts to control it would be fraught with frightful danger."*

In the 1920s, a Christian interpretation came from Father Hugh Benson in a piece titled *In the Convent Chapel* which describes the communion between a nun and the Reserved Sacrament as a spiritual force transmitting itself out across the world, producing beneficial effects. *"This black figure knelt at the centre of reality and force, and with the movements of her will and lips controlled spiritual destinies for eternity. There ran out from the peaceful.chapel lines of spiritual power that lost themselves in the distance, bewildering in their profusion and terrible in the intensity of their hidden fire."* In Benson's eyes, the chapel and nun together acted as a *"centre of reality and force*", the coming together of earthly, human and heavenly powers at the right time and the right place. Here, the spiritual exercises of the nun accomplish the same use of Önd as in the martial arts, and place plays an important part in this.

The recognition, management and channelling of Önd in the martial arts is identical to that in earth harmony: the body of the human is replaced by the body of the Earth. Certain places in the landscape have Önd, the life breath, and the craft of the harmoniser is to discover these places and ascertain their special individual qualities. These qualities are explained as places where Önd accumulates, stagnates or is lost. Techniques exist to manage the flow of Önd to ensure that it is to the benefit of human beings. Each tradition has its own description and explanation of the underlying reason for the perceived differences of places, each the result of its own cosmological view. But despite these differences in terminology, comparison of the systems shows that they are dealing with the same reality. Also, it is apparent that ultimately the character of a site is discernable only by its effects and not by analysis. Earth Harmony sees the characters of sites as depending upon and affecting each other in a series of interactions between the living and non-living components of the whole environment. Here, it is not possible to state that one site is more valuable than another, for value exists only as a judgement which can be answered only in terms relative to the particular requirement of the moment. Any system that views sites from a pre-conceived system of values distorts this subtle network of relationships. These relationships are a web of complex interrelationships that cannot be explained in linear terms, nor can be arranged in a pyramidal, hierarchical manner or structured according to human ideas.

If the character of a site can be understood, or an appropriate site recognised, by whatever means, then harmony can be attained. The aim of Earth harmony is the attainment of oneness - harmony, the state in which essence and form are identical - by way of the many, various methods, techniques and practices. It is based upon a recognition of the harmony of the universe, and humanity's identity with the universe. This harmony involves all matter, both inanimate and animate, visible and invisible, for if humans are in harmony with nature, then they can do only good. Thus there is no bad site - every site has its own qualities with which we can harmonise - every site is good for something!

The Human Body and Önd

Although modern medicine's view of the nature of the human body is so successful and widespread, it would be a mistake to ignore these traditional concepts or perceptions of the nature of the human body. The traditional view of the body in European occultism is that the human frame is an embodiment of all of the significant energies and characteristics of nature. In medieval Europe, each bodily organ reflected one of the twelve signs of the zodiac, which were understood as expressions of particular configurations of forces and qualities active in the cosmos. For more details of this system, see my book *Secret Signs, Symbols and Sigils* (Capall Bann, 1996). A similar correspondence system exists in Indian Tantra, where each chakra or energy centre in the body corresponds to a male and female deity. These deities each symbolise a quality or force present in the natural world, all of them various manifestations of Önd. These correspondences of body with the cosmos also contain correspondences in the physical world. When built according to the ancient canons of structure, form and dimensions, temples and churches are simultaneously images of the cosmos and of the human body. Likewise, similar correspondences exist within the natural landscape.

Because of these correspondences, pilgrimage to a place of power involves a dynamic interaction between pilgrim and place. Here, the earthly location becomes identified with some component of the religious discipline, usually with a region or an organ in the pilgrim's body. By meditating on the place of power through visualisation of its presiding deity in the prescribed manner, the point of concentration in the devotee's body becomes charged with the spiritual energies of that place.

Sanctification and On-Lays

Sanctity - the physical manifestation of the essential nature of a sacred place - comes into being when the Anima Loci is recognised. At such loci, the Önd is patterned and coloured in conformity with the qualities of the Anima Loci. These patterns, never fixed, flow and change according to the qualitative changes of the Anima Loci. There is no dissonance. When the Anima Loci is recognised by human beings, then perfect harmony arises if human actions at the place reinforce, enhance and develop the previously-imperceptible potential. This enhancement comes about when the development takes to form of self-similarity, promoting the evolution of the hitherto unmanifest qualities of the Anima Loci.

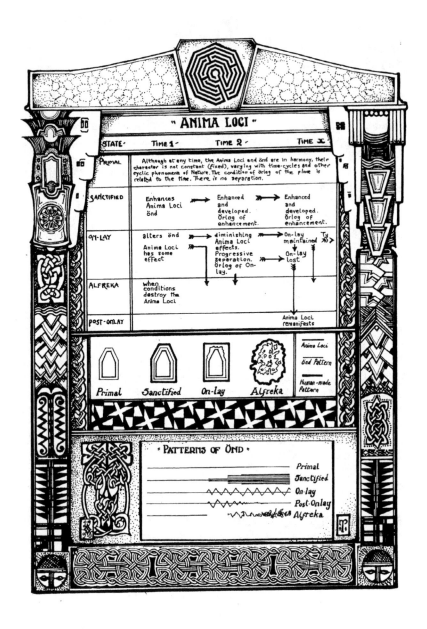

The Anima Loci, On-Lay and Alfreka.

Enhancement is brought about by human activities which are in harmony with the Anima Loci. They are those things that repeat in a self-similar way the pattern-quality of the Anima Loci. They include pleasing artifacts, ceremonies and activities that elicit a similar harmonious response in humans. Enhancing the Anima Loci is spiritual gardening, not trying to 'command and control', but consciously participating in a self-ordering system. At places of sanctity, fully-developed human beings can become outward expressions or embodiments of the Anima Loci. As time passes, through repetition and evolution, the place's orlog is sanctified: the qualities of the Anima Loci are intensified.

By these means, the latent spirit of the Anima Loci can be brought forth into manifestation on the material level. Then, a truly sacred place has come into being. The invisible is made visible. There is the revelation of Paradise. Sanctity does not merely acknowledge or reproduce some specific perception of the Anima Loci. It creates an unique presentation of the Anima Loci that does not act as an intermediate filter, interpretation or representation. Rather, nothing comes between; it is an enhancing gateway to the divine. An on-lay comes into being when the Önd of a site is altered by an act of will. This can either be a ritual act, such as exorcism or consecration, or an act of will that would not normally be considered magical, such as the unmindful construction of a secular building or even intentional but mindless vandalism. Under an on-lay, the qualities of the of the Anima Loci are suppressed, yet still present. Because the patterns of the on-lay are (by definition) different from those of the Anima Loci, there is a conflict between the Önd patterns of the Anima Loci and those of the on-lay. Thus, on-lays must be renewed periodically, or the Anima Loci will re-manifest, bringing the quality of the Önd back into line with the quality of the Anima Loci.

Alfreka and Post-Onlay Sites

A place is rendered alfreka is when the spiritual beings of the land are driven away. It is complete desacralisation. The Anima Loci is destroyed. This can result from a too-powerful on-lay, maintained over a long period. It is the ultimate result of an on-lay which is in direct conflict with the Anima Loci. A place can also be rendered alfreka by physical destruction: if a holy hill is bulldozed away, or a hole for a metro station entrance excavated where once was a sacred place, then the actual locus is no more, and it can have no anima. This type of alfreka is common in cities where the original awareness of natural ground levels has been abolished. If a place is rendered alfreka, this does not extirpate the Önd present there. It will be affected by whatever influences are present there. For example, there can be an on-lay upon an alfreka site. This gives us the means to do some sort of geomantic remedial work at alfreka places. Places where an on-lay once existed, but where it is no longer operative, are post-onlay sites. If the place is not alfreka, then the Anima Loci is still present, even if weakened. She can re-manifest if the site is not overlain by a new on-lay, or rendered alfreka. A post-onlay site that is alfreka is open to any influence, conscious or unconscious, that might come into contact with it. The Önd of the site will be patterned randomly, according to these influences. Alfreka post-onlay sites are particularly prone to destructive influences, and new on-lays, which will be more powerful because they are not in conflict with the Anima Loci, which has been driven down.

If a place is not alfreka, then human actions can accelerate the return of the full influence of the Anima Loci. To do this, it is necessary to remove deteriorating on-lay remnants, and to replace them with harmonious artifacts and activities. Remains which are neutral should stay as a witness to the orlog of the place. The orlog of the on-lay will always be present, but the dwindling of its effects can be accelerated and obliterated. Then the character of the Anima Loci can shine through once more.

Chapter 4
Recognitions of Subtle Landscapes

"We possess beauty when we are true to our own being ugliness is going over to another order" - Plotinus

The Anima Loci at a place can take many forms, and be caused by various phenomena in combination. Places are felt important because some supernatural being has manifested there, or some important person lived or died there, or even because a novelist described the place in a popular work of fiction. Thus pilgrims visit Lourdes, where an apparition of the Virgin indicated a sacred spring, or Gracelands, where Elvis Presley is buried amid his memorabilia. Such places have existed since time immemorial, the shrines of gods and heroes which possess the character of the person or entity commemorated there. They are places of power which must be understood within the context of their surroundings.

Rarely have people with a deep knowledge of the countryside analysed their way of passing through a tract of country, and their vision of its structure. Alfred Watkins, author of *The Old Straight Track*, is one exception. Throughout his long life in Herefordshire, he travelled through that and surrounding counties in an age before the great expansion of towns, the mechanisation of agriculture, the erection of power lines and the construction of motorways. His writing recalls a more leisurely era, when the walker or rider could more easily than now come into direct contact with ancient times. In 1925, he wrote that when the 'outdoor man', walking across country, taking in the uplands, lingers over his mid-day sandwich on the earthwork of some hill-top camp, he will look all round "to get the lay of the land". First, he will determine the hill-points, one perhaps with a bare top, another marked by a clump of trees, or less frequently by a single one. Sometimes one or more mounds or tumuli will appear as points on a hill ridge against the skyline and he will remember similar ones which he has passed along his valley route. Perhaps these will, he mused, be surrounded by a water moat, built for a purpose so obscure that no one had yet explained it. Watkins explained that his hypothetical hiker will not fail also to look for any entrenched hill-top camp he may know. Sometimes he will see blunt notches on the skyline where the earthworks run, but often these ancient markers of place are overgrown by trees, and cannot be seen. This intimate structure of the countryside, that sympathetic human modification of the landscape to create something beyond and greater than the natural, which is an expression of the forces inherent within the land, can be understood still.

The appreciation of earth harmony, which is the appraisal of the nature of a landscape in all of its aspects, material and subtle, is a matter of a certain state of consciousness. Many of those who have possessed a deep understanding of the landscape have awakened this aspect of consciousness, enabling them to see things in what was to them a new way. A modern representative of this is Philip Heselton. Writing in 1982 in the long-established and respected geomantic magazine, *Northern Earth Mysteries*, he described the process of recognition and reinforcement of such places. Looking at the landscape as filled with energy, these are especially powerful locations: "Channels of energy flow will be perceived, with lesser and greater concentrations. Over all a tide is ebbing and flowing with all the natural cycles of life. Perhaps we now imagine a trackway, winding across a hillside, no more than a sheep track, perhaps, or an ancient drove road. Here, a new experience confronts us. We see lines of energy following the path, laid down by those who have passed this way before us. At intervals along the path, the energy intensifies - certain spots sanctified by time - where individuals have paused for a moment to contemplate. Each reflecting moment here builds up the energy store until, after generations, it is noticed more consciously. Here animals stop to rest or to give birth. A wayside seat is erected, or a cross, a standing stone, a church, inn or village. Or perhaps the subtle energy with which this place is charged will encourage the growth of a tree or the thickening of a hedge."

Here, Heselton recognises an important factor - the interaction between people and the landscape. Many people report similar experiences when they visit certain places for the first time, and naturally, this phenomenon has attracted the attentions of many investigators of paranormal events. It is a widely-held belief that a place can trap or record a memory, and that a sensitive person in the right frame of mind coming into the place at the right time.will experience a 'replay' of the memory. In a report issued in 1972 by the Bishop of Exeter's commission on exorcism, 90% of hauntings were blamed on 'Place Memories'. The commission believed that these are impersonal traces of earlier personal action, which seem to be caused by either habitual actions, or by actions accompanied by violent emotion. According to the churchmen, it is possible to obliterate these place memories by means of the ritual of Christian exorcism.

The theory behind exorcism appears be that certain places have 'vibrations' which are somehow recorded or left behind when some violent emotion occurs there. Many theories have been forwarded to account for these 'vibrations', ranging from the trapping spirit entities to the existence of electrostatic fields. What makes analysis difficult is the many kinds of experiences ascribed to place memories. They range from feelings of unease or threat, noises and voices, to smells or visual manifestations including lights and 'ghosts'. Most are just feelings or emotions which are elicited when someone enters a house, or a certain room within that place. Although it is less common, certain natural places also elicit similar emotions.

One interpretation of the factor which gives certain places special qualities which is popular at the present moment is the idea of earth energies. As I outlined in the introduction, this idea of earth energies is very old, and it has been called by many names. Since the 1930s, dowsers, whose craft was developed originally as rhabdomancy for detecting underground veins of minerals and water, have branched out into what is now known as 'energy dowsing'. The ramifications of dowsers' claims and beliefs need not detain us here, but the development of certain areas of Earth Mysteries has come about through the application of dowsers' findings to archaeology and folklore. At the end of the 1960s, the publication of two books, *The Pattern of the Past* by Guy Underwood, and *The View Over Atlantis* by John Michell gave independent yet complementary views of the nature of ancient sites. Underwood was a dowser, and his work claimed that beneath ancient stone circles and cathedrals he had found ramifying spiral patterns of underground water of different types. These patterns, he believed, were detected by the locators of these sacred places, and used to determine their design Michell's book looked at ancient traditions and religious beliefs and correlated them with the design of sacred places as receptacles of spirit or energy.

Since the publication of these books, several other works have emerged, building upon them and now there is a whole school of dowsing dedicated solely to earth energies. According to this viewpoint, ancient mystical sites are places where this power is manifested: either as inner feelings of peace or reverence, or as manifestations of spirits, demons, Our Lady or lights in

Traditional water divining according to Suffolk custom demonstrates the usually-hidden powers that exist within most human beings.

the sky, the type of manifestation depending upon the state of consciousness and expectancy of the witness. Obviously, this viewpoint is incompatible with a belief in the objective existence of these beings. The theory asserts that the ancients knew this power, and manipulated it according to well-defined methods to create the sacred energy centres we know today. This viewpoint likens the dowsing patterns perceived around standing stones to the electrical effects on the human skin induced by the acupuncturist's needle. According to this view, these 'needles of stone' were inserted, millennia ago, into nodal points on the supposed energy-matrix of the earth in order to produce effects in the earth's body comparable with the effects of acupuncture in the human body. By so doing, it is theorized that the currents induced in the earth by celestial phenomena were enhanced, diverted or blocked for human benefit. At appropriate times, these energies would be added to or characterised by symbolic human observances. These might take the form of religious services, meditation, sacred dance or sacrifice, serving the function of aligning the members of the community with the energies in the earth and the forces of the unseen.

Places of power are not distributed equally across the landscape. Powerful qualities occur at certain classes of natural feature, such as waterfalls, springs and streams, various trees and parts of woodland, deserts, moorland, mountains and sea-shores. These are the classes of natural place traditionally associated with nature spirits. The noted archaeologist T.C. Lethbridge, who was an important figure in this investigation, did not believe that these spirits were actual conscious entities, but energy fields. But in recognition of this traditional perception, Lethbridge called his fields after the nature spirits of the ancient Pagan Greeks. The qualities and character associated with waterfalls he called Naiads, those at trees and woodland, Dryads, Oreads at mountains, and Nereids at the sea. Lethbridge asserted that each person is surrounded by an aura, whose condition depends on the emotional state of the person. He theorized that the interaction between this field, which he described as 'electromagnetic' and 'static', and other fields of force present at certain places, created the reported effects.

This perception of nature spirits as energies is the modern view of the matter, which, unfortunately, adds more confusing terminology to the already-cluttered area. The concentration or generation of energies at certain places on our planet's surface, he believed, can under certain conditions, be perceived as gods, saints, nature spirits, elementals, fairies, ghosts, boggarts or demons. Those who do not believe there is evidence for either energies or

48

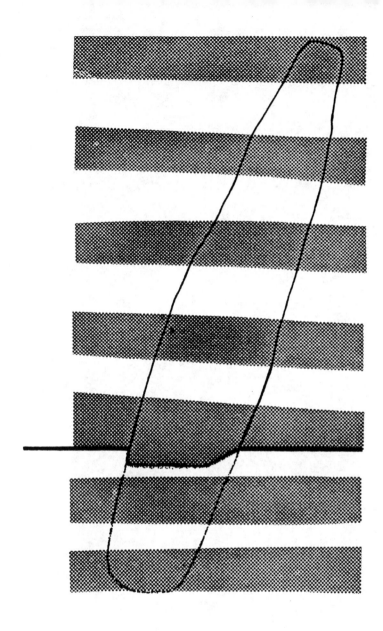

Dowsers can find serpentine bands of 'energy' on megaliths at certain times.

The Anima Loci

spirits, but who recognise some genuine effect, explain these observations in terms of the psychological imprinting or instinctive theories.

The interpretation of ancient sites and ritual in this way is a coherent way of looking at the interaction of heaven, human and earth, but because it is based upon the intrinsically subjective assertions of dowsers, it runs the risk of being dismissed as wishful thinking. As a genuine human detection of scientifically-measurable fields, dowsing has been demonstrated successfully in France by Yves Rocard and his associates and by various researchers in the former Soviet Union. The possible energies associated with ancient standing stones were investigated in Britain by several workers using technical instrumentation, but few convincing results were obtained. However, it was proven that the sites studied had some measurably qualitative difference from their surroundings which may interact with human beings present there at the right time to produce the whole gamut of reported experiences. It is likely then, that dowsers are picking up certain elements or components of these fields at standing stones or on ancient trackways, but because different dowsers at the same site may come up with completely different patterns, interpretation is very subjective and personal. The quest for a coherent explanation, which at present appears lacking or unconvincing, does not mean that any experiences people may have at places of power are not real or reproducible. It just means that, like the appreciation of beauty, or religious experience, the qualities of these places are subjective, that is, they relate directly to singular perceptions which may differ from person to person, yet which have an overall genetic or cultural basis.

When our perception of the world over the greater part of human existence is considered, it is apparent that people have used the intuitive way for the greater part of that time. The modern view has existed for only about three centuries, but has largely superseded the old ways of thought. A compartmentalised view of things has been substituted for the older holistic vision of existence, reinforced by an education system that sees itself as having the function of producing the next generation of workers. The practice of earth harmony combines these two apparently differing perceptions of the world in a single new vision. This awareness is suppressed in modern consciousness. But it has never been suppressed in some cultures, even surviving into the recent past as the official way of doing things. Thus our perception of earth harmony today comes from several sources: the study of traditional systems; contemporary research into the remote sensing of subtle qualities in the earth by techniques like dowsing,and, perhaps most importantly, by that intuitive faculty which exists within all of us.

As most of us live in the urbanised environment, which has obliterated the natural distinctions between times of day,we have to re-learn the idea that times of day have their own character.The time of day or the season, are elements in our experience of landscape, but often the variations have been explained in terms of painting. For example the light of sunrise and sunset are spoken of as being times of heightened emotion, more so than at midday, yet the interpretation is one of illumination rather than time. Time of day has a real meaning, for if we have not just arrived from another continent, or have an unnatural cycle of sleep and wakefulness, we will be in tune with the cycles of day and night. At dawn and dusk, the appearance or disappearance of the sun has a physical effect, for we are no longer receiving direct radiation from it. The subtle changes in solar radiation, the Earth's magnetic field and other forms of energy in and around the Earth affected by the sun, alter at sunrise and sunset, and we perceive this in subtle ways.

Chapter 5
Places of Power

"Do not make a custom, and do not break a custom" - Old Irish Proverb.

Seeing our Earth symbolically as a sacred living being rather than an inanimate sphere of rock, water and gas spinning aimlessly through the cosmos is fundamental to our understanding of Earth Harmony. Natural religions revere the world, and the places of power within it as locations where the Gods manifest. Whether or not this is a correct interpretation of these places, such sacred sites are recognised by devotees of the nature religions as possessing numinous qualities. They are those places where, by meditation, prayer, ritual and ceremony, one may attain inner spiritual harmony.

One must be conscious of this when attempting to understand the significance of places like sacred springs, stone circles, holy rocks and similar places of power. The qualities of such places can be only partly understood by intellectual analysis, for it is only by means of a holistic vision of the universal continuum that the many qualities of a place of power may be comprehended. These qualities do not lend themselves to intellectual or scientific explanation, for an understanding of them comes only from a liaison between the analytical and intuitive faculties of the whole human organism. Investigation of places of power on the Earth must be approached from an holistic angle. The linear, analytical approach that underlies scientific thought and hence modern technological civilisation is inadequate to describe the qualities present at such a place.

Leaving aside the actual nature of the energies or qualities present at these locations, many geomantic researchers have recognised particular elements in the landscape which combine to create special or sacred places. These are:

1. Sources of Önd within the landscape, including streams, springs and waterfalls; the coastline, especially rocky shores; windy hilltops; and rocky areas which are electrically- or radio-active, such as quartz bearing rocks. Underground water in streams and deeper structures, such as fault lines and areas of tectonic activity.

2. A complex landscape with great variety: small valleys and hills, and serpentine watercourses, where all aspects are in balance, neither flowing away or dissipating too rapidly, nor accumulating in stagnation.

3. Woodlands, and small groves of trees, especially hilltop tree clumps with a variety of types of tree and where there is some space between the trees.

4. Astronomically-important points where the phenomena of the yearly cycles of sun and moon are particularly apparent. When these viewpoints are at locations which have other qualities, the overall site is enhanced.

A combination of the above features, such as a tree over a stone, or a waterfall in a geologically active zone. These factors and combinations, whilst real, are only consciously recognised and appreciated by human beings. Popular natural places for tourists, which many people visit for 'recreational' purposes, that is, as places where they can escape from and forget the environment and pressures of everyday living, are places which have some character which promotes this end. Usually, they are those places where some approximation to natural conditions is still present: the seaside, the last place most people can encounter primal nature in the form of the sea, is perennially popular; lakes, rivers and waterfalls, high points, especially with good, distant views of the countryside around; rocky promontories and outcrops; spectacular changes in the landscape or unique geological features such as the Giant's Causeway in Northern Ireland or the Cheddar Gorge in western England; grassed slopes with occasional trees and bushes, woodland and spectacular tall trees are all examples of this.

The 'landscape architects' of the past who created 'parkland' recognised these features and incorporated them into wholly artificial landscapes. How well these work depends upon one's viewpoint, and personal preferences play a large part in our experience of artificial landscape. But underlying personal preferences are the deeper layers of subconscious perception, which may be completely at odds with our conscious experience of the place. Where these conflict, unease and uncertainty enter, and the artistry of the landscape engineer is negated. When a theoretically beautiful piece of landscape gardening generates harmful energies, then it is our unconscious detection of these energies that will condition our feelings, not our delight at a place pleasing to the eye or fitting the fashion of the day.

If we visit various places and types of landscape, and record our feelings and experiences, we can build up an understanding of how we relate to landscape as individuals. Once we know something about these feelings, we can begin to understand why we feel good or bad in certain places, and what we can do about it. We can look at our own surroundings with a new perspective, and change those things which are causing disharmony. By examining traditional methods, we can see how our ancestors dealt with these matters, gaining knowledge which can be applied in our own lives.

Coming-into-being, Sanctification and Later Effects

"The holy places of the Gods are open to the righteous, nor have they any need of lustration; no defilement touches virtue. But thou who art evil at heart, depart; for never by sprinkling thy body shalt thou cleanse thy soul" - An Oracle of the Pythia of Delphi.

The nature of sanctification and desacralisation in the world can be described well in terms of the Northern Tradition model. This sees existence in terms of subtle elements which embody natural qualities, but which can also be affected by external actions. Naturally, everything that humans describe are explained in human terms. These descriptions are interpretations of reality according to the structure and function of human consciousness. We should always bear in mind, that, whilst the descriptions fit very well into the perceived reality, we should never take them literally. Once they are taken literalistically, these perceptions degenerate into spectacle. But, as Alfred Adler warned: *"What makes madness is literalism"*. The world's fundamentalisms - and their results - richly attest to the correctness of his assertion. *"For hard are the Gods to him who sees them manifestly"* - Homer.

The Northern Tradition views the world symbolically, as attested by the old Norse poets' predilection for kennings and allusions. Accordingly, the Nordic 'creation' myth describes symbolically the processes of coming into being. Once the formless power of the cosmos had produced order out of chaos, it tells how the Elves were called upon to facilitate the evolution of the material world. Thus, their activities are essential for the Earth's well-being, and if they are interfered with, then serious problems will result. Woe betide us if we drive them out, knowingly or unknowingly, for then the land becomes alfreka, desecrated and barren, order and plenty cease, and are replaced by chaos and destruction.

The Younger Edda narrates the accounts of how these beings or archetypal qualities created all of the instruments, tools and weapons that the gods and goddesses needed for their functions. They made Frey's gold-bristled boar, Gullinbursti, upon which he rides, also the sacred gold ring, Draupnir, from which, every ninth night drops eight new rings of the same weight; they crafted Mjöllnir, the hammer of Thor, and created Brisingamen, the amber necklace of Freyja. Symbolically, these artifacts represent aspects of divine power acting through their corresponding physical manifestations. It should be noted that all of the Elven artifacts have names - they are individually ensouled. But if and when these functions are reduced to no more than the impersonal, material level, as they have been by the modern industrial culture, then the craft of the Earth is eliminated, and they, too become alfreka, nameless, soulless tools of a dehumanised, mechanical world.

The Elves are a symbolic means of describing the Anima Loci, those pluralistic qualities which may be experienced at any place by any person who has not cut off her- or himself from the cosmos. In countless ways the Anima Loci has manifested throughout history: apparitions, revelations, alterations in consciousness, inspiration and genius, even divine madness has resulted. At such a places, the human psyche, interacting with the subtle qualities experienced as the Anima Loci, brings forth revealment, a mystic event which renders surrounding events intelligible. The soul's essence is disclosed: all things display their innate nature: they shine forth with undiminished clarity. Places where the Anima Loci has manifested directly have always been marked and honoured. Around the year 253 AUC (500 BCE), Princess Hagelochia of Sparta erected an image of Artemis, with the following inscription:

> *"This Artemis in the cross-ways did Hagelochia*
> *the daughter of Damaretus erect*
> *while still a virgin in her father's house;*
> *for the goddess herself appeared to her,*
> *by the weft of her loom, like a flame of fire".*

Artemis's appearance to Hagelochia is a classical instance of a spontaneous manifestation of the Anima Loci. Many holy places have gained human recognition through such epiphanies. Thereby, truth to the Anima Loci is truth to the nature of the place. But the Anima Loci is also quite fragile. She can be dislocated in many ways, on both the subtle and physical levels. These dislocations take a number of forms, all of which, unfortunately, are common to contemporary civilisation. Even on a spiritual level, there are religions which pointedly deny the Anima Loci. Their doctrines deny explicitly any validity to the Anima Loci as a manifestation of Mother Earth, or the Anima Loci as a manifestation of the female force. Their spiritual practices are one-sided, and, if applied at a place, succeed in suppressing the Anima Loci there. If unchecked, such religious practices lead inevitably to the next level of dislocation, which is materialism. Materialism is often raised to the status of a faith, and, not without reason. In symbolic terms, this materialistic destruction of the world is represented by the being of Mammon, who, according to John Milton in *Paradise Lost* was cast out of Heaven along with Satan. Mammon is the personification of selfish greed, for

> *"By him first*
> *Men also, and by his suggestion taught,*
> *Ransack'd the centre, and with impious hands*
> *Rifled the bowels of their mother earth*
> *For treasures better hid. Soon had his crew*
> *Open'd into the hill a spacious wound,*
> *And diggèd out ribs of gold. Let none admire*
> *That riches grow in Hell; that soil may best*
> *Deserve the precious bane."*

The materialist view of the world implicitly states that nothing is holy or sacred - the only significant factor about anything is its price. To knowing and unknowing devotees of Mammon alike, holy shrines and sacred places have no intrinsic value. They are worth only what money they raise when they are put up for sale to the highest bidder. Heritage organisations, set up to guard these places for the commonweal, have betrayed the trust of those in whose name they act. Holy or sacred places entrusted to them in perpetuity are put up for sale, perhaps to be destroyed by their new owners. The traditional collective trusteeship of holy places, once universal, has been appropriated by state organisations - and now that the state is abdicating its trusteeship, these places of spiritual peace and harmony are being sold to private owners in the same way that the common lands were 'enclosed' by private landowners at the beginning of the industrial revolution. Even if a few if them come into the ownership of 'trusts' set up specifically to look after them, the local, collective, links are no longer in existence.

There is also ever-present risk that outsiders will press their own on-lays on such holy places. However well-meaning, the new 'trusts' are just another kind of owner, part of the syndrome that enslaves Mother Earth into Real Estate. Whatever happens, these sacred places are being rendered alfreka. The Anima Loci is driven down, never to return.

The myth that the present is inferior to the past, that we are human dwarves standing on the shoulders of giants, is a potent syndrome. It diminishes the vibrant, living, present to a pale shadow of a golden age. It belittles anything done now as worthless in comparison with the past. In geomancy, this worship of ancient places which are already alfreka diverts attention and energy from the living, spontaneous, manifestations of the contemporary Anima. This myth serves only to fuel the 'heritage industry', and the fixed myths of spectacle, which grade rapidly into varieties of fundamentalism. This myth derives from the orthodoxy that worships literally some pseudo-historic event in the past as possessed of primary importance to all time.

Whether it be the writing of a religious text, the birth of a prophet, the planting of a flag, the painting of a picture, or the erection of a building, this event is made into a spectacle which denies any change of perspective. It is presented as fundamental, and fundamentalists are charged with its preservation, literalistically, unchanging, throughout time. In the pursuance of this cause, they deny the ever-changing flux of existence, and fight in vain against Nature. This narrow, sectarian, view serves only to promote the doctrines of a rigid, orthodoxy that has long since lost its spontaneity and degenerated into empty spectacle. Unlinked with the flows of Manred and the spirit of the Anima Loci, its protagonists are unaware of the spirit that is present *now*.

Manred, the Middle Ground and Self-Similarity in the Cosmic Order

"Form arises out of the mystic abyss" - Hans Poelzig

The word Manred comes from the ancient Bardic teachings of Britain. It refers to the underlying matrix of matter, the atoms, molecules and geometrical relationships that compose physical reality. Ancient Celtic art displays the ever-changing patterns of Manred. The geometric matrices upon which Celtic tesselations, spirals and knotwork are based are continuous. In their plurality, tesselations, spirals and knotwork are interchangeable. They fade into one another. These patterns are fixed artistic representations of the ever-flowing particles of Manred, for all is flux, and the patterns we see at any one time are the patterns of that time, not eternal and unchanging.

In modernism, the middle ground is ignored. This wilful denial of Nature was actually promoted for the larger part of the twentieth century as 'the only way'. Its seeds were sown before the First World War, in 1908, when Adolf Loos published his notorious work that linked ornament with crime. This led directly to the doctrinal basis of the modern movement in architecture, in which the middle ground, traditionally the most accessible place of spirit, is a blank, barren, sterile void. In the early part of this century, the oppressive walls of concrete, known everywhere to our cost, were promoted by the fanatics of Futurism, whose anti-Nature polemics were the roots of totalitarianism in all its manifestations.

As the opposing armies in the Great War blew each other apart in the battle for no-man's land, another battle was waged in Holland, a country fortunate enough not to be involved in the collective frenzy. This was the spiritual and political battle for the middle ground between the ensouled artists and architects of Amsterdam and the sterile Loos-followers in Rotterdam. The Amsterdam school was pluralistic, based upon a recognition of the middle ground. In Rotterdam, exponents of the mechanistic straight line of De Stijl (THE Style - promoted as the only style permissible) vilified the architects of the Amsterdam school without understanding what they were trying to do. Such was the lack of awareness of spiritual and even physical ecology of some De Stijl extremists that the painter Piet Mondriaan could look forward seriously to the day when plants would be abolished. History teaches us that such single-minded fanaticism has always led to misery and destruction.

The pluralistic, multicultural tolerance of Amsterdam, incorporating elements of indigenous Dutch and Frisian folk-tradition, Balinese Hinduism, Jewish and Surinamese mysticism could never promote such a fanatical, narrow, view of existence. Unfortunately, the Rotterdam school was triumphant, and, with International School architects in other lands, attempted to sweep away the middle ground throughout the world. In the view of modernism, nothing is ensouled. The Anima Loci is denied, and means sought to render everywhere alfreka. That the self-styled International School has been very successful at this is all too apparent.

The principle of self-similarity at different scales, but precisely related, was re-established by the Benoit Mandelbrot's brilliant discovery of fractal mathematics in 1980. Self-similarity means that structure is repeated at different levels. There is no void. Structure is present at every point, reflecting at once both the structure on a smaller and a larger scale. All is an integrated, inseparable part of the whole. Self-similarity is integral at every level, manifesting as repeating patterns from the smallest to the largest. Microcosm is linked to macrocosm, not by crude reflection, but by ordered repetition through the middle ground. There is no place for a void middle ground in Nature. There are no blank spaces. Every part of the cosmos is ensouled. The Anima Loci is honoured.

Underlying everything in existence are the so-called 'laws' of Nature, that are actually the ways that natural processes occur: the process of trans-volution, the underlying structures and causes. Often, scientists and priests assert that their hypotheses are actually eternal and immutable 'laws', rather than speculations based on tradition, observation and deduction. Regarding these views as 'laws' leads to conflict between protagonists of differing hypotheses who regard other suggestions to be in opposition to their own views. Suspending consciousness, they promote their own views as objective truth, whilst disparaging the others as erroneous. This dualistic attitude tends to elevate hypothesis to dogma, thence to orthodoxy, which is hypothesis transformed to spectacle. Then this position is defended with violence. It may even go on the offensive. But all of this is unnecessary. The orthodox fail to recognise that essentially all knowledge is incomplete, that the cosmos is pluralistic, and that all things have a built-in failure rate. These 'laws of Nature' are best viewed as hypotheses that enable us to deal with the phenomena in limited and circumscribed circumstances: essentially, they are in continuous flux, acting pluralistically on many levels simultaneously throughout the cosmos.

Literally, the Greek word *Cosmos* means the right placing of the multiple things of the world according to their proper order. It is the aesthetic, polyvalent, polytheistic arrangement of the things of existence. The right orderliness of things, so that all things work in harmony - the divine harmony. One of the maxims of Freemasonry, *Ordo Ab Chao* (order out of chaos), expresses the understanding that the cosmos is a self-ordering system, which, in a state of balance, has produced life and consciousness. The spiritual conception of Cosmos is far more than the narrow, reductionist view of 'Universe', Unus-versus, everything circling around one point, or, by reduction 'turned into one'. The actual concept of 'Universe' denies the plurality of existence. 'Universe' is dualistic, presented as being in opposition to Chaos, which is perceived as disorder, displacement and derangement. But, as recent developments in Chaos Mathematics have shown, order arises out of chaos - *Ordo ab Chao* - not through some mysterious opposition to it. Pluralism is the essence of the world, and manifestations of the Anima Loci within it.

Stones in the Landscape

Modern attitudes to the landscape are the result of an historical process which can be understood by looking at the rediscovery of standing stones. On 7 January 1648, during a foxhunt, the antiquary John Aubrey (1626-97) rode through 'the Country about Marlborough' where he noticed that '*These Downes looke as if they were Sown with great Stones, very thicke.*' His ride took him through the Village of Aubury, into the Closes there: "*where I was wonderfully surprised at the Sight of those vast Stones, of which I had not heard before; as also at the mighty Banke and Graffe about it . . . This Old Monument does as much exceed in Greatness the so renowned Stoneheng, as a Cathedral doeth a Parish Church: so that by its Grandure One might presume it to have been an Arch-Temple of the Druids*".

As this quote shows, Aubrey's time was an age when learned people started to take an interest in the ancient relics then common in the landscape. Of course, to local inhabitants, the great standing stones were part of their everyday world, objects of reverence, fear, or even just a nuisance to agriculture. Local lore and legend told of the supernatural origin and properties of each stone, but little else was known about them. The new antiquaries, however, sought verifiable information and, when this was not forthcoming from the locals, put forward their own theories to account for these enigmatic relics of a bygone age. Of all the ancient megalithic remains of

Europe, the most investigated is Stonehenge which, since the time of Geoffrey of Monmouth in the thirteenth century, has been identified with the legends of King Arthur and his knights. It was said that the wizard Merlin had transported the stone circle from Ireland magically, 'not by Force, but by Merlin's Art', to commemorate a massacre of British noblemen by the Saxons. But no one was interested enough to bother to investigate the site. Even when it was mentioned, its characteristics were vague for example, the earliest known illustration of Stonehenge shows it as rectangular! Shortly after his accession to the English throne in 1601, King James I visited Stonehenge and afterwards instructed his architect, Inigo Jones, to investigate the origin of the structure. Jones did so, although his results were not published until 1655, some years after his death. The volume, entitled *The Most Notable Antiquity of Great Britain, Vulgarly Called Stone-Heng, Restored,* mistakenly described the monument as a Roman temple of the sky-god Coelus. Educated architects of the seventeenth century could not imagine that the ancient Britons, those rude savages described in the works of Julius Caesar, could have built such a sophisticated structure as Stonehenge. Nevertheless, the book drew attention to Stonehenge and megaliths in general, and all later research, even to the present day, can be traced back to this era.

Many antiquarian researchers investigated the relationship between the layout and location of standing stones and celestial phenomena. Once investigation began, even the earliest antiquaries had some idea that there was a celestial connection, information which may have been derived from the oral tradition of local residents. Although, since time immemorial, local people had gathered at Stonehenge to view the rising sun at midsummer, it was not until 1740 that anybody wrote about it. In that year, William Stukeley recorded that the axis of Stonehenge along the earthwork known as The Avenue points towards the quarter of the sky *'where abouts the sun rises when the days are longest'*. He added that this was in keeping with classical techniques of orientation found in Roman temples. Because of his great learning, Stukeley was able to draw parallels with classical tradition in his book, *Stonehenge, a Temple Restored to the British Druids.* In this, he became one of the first writers since classical times to note the relationship of an ancient monument to the landscape, remarking that The Avenue is aligned towards an ancient earthwork on the brow of Haradon Hill. The astronomical element in the ancient landscape was recognised as significant by these early researchers and, ever since, it has been an important dimension to the study of ancient standing stones.

From the eighteenth century, the recovery of the lost knowledge preserved in the stones' location and layout has played an important role in the British Mystery Tradition. The mystical architect, John Wood the Elder of Bath, was one of the students of the works of the Stone Age skywatchers who altered the landscape in accordance with their findings. Wood believed that the ancient Druids had built Stonehenge and the other megalithic monuments, and placed them in symbolic relation to one another. He used the astronomical truths he discerned in their geometry and numerology in his designs for the development of the city of Bath, altering the face of the country in accordance with mystic principles. Although some of the more complex calculations and numerological contortions ascribed to Stonehenge by eighteenth-century mystics may be fanciful, the basic observations of celestial phenomena are not. The eighteenth century antiquaries who, of necessity, walked the countryside with a direct experience impossible since the Industrial Revolution, took direct observations of sun, moon and stars at the sites themselves. They did not rely upon tables and maps, for none was accurate enough, if they existed at all. The antiquaries' intimacy with the landscape can be gauged by reading any of their works. For example, in his book Stonehenge, published in 1796, the antiquary H. Wansey wrote:

"Stonehenge stands in the best situation possible for observing the heavenly bodies, as there is an horizon nearly three miles distant on all sides; and on either distant hill, trees might have been planted as to have measured any number of degrees in a circle, so as to calculate the right ascension or delineation of a star or planet".

It is possible that, in 1796, the direct observation of the sun-over-horizon markers was still being carried out as a means of time-telling by people in remote districts of England, and that Wansey had knowledge of this. Unfortunately, any local knowledge of the time-telling functions of standing stones was lost with the arrival of cheap clocks and 'railway time' in the Industrial Revolution. Since then, many people have investigated the standing stones of northern Europe, observing and calculating their arrangement with regard to celestial phenomena. Among the many eminent people who have devoted their time to this study, we may note Sir Joseph Norman Lockyer, Gerald Hawkins and Professor Alexander Thom. Lockyer, founder of the scientific journal *Nature* and discoverer of helium, studied the temples of Egypt and the stone circles of Britain to deter mine their astronomical features.

In northern Holland are impressive megalithic structures called Hunnebed (Hun's Beds), which attract the attentions of local dowsers.

In 1906, Lockyer published his major work, entitled *Stonehenge and Other British Stone Monuments Astronomically Considered*, in which he claimed that the megalithic remains had been laid out to mark sunrise or sunset at the times of the equinoxes and solstices, as well as the 'cross-quarter-days' of May Day, Lammas, All Hallows' and Candlemas. In a later edition, Lockyer gave further information on how outlying sites in the surrounding country side had astronomical relationships with the main sites. Subsequent to Lockyer, many others followed his example and surveyed megalithic sites for astronomical phenomena but, in 1965, Gerald Hawkins published his book, *Stonehenge Decoded*. This was the first computer-aided study of Stonehenge and showed that the arrangement of the stones had enabled the ancients to view celestial phenomena and to predict eclipses, among other things.

This book, which attracted vigorous opposition and equally vigorous defenders, spurred further study of the enigmatic stones. Of these, the most notable was that of Professor Alexander Thom. Thom's meticulous surveys, analysed statistically according to the best mathematical models available, showed that many of the stone circles he surveyed were masterly examples of accurate geolocation. Their geometry and orientation, determined by astronomical factors, were located at appropriate sites in the landscape where natural features, interacting with the stones, would make the entire area a vast observatory. Thom showed that stone observatories were located at places where lines towards sun and moon rise and set, at important times like midsummer, crossed one another. The local alignments, slopes, hills and mountain peaks were incorporated into the geometry of the stone circle itself, an intrinsic reflection of the entire landscape therefore, the epitome of earth harmony.

The skills required to locate such a place are considerable and Thom's discovery, therefore, has implications which range far beyond the realm of stone circles. The location of important places should be seen in terms of the whole country side, an overview unfortunately lacking in many archaeo-logical analyses of ancient sites. The scientific analysis that Thom made of stone circles was undertaken in a specialised area which was amenable to such statistical methods, and produced startling results. These methods are applicable to orientated structures like churches and even ancient, regularly planned towns, but they are not available to us when we look at less well-defined classes of site. A more intuitive approach must be used with the landscape as a whole.

Chapter 6
Looking at Landscapes

To work out the character of a site in the country, or an individual building in a small village in direct connection with the landscape, we need to examine several aspects of the area. These are examined with relation to the site in question, their character and direction, and also with regard to the directions of the world.

In a landscape, the most immediately important features are the hills or mountains, which with the watercourses, give the land its form. These mountain ridges or hills, looked on more poetically as "the bones of the Earth" in the Northern European Tradition affect the local area for considerable distances. Since the remotest antiquity, the sacred qualities of certain hills, peaks and passes have been recognised, and even today, deities or saints are honoured there. The attributes and character of these beings give us an indication of the nature of the forces present there, or which are channelled through those hills. Traditional Earth Harmony in the northern hemisphere has seen the most favoured site as one which has the highest mountains or hills to the north, shielding the place from the cold northern winds as well as benefiting from the general tendency of subtle forces to flow from north to south.

Basic geomantic perceptions of hill ridges tell that good places occur largely at the end-points of ridges, especially at confluences of watercourses. It is thought best if the landforms surrounding beneficial places should be like a curving wall that embraces the location. But most places are not ideal, and it is necessary to balance the various characteristics of the landscape. The form, direction of flow, capacity, speed and quality of watercourses have a fundamental effect upon the character of a site. Apart from the utilitarian considerations of water supply, ground quality and flooding, the physical shape of watercourses can determine whether a place is good or bad for habitation. Sites considered good for habitation can be shown by dowsers to be located at places of beneficial energy, and the numerous folk traditions concerning the relationship between health, illness, magic and running water demonstrate a practical knowledge of these matters in former times.

The juxtaposition of watercourses with hills and mountains is fundamental to the physical structure of the land itself. To harmonise these, there are specific remedies, which were used widely in former times in Europe. Geophysically, watercourses and hill ridges are two sides of the same phenomenon. Places where they interact are regarded as favourable. When mountain and watercourse come together, positive and negative elements are joined, and a certain quality of Anima Loci is apparent. When the hill-ridge curves to the left, then if the place is to be harmonious, the watercourse should curve to the right, and vice versa. When the two forms embrace one another, then there is balance, which is favourable for human activity. Any water that surrounds a place gives it a defensive quality, both physically and spiritually. Strategically, a river bend or a moat around a place prevents intruders from getting in easily, whilst on the more subtle planes, it has the magical effect of preventing the entry of evil spirits, entities and harmful forces into the location.

In traditional European landscapes, the dwelling-places of wise women, cunning men, priests, wizards and alchemists, those people whose lives interact with the world of the supernatural, often possess special qualities. Many are surrounded by water, which has a twofold function of preventing the entry of harmful people and spirits, and of keeping in the spiritual power generated by the magical practitioners themselves. It is common folk-knowledge in Britain that evil spirits or the Devil cannot cross water, and it appears that people believed that magical powers were contained or enhanced by enclosure by water. This tradition was carried on until well into this century in country areas of Britain. The dwelling of Old Mother Redcap, a famous nineteenth century witch, was the only house on Wallasea Island, off the Essex coast, and the famous Daddy Witch (who was a woman) of Horseheath, Cambridgeshire, lived in a house inside a water-filled moat known as Daddy Witch's Pond. The medieval Bishop's Palace at Wells in Somerset is similarly enclosed by water.

Certainly, enclosure by water is a common feature of medieval house sites in the former forested areas of England and Wales. Most of the moats are around twenty to thirty feet in width, with no internal earth banks, the interiors being at the same level as the surrounding land. Livestock was kept in adjacent yards, which makes it clear that they were not for animal containment or exclusion. Of course, the size and structure of these moats is inadequate for protection against marauders, so it is likely that their function was primarily for magical protection.These protective moats have been classified into three categories: Level Moats; Perched Moats, and Valley Moats. Level Moats are moats dug in level ground, generally permanently wet ground filling the ditches by seepage. Perched Moats occupy valley sides, and are filled with water from leats linked to nearby rivers or streams. A series of four connected perched moats exists still at Bottisham, Cambridgeshire. Here, the moats are arranged on the side of a shallow valley in a line 50 - 100 yards apart, and with the original complex of watercourses connecting them to an adjacent stream. Valley Moats are at the bottom of the valley, and either on old stream lines, or linked to streams by leats. At Caxton in Cambridgeshire, a moat was built using the bed of a stream as one side, and at Orwell, the river forms one side of the watery enclosure.

Traditional European water-management techniques were extremely sophisticated. Most moats were fed by water pounded up behind a dam across an existing or diverted stream, and a system of sluices was required to keep the levels correct. Conduits and ditches conducted the water to wherever it was needed, altering the geomantic character of the houses' sites. Many of these feature exist today in the landscape, and studying them has revealed the high level of sophistication that the locators possessed in former times.The overall form of the landscape, its watercourses, slope, depressions and eminences, determines the accumulation or dispersal of the energies discussed above, and hence the character of a locus. Depressions in the ground tend to collect cold air, certain electrostatic charges and other energies, and their character is such that, if unfavourably placed, these will have a detrimental effect upon people there. A site which is exposed suffers from the cold winds, is more prone to lightning strikes, and loses energy rapidly, especially if water is flowing away from it. According to traditional perceptions, the depression is harmful through positive imbalance, whilst the high point suffers negative imbalance.

To find out what is going on in the landscape now, we must look at the reasons why it is like it is. This means looking at its history, especially in relation to the ancient sites within the landscape. These places range from places of natural origin used in ancient times for human purposes, to artifacts of antiquity. These are the places of power which give the landscape its human point of reference. A very important aspect of reading the landscape is the location of what are called places of power, with attention to their specific character and orientation. These so-called places of power range from sanctified natural features to fully-developed sacred

This allegorical illustration of The Rose Garden shows the shapes of hills ascribed to the planetary powers in the European tradition.

complexes like temples and abbeys. The types of site are familiar in every landscape which once was sacred: holy hills; former sacred woods and groves; isolated sacred trees; holy wells; ancient mounds and earthworks; dolmens and menhirs; labyrinths; wayside shrines; temples; crosses; calvaries; chapels and chantries. The major features like castles, churches, monasteries and cathedrals have a much larger effect, as do the major holy hills like Croagh Patrick, Glastonbury Tor and Mont-Saint-Michel. These places of power were recognised in the past, appropriately sanctified by the prevailing religion of the day, and, in many cases, maintained in an active spiritual condition to this day.

The various general shapes of hills and mountains have certain qualities which are associated with gods and goddesses, demons, saints and heroes. The shapes of mountains and hills are the result of their geology and history, but the effect they have upon humans and in the transhuman realm is well understood by Earth Harmony. There is a general rule-of-thumb one can use to describe these qualities, classifying hills and mountains by shape. The basic form of a hill is either rounded, pointed, flattened or irregular. Rounded-top hills are assigned to the female principle, the planet Venus and the element water. They are especially powerful when associated with a medicinal spring. Goddesses worshipped at such places include Cerridwen, Erda, Frigg, Hlin and Our Lady. Pointed hills are assigned to the male principle, the planet Mars, and the element fire. Allied to these are hills with a round head and a long body which are assigned to the male principle, the planet Jupiter, fire and metal. In Europe, these are the powerful hills of the sky-god Zeus, Jupiter, Taranis, Daronwy, Perkunas and Thor. These are hills of strategic defence, and many a hill-fort or castle remains on top of such sites, whose innate power was channelled by the martial arts of the warriors who garrisoned the hills. Mountains of the Sun have a ridge or ridges just below the summit. In the Christian interpretation, they are dedicated to St Michael, who is the body of the Sun. Square headed hills are assigned to the planet Saturn and the Fates. Irregular hills are assigned to the hermaphroditic planet Mercury, being alive, crooked and moving, the dragon form. These are the hills of Woden, on parts of which executions took place. Such minor promontories on larger hilly areas are often called Gallows Hill, Galley Hill, or, in Scandinavia and German-speaking lands, Galgenberg.

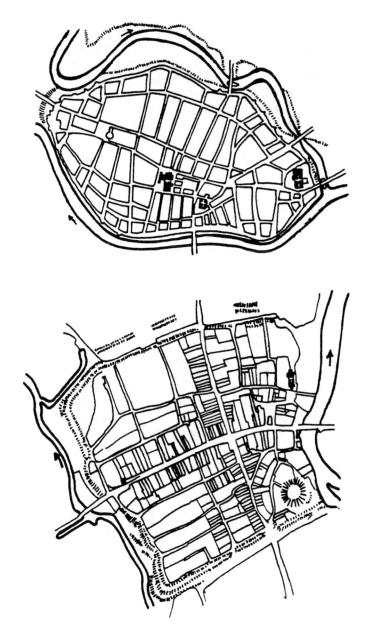

Rivers in European geomancy; (left) Wareham, England; (right), Lübeck, Germany.

The local folklore and traditions of places are their memory, living in the people who inhabit the land. These geomythic accounts are of two kinds: legendary stories about places and actual observances and observations. Legendary tales of dragons, spirits, giants, witches and ghosts tell of places of power where the events which occurred there are lost in the mists of history. Observances and observations include traditional ceremonies conducted annually at a site as well as the visions, apparitions, fireballs and phantom beings that have appeared and continue to manifest at such places. By investigating, cataloguing and analysing these phenomena, we can find out the character of the site we are dealing with, and gain a deeper understanding of the nature of the landscape we are investigating.

These places of power have certain relationships with one another, which often appear to make landscape patterns of various kinds. Landscape patterns can take many forms: the best known are leys or ley lines that people draw between certain classes of ancient sites. Other, more complex, forms have been discerned, forming a kind of 'landscape geometry' which some take into account when practising geomancy. In former times, landmarks visible on the horizon were taken into account when determining the character of any place. The augurs of ancient Europe were aware of the critical importance of these features, not only for the practical aspect of time-telling by the sun, but also because of the necessity to harmonise the structure with the subtle character expressed by these features. In ancient northern Europe, natural or, if absolutely necessary, artificial features on the horizon marked the passage of the sun. Each *Dagsmark* or *Eyktmark,* however far away, thus related to the structure and orientation of the house from which it was viewed. The actual 'house stone', usually the doorstep outside the south-facing door, was the place upon which the householder stood to view the position and elevation of the sun. This natural integration of human habitation with the qualities inherent in the landscape and the heavens is the goal of Earth Harmony. It is no less than the creation of balance and reunion with the cosmic whole. Thus, in the European tradition of location, the attributes of the eight winds or directions gave the locator a good idea of which beneficial or harmful influences could be expected at any place, and what precautions ought to be taken against them, should they prove unfavourable.

Skill in the art of location was essential in former times for the design of successful fortifications, which required a considerable understanding of the landscape. Many sacred places are also strategically important, and the

72

fortified monastery or temple complex is a well known structure in many countries. In western Europe, the great Celtic hillfort complexes are masterful examples of the ancients' skill in location and design. Constructed on high points, where the occupants could see approaching danger with time to prepare against it, hillforts made use of the natural features of the terrain to place any would-be assailant at an immediate disadvantage. Although they are called 'hillforts', excavations at major sites have shown that some at least had permanent settlements built within them.

The hilltops were defended by ditches, inside which the earth was built up to form ramparts. Entrances to the hillforts were by gaps in the rampart: sometimes no ditch was dug at the entrance point, but in others a bridge of sorts was necessary to cross the ditch at the entrance. In several important hill forts like Hod Hill, Danebury and Maiden Castle, the entrances were made complex by additional mounds which prevented direct access to the entrance. These complex entrances have been shown archaeologically to be later additions to the main earthwork, inserted when tactical techniques had advanced. Their design, however, is tailored to the contour of the hill.

Associated with hill forts and lookout points are the ancient beacon sites of Britain. Until the invention and deployment of the Admiralty shutter telegraph system in 1796, bonfires on hilltops were the only means of rapid signalling over distances. The origin of the British beacon system is lost, although it is known that the ancient Greeks signalled over distances using flaming torches at night. One of the earliest students of beacons, William Lambarde, wrote in 1570 that :"*Touching the Antiquity, and Name: it seemeth they came from the Saxons, for their Word Becnian, which is to call by Signe (or to becken, as we yet speake), they are named Beacons: and I find, that before the Time of King Edward the Third they were made of great Stacks of Wood..but about the XJ(11th) yeere of his Raigne it was ordeined that in our Shire (Kent) they should be high Standards with their Pitch-Pots*".

It is clear from their association with ancient earthworks, however, that beacons must be of greater antiquity than this. The beacon hills are high points which are intervisible with each other as well as having a good view of strategically important roads, passes, rivers, fords, bridges and ports. In times of war, each beacon was manned with lookouts. When an approaching enemy was sighted, the beacon was lit, and lookouts at the other beacons would fire up their material on seeing the first one lit. In this way, the

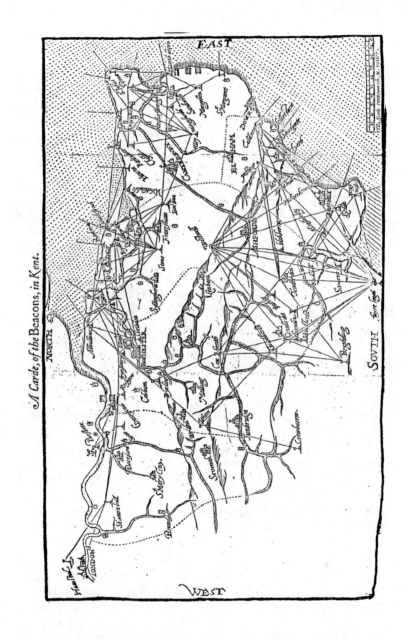

The Lambarde Map (1570), the first map to show the location of the hill-top beacons in Kent and the lines-of-sight between them.

beacons of the whole country would be fired up, and everyone in the land, military and civilian, were warned of impending attack. In peace time, the beacons served the alternative function of carrying the bonfires celebrating the fire festivals of May, Midsummer, Lammas and All Hallows. They are also lit to celebrate royal events like the 1977 Silver Jubilee of Her Royal Highness Queen Elizabeth II.

The location of hillforts and beacons was not a simple task. In the absence of contour-maps, it required an intimate knowledge of the landscape, and in the case of beacons, an appraisal of the relationship of one hill to another, perhaps ten miles away. Carried out in an age when maps were inaccurate, if they existed at all, the location of beacons was a remarkable feat of harmonising a human need with the natural landscape. In later times, many of these hills were used by the Admiralty telegraph systems, which depended upon the operation of mechanical shutters to communicate visually their message to the next station on the line. Even today, the towers of the microwave telecommunications network stand on ancient beacon hills, using the same lines of sight as their prehistoric forebears.

Integrated within all of these factors was the traditional life of the countryside, now largely disrupted by modern machine-life. This integrated vision is not lost, however, for it is preserved within the very fabric of the landscape, and the human constructions that relate to it. Study of the traditional house design in the locality where the modern practitioner lives is necessary to determine the practicalities of Earth Harmony as they were perceived in the past. The vernacular design of houses varies from locality to locality, but the general underlying principles can be rediscovered if one approaches them using the basic concepts. The relationship between the design and its surroundings, once understood, can be applied again today.

Chapter 7
The Name of the Land

"*Without a language, there is no country*" - Old Irish Proverb.

The traditional wisdom of the country innately recognises our relationship with subtle qualities that are present in the land. This is expressed in the relationship between each individual and the earth. Although it manifests its spiritual nature in different places by differing spiritual qualities, we can have a personal spiritual relationship to these qualities. Basically, this experience can be seen symbolically as our personal relationships to the goddess of the landscape, which is Mother Earth in whatever local forms she may take. This may be best described as the Anima Loci, the soul of a place. Like all expressions of the earth spirit, whilst it can only be partially described in words, yet it may be experienced by anyone anywhere. It is essentially personal and ineffable.

When one walks one's own land, one is an integral part of that landscape, and the sum of its total history - its örlog - is part of one's inner body knowledge. Consciousness of place, truly being present in space and time, is a prerequisite for practising Earth Harmony. Anyone who is part of his or her own land does not need a map. The names of places are known locally, without recourse to written or printed records, and walking is the primary form of understanding the subtle nature of the land. In the traditional landscape of Europe, each place has its own Anima Loci, each place possesses its own history, geomythic qualities and anecdotes. According to traditional principles, everything has a name. Thus, the whole body of the land is infused with names of deities, people, sprites, events, qualities and numinosity.

Maps replace body knowledge with an intellectual concept: they separate us from the living body reality of the Anima Loci. Being compiled and printed at some distance from the places they portray, maps contain the official view of the land, which may not concur with its reality. Names may be omitted, misinterpreted or deliberately altered. Official names are the result of a form of conquest, where someone from outside decides what the land's name should be. Official names bring psychic and then physical destruction. Those that use them will tend to drive out the Anima Loci, ultimately rendering the land alfreka - spiritually dead, as anyone who has walked in a hypermarket car park will have experienced. The unconquered land is alive. When we are participants rather than conquerors, we have a personal and collective cultural relationship to the landscape. Then, we are not separated from it, for we are part of the landscape. The reality is what we walk, see, touch, smell and experience. It is the solid, real version of what otherwise is no more than a phantasmal intellectual concept. Removing or changing names demythologises the landscape: no longer is its örlog remembered, or its character recognised. The spirit is driven out - it becomes gast, barren land.

It is an implicit tenet of the materialist belief-system that there can be no spiritual or even physical difference of note between places. This is part of the postmodern portable person hypothesis, that anyone (or anything) is the same wherever he, she or it is located. It is that denaturing of place which leads to the maxim "Nothing is Sacred". The impersonal nature of industry means that the local earth as provider is no longer honoured. Nobody knows precisely where anything comes from, nor who made it. It is delocalised and depersonalised, identified only by a trade name and perhaps a country. Nevertheless, each thing does come from somewhere. It has its own personal history (örlog), for it came into being, then was harvested, processed or made by someone, somehow, somewhere, and transported to where it is now.

In traditional societies, everything has its own name. Everything is animated. It is a subject, not an object. Nothing is impersonal. Every stick, cup, plate, ring, jewel, knife, sword, hammer, drill, hat, shield, door, house, tree, gate, field, rock, stream, sand dune, wind and time of day had its own personal name, reflecting the character of its animated nature and its personal relationship to people. In turn, each name had a personal quality both to the thing itself and to those who lived with and related to it. With the rise of manufacturing industry, most artifacts became anonymous products. Their essential character reflected no longer the character of its maker, use and user. Instead, trade became the main consideration. The spiritual life of materials, their nature and qualities, was subordinated to the profit motive, so that in present-day Europe, the formerly universal naming of the animated world survives only in truncated form in the names of private and public houses, hotels, Dutch windmills, ships and occasionally other personal possessions like cars, knives, guns and guitars.

Another factor in the process which has led to the de-naming of the land has been the rise of a centralised bureaucracy. Centralised control is official geomantic dislocation, where the local is denied for the convenience of the administration. All is ruled from an administrative centre which claims authority over a certain area of land. Then, instead of possessing an identity stemming from a specific locality with a specific character, each person, place and thing is described in terms of and as a part of a centralised nation. As with military occupations, national central authorities claim the exclusive power to name and define, and to punish those who will not or cannot conform. The official name takes over from the local one. It is defined on the official map, issued by the military authorities for the use of armies in time of war or rebellion. The British Ordnance Survey, for the use of government artillery officers, is the archetypal example of this process. The spectacle of the official state map of the country took over from the direct, local experience of land as its official, and therefore 'real' description. This removal of significant subjectivity reduces the landscape to spectacle, where it is described as an 'object', deanimated and commanding no respect.

When the land is de-named or re-named, the Anima Loci is denied. Its historical precedent can be seen in the imperialist adventures of the French Emperor, Napoleon Bonaparte. When Napoleon's armies occupied the cities of central Europe, every building there, known to local people by name, was given a number. In this way, the occupying soldiers could locate anywhere (and anyone) easily, even when they could not speak the local language. The names known to local people, perfectly tailored to everyday life, were meaningless to foreign invaders. In this way, the Empire's imposed control could be absolute. Now every building in every city, town and village carries a number, as do we as individuals. Its location is defined in terms of numbers on both national maps and in the Global Positioning System. The personality of a house, expressed by its name - or a person - is denied by this numerical view of existence. It is reduced to an object, defined only in terms of its relationship, spatial or otherwise, to other objects classified similarly. Thus, its character is no longer recognised - it has been reduced to the domain of measurement and documentation.

Trackways

It is generally recognised that the first step in the modification of a virgin landscape is by the creation of trackways. Although they may be superseded at a later date by surveyed metalled roads and railways, these early lines of communication are the most harmoniously integrated with the landscape.

Generally, such ancient trackways were trading routes. In Britain, from the Bronze Age, trade was an important part of life as evidenced by the many finds of artifacts made from materials absent in the locality of their discovery. Such objects as Irish bronze axes were brought in from outside by pedlars and traders who used the ancient upland trackways during the summer months. The ancient ridgeways that still connect early Iron Age hill-forts which, in reality, were towns, are the fundamental division of the landscape. In places, these tracks were the forerunners of later roads and, in other places, their existence was recognised by the Saxons who used them as boundaries when they laid out the parish system.

These ridgeways kept to the high ground and descended to the valleys only when there was no way round the valley head along the 'high way'. These highways link the ancient earthworks of the uplands in a harmonious symbiosis with the natural landscape. Many of the old trackways were lined by earth banks and hedges during the enclosures when the aristocracy took the common lands to form their own personal country estates. At most places it was not possible to enclose the 'king's highway' so boundaries were made to prevent animals and people encroaching upon the new estates. Where new landowners did enclose the ancient trackway they were compelled to construct new diversionary routes around the new enclosure, leaving the road continuous, for these green roads were the drovers' roads along which livestock were taken, at the appropriate time of year, to the hilltop fairs to be sold, or to slaughter.

From the seventeenth century onwards, new turnpike roads provided more direct and better paved routes. Some of the stagecoach routes remained along the old green roads, however, but, with the advent of powered transport, first the railways and then motor vehicles, they have fallen into disuse. Instead of being driven to market along the green roads, cattle and sheep were transported to the new abattoirs in the cities by rail transport which gave way, later, to road haulage. The tracks remain, fortunately impassable to all but the most rugged motor vehicles, harmonising with the contours and watercourses of the landscape as did the first trackways thousands of years ago. Even the names of the old tracks remain with us: the Great Ridgeway, the Harrow Way, the Icknield Way, Saxon Way, Lunway, Herepath and Ox Drove. To walk the unspoiled sections of these archaic tracks is to reconnect with the spirit and feeling of those people who, so long ago, pioneered them across the uninhabited downlands.

Every piece of country also has its boundaries. These are the natural divisions of the landscape and hindrances to the free passage of humans. They include rivers, lakes, swamp, rocky land, mountainous terrain and forest. In addition to natural boundaries, artificial ones exist in every country which has, or has had, an organised agriculture demanding land measure and allocation of areas to individual farmers or villages. The very existence of any boundaries at all shows that some conscious effort has gone into laying them down, creating markers and systems of maintenance. These artificial boundaries often contain natural features, such as rivers, which form the borders between counties, provinces and even countries. Those laid down with local knowledge of a very intimate kind follow contours, allow for local hills, hollows, streams and small-scale landscape features including places of power. Those laid down from 'on high' by governments tend to be coarser, derived from maps and rectilinear grids.

Designed for ease of abstract mathematical calculation of areas and taxation, these gridded forms bear no relationship to the land and lead, in the worst cases, to a landscape of disharmony. The great imperial powers of ancient Egypt, the Roman Empire and the United States of America used grids across the landscape where they were not totally impracticable. The Roman system was based upon the Etruscan augury and, at least, the centres from which the surveys ran were related to earth-harmony principles. The Rectangular Survey of the United States, however, was carried out from utilitarian motives and produced the familiar landscape of straight roads running north-south and east-west for hundreds of miles without any regard for the terrain. In northern Europe, stone walls and hedges have been used extensively for local boundaries which, almost invariably, have incorporated sites of pagan sanctity. In parts of Britain, such as Cornwall, the word hedge refers to drystone walling, but here I shall use the southern English meaning of a boundary composed of woody shrubs and trees cut and laid to form a stock-proof boundary. In northern Europe (south of the Arctic zone), the high quality and productivity of pastureland has always permitted intensive grazing by domestic animals. In less productive areas, such as highland moor or tundra, animals must be allowed a large range and travel some distance each day to find food; this requires nomadic herdsmen and a different way of life from the enclosed pastoral life of more fertile areas.

Before the predations of mechanised farming wiped out hedgerows wholesale, leaving some areas completely devoid of them, the hedge was a characteristic feature of the landscape. Where animals could be kept in a small productive area of pasture, it was necessary to keep them from straying into arable land or into neighbouring parishes where they might disappear into cooking-pots. Boundaries incorporating ditches and banks seem to have been the earliest type of division, though it must be admitted that when a hedge has disappeared, for whatever reasons, the last trace of it is usually a bank. Some very ancient parish boundaries were double ditches with an earth bank between them on which thorny plants were grown to create an impenetrable barrier. These thorny plants had several functions: they were impenetrable to animals; the intrinsic magical properties of the plants functioned appropriately at the places they were planted; and they provided some firewood, timber and even fodder for livestock. Hedges were planted until the nineteenth century whenever new boundaries were made or common land enclosed. Some hedges existing today (many of which are under threat of destruction) date from before the enclosures of the Tudor period, perhaps as early as the thirteenth century. The trees and shrubs in hedges all possess characteristics far beyond the mere physical function of blocking access. In traditional societies, nothing is redundant. Each piece of land, each plant, each person and each time have their place and function in the overall scheme of things. The function of hedges fits this pattern. Hedge maintenance yielded wood for fire and staves during the annual trimming and laying. Each autumn, fruits such as hips, sloes and blackberries were harvested as a valuable supplement to the diet.

The Winds

Knowledge of the qualities of the landscape involves a know ledge of the forces acting in it and, of these, the wind is the most important. This is recognised fully in early writings. In Book I of his *Ten Books on Architecture*, the Roman architect Vitruvius recommended the traditional methods of dealing with the winds. '*Cold winds are disagreeable,*' he wrote, '*hot winds enervating, moist winds unhealthy.*' He recommended the orientation of town streets in certain directions so that the harmful winds would be excluded. Traditionally, the winds were associated with spirits or qualities, although their actual names varied from culture to culture, and the qualities according to local conditions. Confusingly, too, the winds were held to be synonymous with direction and the names interchange able with the compass points. But it is apparent that, to the ancients, they also indicated other, more subtle, qualities. '*By shutting out the winds*', Vitruvius continued, '*we shall not only make the place healthful for those who are well, but also in the case of diseases due, perhaps, to unfavourable situations elsewhere, the patients, who in other healthy places might be*

This Allegorical drawing includes the Old Quadrant, fundamental tool of the early medieval locators of Europe.

cured by a different treatment, will be more rapidly cured here by the mildness that comes from shutting out the winds.'

The knowledge of wind direction, then, was considered important over and above its connection with the weather. Weathercocks, wind vanes and church cocks are picturesque ornaments to many church towers and spires, yet few who see them realise that they have a function far beyond the decorative, for they are indicators of the direction of one of the most important forces which impinge on buildings and people - the wind. They have been in common use on churches and public buildings in Europe since at least the ninth century, but the earliest known reference to a weathercock is that on the tomb of Flavius at Cillium in north Africa. Long before that Andronicus of Cyrrhus had erected the Tower of the Winds at Athens. This octagonal tower bore on each of its sides a representation of the wind it faced and, on top, was a conical piece of marble bearing a bronze triton holding a rod in its right hand. This was an early weather vane, the rod pointing directly over the representation of the wind which was blowing at any time. With a knowledge of the direction of the wind, it was possible to carry out acts connected with that wind, or not to do things which were inappropriate. Folklore records a tradition that one's destiny depends upon the direction of the wind at one's birth: an ancient Irish poem, *'The Winds of Fate'*, recounts the qualities of life to be expected from the various winds:

> *The boy who is born when the wind is from the west,*
> *He shall obtain clothing, food he shall obtain;*
> *He shall obtain from his lord, I say,*
> *No more than food and clothing.*

> *The boy who is born when the wind is from the north,*
> *He shall win victory, but shall endure defeat.*
> *He shall be wounded, another shall he wound,*
> *Before he ascends to an angelic Heaven.*

> *The boy who is born when the wind is from the south,*
> *He shall get honey, fruit he shall get.*
> *In his house shall entertain*
> *Bishops and fine musicians.*

Laden with gold is the wind from the east,
The best wind of all four that blow;
The boy who is born when that wind blows
Want shall he never taste in his whole life.

Whenever the wind does not blow
Over the grass of the plain or mountain heather
Whosoever is then born,
Whether boy or girl, a fool shall be.

This is not the only ancient literature containing the attributes of the wind, but it is an example of the widespread belief, doubtless gained through observation over the years, that the direction of the wind had specific effects. A more practical example of this knowledge can be seen in the design, location and use of windmills. The location of anything which relates to natural sources of energy must be arranged to tap that energy in an optimal way, which necessarily means harmonising with the landscape. Although wind power is little used today, formerly in many places it was the only source of energy which did not come from the muscle power of humans or animals.

The classic windmill is a perfect example of earth harmony for, by its design, location and use, it harnesses the energy of the wind in an ecologically sound way. The earliest known reliable report of a windmill comes from about the year 947. This is of an Asiatic horizontal mill, that is, with the axis of rotation in the vertical. As far as is known, the more familiar vertical wind mill was invented in northern France in about 1180 and spread rapidly throughout Europe in the next few years. Because of the mystical attributes of the winds, and the more mundane wish of Church and lords to gain taxation, it was usual that mills could not be erected without a license. The rulers of an area held the wind rights and, to make use of the wind, permission had to be obtained. In many European countries, mills belonged to the major landowner in any event, and flour was produced for the people living within a certain stipulated area around the mill. This was the so-called Molenban (Mill Ban), which restricted the number of mills on a geographical basis. Within the area of the Molenban, it was forbidden to erect another mill without express permission of the lord. As the earliest mills were erected at a time when the craft of location was at its height in Europe, their siting shows a masterly understanding of the interaction between the winds and the local topography. The Molenban meant that they were placed at sufficient distance from one another so that they did not block each others' airflow.

Like sailors, millers attained a subtle rapport with their machines' interaction with the winds, and the operation of a mill has been compared to sailing a ship. Although most mills have vanished from the face of the earth, the knowledge of millcraft is not dead. In Holland today, water-pumping mills still have shutters which are opened when the mill is in operation. The sound that the wind makes when it blows through these shutters shows the mill operator whether it is in perfect alignment with the direction of the wind. When the note changes, then it is time to move the mill's sails into the wind. This technique, known and used today, is perhaps the last survivor of a much more comprehensive craft knowledge of the nature of the winds on land.

Local knowledge of the nature and qualities of the prevailing winds, essential for the erection of a windmill, was also necessary for the optimal orientation of buildings but, today, the only relics of this knowledge survive as windmills, weathercocks and wind vanes which are now seen as merely decorative elements. Even objects with obvious functions, however, such as the sails of windmills, can have more symbolic uses. In various districts, the angle of the sails of a mill at rest signified certain messages, so someone with a knowledge of millers' codes could read the state of the miller's work or his family without visiting the mill. Integrated within all these factors was the traditional life of the countryside, now largely disrupted by the modern industrialized culture.

This vision is not lost, however; it is preserved within the very fabric of the landscape and of the human constructions that relate to it. Study of the traditional house design in the locality where the modern practitioner lives is necessary to determine the practicalities of earth harmony as they were perceived in the past. The vernacular design of houses varies from locality to locality, but the general underlying principles can be rediscovered if one approaches them using the basic concepts. The relationship between the design and its surroundings, once understood, can be applied again today.

Chapter 8
Trees

Wherever it is possible for them to grow, trees form an important feature of the landscape. They provide shelter, materials and fuel for human use, and indicate the character of a place by their location and shape. Trees have a dynamic interaction with the environment. Every tree is a living watercourse; its roots, trunk and branches conduct water up from the soil to the leaves, from which it evaporates into the atmosphere. This process of transpiration, transports the water and nutrients necessary for the leaves to make the food that the tree needs. Microscopic organelles in the leaves build up sugars and starches through the transmutation of light and water. The light comes from the sun - the heavens - and the water from the soil - the Earth. Thus the tree, like the human, is a mediator between the Earth and the Heavens. In order to get as much light as possible, the branches and leaves are arranged according to precise geometrical laws which reflect the universal order implicit in all things. Similarly, the form of the tree's canopy depends on many factors which reflect the interaction between its genetics, the place it grows, and events occurring during the life of the tree.

The tree is a balanced functional system, and the root and branch system develops in harmony. Beneath the ground surface, the roots radiate out in a shallow layer of the subsoil, rarely deeper than four or five feet. Some species of tree have a deeper taproot for anchorage, but only relatively shallow roots can collect the water required through a fine network of fibrous roots. These are related to the structure of the tree above ground, as most of these fine roots fan out at the edges of the root system beneath the tips of the branches where rainwater drips from the leafy canopy.

The shapes of trees depend primarily upon the genetics encoded within the species; but as organisms which exist in natural conditions for the whole of their lives fixed in one place, they are constantly subject to the prevailing influences of that location. When looking at the landscape for any indications of the influences present there, one must examine tree type and shape. For different reasons, the British Army long had a simple but effective way of classifying tree shape. Only three types of tree were recognised: 'fir trees', 'poplars' and 'bushy-top trees'. Whilst such a classification might enrage botanists, it was sufficient for military purposes.

Using army terminology, so-called 'fir' trees are the typical 'Christmas tree' type plant, with a prominent and straight main stem being short and almost horizontal side branches, often drooping. 'Poplars' are vertical trees with ascending side branches, and 'bushy-top' trees are the characteristic type of most non-coniferous species, with the main stem almost indistinguishable at the crown. These three categories can be visualised easily by anyone, and they are valuable because they give an image of the 'perfect' shape of the tree. This army terminology can be used when first noting down the forms and location of the trees in a landscape. Looking at trees from this simple viewpoint, we can check whether they conform to any of these shapes, or whether they are 'distorted' in some way. When we try to determine the character of a site, the type of trees there and their shape can be useful guides.

Tree shape depends upon many factors. The basic form is that 'typical' for the species, but as in most things, the 'ideal' or 'typical' shape is relatively uncommon. Soil conditions, competition from other trees, slope, shade, wind and lightning are some of the natural factors that affect tree shape. Of course human intervention in the shape of accidental and deliberate mutilation, or the secondary effects of air pollution and acid rain is one of the major factors in the urban and suburban environment.

The augurs of ancient Europe used to examine the shape of trees to determine various facts about the location. Distorted shapes showed abnormal forces acting at that place; shattered trees were magnets for lightning, and stunted trees indicated poor soil quality. In a less scientific age than ours, this examination was discounted as 'superstition' and discarded as unworthy of study, yet today it can be seen that such examination was indeed a way of obtaining valuable information about a site. Whether a tree grows to its full potential size depends largely upon the quality of the soil and the consistency of the water supply over the years. Its shape can be distorted because of underground factors, by extreme weather conditions during its growth, or by constant factors such as the wind. Trees are living organisms which link the underworld of the ground, with its serpentine watercourses, the surface of the ground upon which we live, with the sky and air. Dowsers have noted that the forms of trees are affected as they grow over underground water, especially blind springs. They develop twisted trunks, double forms, and branches grow back into the trunk, making contorted shapes, living indicators of an active place.

Twisted trees were revered as sacred by the ancient Pagans, and the spiral wands used by journeymen, witches and druids are a reminder of this. As indicators of the character of site, twisted trees are valuable. The nature of the ground is indicated by the types of plant growing there, and the most permanent of plants are trees, which require a considerable time to grow, and hence relatively stable conditions over a long period. In northern Europe, damp or wet places are indicated by certain trees, alder, black and grey poplars, the osiers and willows. In other parts of the world, likewise, the local species of tree indicate wet places. Wet places are obviously not good for building or human health, so it is important to identify them. Riversides are obviously wet places, but less obvious are the local depressions which may be wet only intermittently. In the countryside, such wet basins are often indicated by the trees growing there, even when ground water is not apparent.

Because the wind is a major factor in the geolocation of human habitation, the shape of trees can be a valuable indicator of the prevailing local conditions. Tree clumps often have the form of a unified overall canopy, making the whole wood look like a single massive tree. Such clumps are most prominent in rolling hilly country, where they occupy small hilltops, knolls or ancient burial barrows. Trees growing in very windy places, such as near the sea, have longer and better branches on the side away from the prevailing wind. These 'wind-cut' trees look as if they are blowing in the wind like a frozen banner. In fact, this effect has been produced by the death of buds and young branches through drying out on the windward side, though constant wind pressure on the main stem or trunk during growth does cause it to lean away from the wind. 'Wind cutting' is more marked close to the sea, where salt spray increases the desiccatory effect. Growth takes place only on the leeward side, and is more vigorous because these branches obtain more nutrients than they would if all the branches were growing normally. From a 'wind-cut' tree we can find the prevailing wind-direction, and estimate its strength.

The higher we go, the stronger the average speed of the wind, and the harder the effect of driving rain and snow. Often trees cannot grow on exposed hillsides and the tops of ridges, because of these factors. When growth is not impossible there, tree shape is highly modified, and stunted or shrubby forms are common. Both the direct physical effect of the wind, and the climatic effect of lower average temperatures conspire to prevent vigorous 'typical' growth. Frost and snow are more prevalent on exposed hills and mountains, begin earlier in the year and last longer. Observation of trees in these conditions can indicate areas with more (or less) favourable microclimate than nearby locations. It is in these areas in hilly or mountainous terrain that shrines and hermitages have been located.

Frost damage in exposed places leads to changes in tree shape, and individual species of tree have varying tolerance. If late frosts kill the first shoots or leaves of spring, then regeneration produces 'misshapen' branches, and repeated loss of leading or side branches at high altitudes or in 'frost-hollows' may result in a many-branched plant. In northern Europe, aspen, birch and rowan are unaffected by late frosts, whilst oak and scots pine are less resistant. Ash and beech suffer badly, and cannot grow on very exposed hillsides. These innate qualities of trees are part of the traditional lore to which we can refer today both to understand the character of a site and when choosing which trees to plant.

As large objects which carry an electric charge, trees are sometimes struck by lightning. The oak, sacred tree of the ancient Indo-European sky god Deivos and later revered by the priests of Zeus, Thor, Perkunas and the Druids, is commonly stricken by lightning, the force wielded by these deities. Lightning-damaged trees have a characteristic furrow down one or more of the upper branches which continues down the trunk. Often the furrow takes a spiral pathway down through the tree, and many of the venerable hollow oaks have originated in this way. Although any tree can be struck, there is a tradition that some trees "court the flash", that is attract lightning. These may be trees whose structure and physiology create stronger fields around them. Oaks are particularly prone to lightning damage because they are very deep-rooted, often stand in isolation and as rough-barked trees conduct the lightning through the woody parts. Smooth-barked trees when wet provide a good pathway for the conductance of lightning over the surface, but with the oak this is not possible and the charge takes the line of least resistance. Travelling through the wood, the lightning causes explosive vaporisation of the water inside, ripping open the trunk and sometimes blowing off branches. Trees stricken by lightning often regenerate in a shape known as 'stag-headed'.

Abrupt changes in the character of a place may be 'read' by looking at the vegetation. This ancient way of looking at things was part of the everyday lives of the wise women and cunning men of the countryside, who knew where they could find the herbs or woods they required for their protective magic and folk medicine. The dismemberment of the traditional landscape by mechanised farming and urbanisation has destroyed the intimate balance of many areas with the resultant depletion of the vegetation. But this, too, is an indication of the character of an area as it is now. Rubbish tips, polluted ex-industrial areas and motorway service stations are as disruptive of Earth Harmony as sacred places are harmonious with it. Appropriate planting can diminish the harmful effects of such places, screening them from the surrounding environment and helping to re-integrate them. Even the restoration of the traditional hedges has a markedly beneficial effect, especially when ancient places of power are recognised again.

Within the hedges of the traditional landscape are Standard trees, trees that have been left to grow to full size. These Standards, many of which are actual markers of changes of direction in the local boundaries, or upon which footpaths are aligned, are often growing at places of power. The most notable of these hedgerow standard trees are the customary Gospel Oaks, several of which still exist. The parish priest would read a religious text at such oaks during the ceremony of Beating the Bounds, and also marriages were solemnised beneath their branches where marriages in the tradition of the Elder Faith. After a Christian wedding in church, couples would go to a Marriage Oak to have their union blessed according to the handfasting customs of the Old Religion.

Also among unusual hedgerow standards are the mysterious Fairy Trees, strange hybrids where oak, ash and thorn have grown together by means unknown. Fairy Trees, and other standards characterised by special shape or location, are still resorted to in country districts for sacred or therapeutic purposes. In Northern European lore, each common species of tree has its own virtue and character, corresponding to a direction, astrological planet, day of the week, period of time, colour, deity and use. The modern western materialist view of these correspondences might consider these attributes as mere customary or superstitious use, with no "real" meaning. However, morphologically and biochemically, the species of tree vary from one another: their shapes create different electrostatic fields around themselves; they attract statistically different amounts of lightning, and react differently to it; they modify airflow in ways depending on trunk, branch and leaf form; local variations in the mix of gases in the air around certain trees are known; and there are the aesthetic and psychological effects upon humans, too.

The traditional attributes of Day, Planet, Tree and Deity in the Northern Tradition are as follows:

Day	Planet	Tree	Deity
Sunday	Sun	Birch	Sól/Ogmios
Monday	Moon	Willow	Mani.
Tuesday	Mars	Holly	Tiw/Teutates
Wednesday	Mercury	Ash	Odin/Gwydion
Thursday	Jupiter	Oak	Thor/Taranis
Friday	Venus	Apple	Frigg/Freyja
Saturday	Saturn	Alder	Saetere

In the Celto-Germanic cultural area, in addition to the day/planet/deity attribution, thirteen species of tree are related to thirteen time-periods in the year, and hence the circle of the directions. The number thirteen refers to the annual cycle of the thirteen lunar months. The wood of each tree also has a traditional use, related both to the practical qualities of the material, and to mystical considerations:

Tree	Dates	Use of Wood From Tree
Birch	Dec 24 - Jan 20	Cradles, Maypoles
Rowan	Jan 21 - Feb17	Lintels, Mantelpieces, Speer-posts, "witch wands", dowsing rods for metal, protective amulets.
Ash	Feb 18 - Mar17	Fence posts, weapon handles, the High Seat Pillars of the Lord's hall, spiral wands of wizards.
Alder	Mar 18 - Apr 14	Foundation piles.
Willow	Apr 15 - May12	Stockade fencing, support for thatch.
Hawthorn	May 13 - Jun 9	Hedging around sacred enclosures.
Oak	Jun10 - Jul 7	Doorposts and doors, structural house timbers.
Holly	Jul 8 - Aug 4	Sacred staves and clubs.
Hazel	Aug 5 - Sep 1	Ceremonial shields, water divining rods.
Vine	Sep 2 - Sep 29	
Ivy	Sep 30 - Oct 27	Bindings
Water Elder	Oct 28 - Nov24	
Elder	Nov 25 - Dec 22	Witch's Tree, to be used only outside the house.

A complete symbolic harmonisation of a country house or cottage and its surroundings might use appropriate species of trees planted at positions corresponding to the directions and qualities of the location. The Celtic tree year circle has been planted recently at Glastonbury and also at Wingen-sur-Moder in France, near the German border. The thirteen trees in their correct order and orientation can be used to create a sacred space for meditation or rituals connected with personal harmony, for they reflect an aspect of the cosmic order, giving us access to it at a material level.

Harmonisation can be carried out at many levels, from techniques which incorporate every nuance of symbolism, such as woods, sacred geometry, canonical dimensions, symbolic colours, appropriate signs and artifacts, to a simple system hardly involving the rich symbolic dimension at all. The latter method is more in tune with modern interior (and exterior) design, and the simplified, non-ornamental approach towards modern artifacts, and it is obviously better to be aware of harmonisation than not to attempt it at all. But to ignore the spiritual dimension, and leave out the symbolic aspects, is to deny an essential aspect of Earth Harmony. By taking the traditional qualities and correspondences of trees into consideration, we can create this harmonisation almost imperceptibly. Just by using correct orientation and materials, we can get close to that harmony we seek.

Although they have many valuable qualities, trees are not always beneficial. In relating our living quarters to Earth Harmony a large tree growing close to the front is harmful because it obstructs the entry both of people and beneficial energies. It may obscure the view of the door and thereby assist intruders who cannot be seen by passers-by. Also a large tree blocks the householder's view outwards. Its roots may undermine the house structure, physically damaging the foundations, and altering the flows of underground water beneath the floor. In traditional house-orientation, a large tree at the front blocks out a view of the sun from the house-stone (doorstep). In windy weather, falling branches or perhaps the whole tree threatens to damage or destroy the house, and large trees charge up and attract lightning, bringing the danger of fire. As a rule, only the smaller trees are appropriate close to the front door, planted as a wind barrier if necessary. Many common trees have certain qualities ascribed to them. The following lists those most commonly encountered:

Apple *(Malus spp.)* Symbolic of the solar power, kingship and rebirth. Planted traditionally in orchards which were a special kind of sacred ground.

Ash *(Fraxinus excelsior)* the Cosmic Tree in the Northern European tradition. According to folklore, the ash attracts lightning.

Bay Tree (*Laurus nobilis*): planted near a house will protect it from the plague, and general infection. Said to provide protection from lightning.

Birch *(Betula pendula)*, the tree of purification.

Blackthorn *(Sloe, Prunus spinosa)* is a plant whose wood has been used for magical staves, and protection against harmful magic. The drink derived from its fruit, Sloe gin, has medicinal qualities.

Elder *(Sambucus nigra)* the witches' tree or Bourtree, is reputed to ward off lightning.

Hawthorn *(Crataegus monogyna)* the May Tree, is a useful psychic shield for sacred places and cemeteries. A sacred tree of the god Thor, it is supposed to give protection against lightning. There are three main species of this: the Common Hawthorn, the Midland Hawthorn, and the Glastonbury Thorn, each of which have slightly different qualities.

Hazel *(Corylus avellana)* promotes fertility, poetry and wisdom.

Holly *(Ilex aquifolium)* protection against witches, demons, the evil eye, lightning.

Ivy *(Hedera helix)* growing on a house wall is a customary protection against witchcraft and evil.

Linden *(Lime, Tilia platyphyllos)*, is a tree used as a central marker, found as the Dorflinde, Village Tree in Germany and surrounding countries. In medieval times, it was the Law Tree, under which judgement was meted, and upon which those found guilty were hanged - the gallows tree.

Oak *(Quercus robur)* is a mark tree in countryside boundaries, sometimes a Marriage Oak or Gospel Oak. In the European Pagan religions, it was sacred to Jupiter/Taranis/Thunor/Thor, gods associated with thunderbolts and lightning. The oak is reputed to give protection against lightning, probably because it "courts the flash" itself.

Rowan *(Sorbus aucuparia)* by the gate will ward off harm of a magical kind.

Yew *(Taxus baccata)* a very long-lived tree, is a protector of sacred ground, and used in shamanic practices. On warm days, the Yew gives out a toxic vapour which lingers in the air and can cause hallucinations and out-of-the-body experiences in people who stop under the branches for any length of time. Sometimes, its leaves have been used by Druids for ceremonial suicide.

Holy Groves

Until the advent of tree plantations for the timber industry, the only large, artificial plantations of trees were the holy groves of Pagan religions such as Druidism, Asatrú and Ushmari-Chinmari, and orchards of fruit-bearing trees. Both of these types of plantation were at consciously-chosen locations, and both traditional lore and modern research concur that they are indeed special places - holy ground. Although most of the ancient Heathen groves were destroyed by Christian priests long ago, orchards, having valuable fruit trees, were not. Even today, the destruction of an orchard is rightly looked upon in some places as an act of sacrilege, and not only because a valuable living resource is being wiped out. The tradition of wassailing the orchards at midwinter, when offerings are made to fruit trees, and shotguns or party poppers fired into the air to ward off evil in the coming year, is a continuation of the traditions of the days when orchards were also holy groves.

The sanctity of orchards is enshrined also in common law under the Privileges of the Free Miners. These men, from Cornwall and parts of England including Alston Moor in Derbyshire, the Weald of Sussex and the Forest of Dean (where they still operate despite government attempts to suppress their rights), belonged to chartered associations of independent miners. Their royal charters gave them the right to dig for coal and minerals on any land, with three exceptions. These are sacred ground - the King's Highway, churchyards and orchards. Roads, churchyards and orchards are places where dowsers say that earth energies are strong, and from which it is dispersed to other areas.

Digging in such ground, and the removal of minerals might cause serious alterations in the character of a whole area, causing imbalance and hence other problems. The destruction of sacred trees was a universal geis, whose breaking was held to bring misfortune not only to the perpetrator of the deed, but also to the locality in which the tree stood. Cutting down a sacred tree on a place of power would lead to the release of harmful spirits or

95

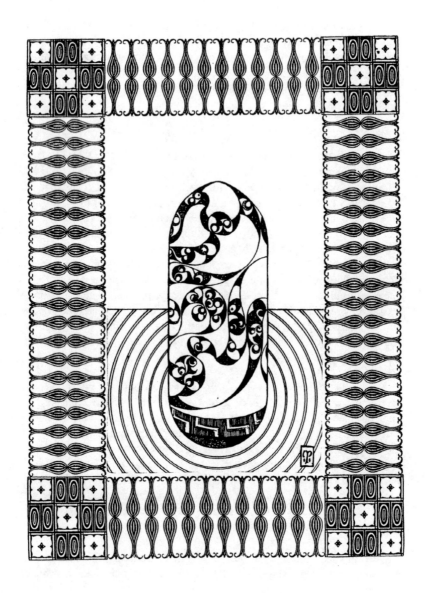

The Omphalos, centre of the world

energies held in check there by the tree, causing an imbalance which would be manifested as poor crops, sickness and general misfortune. Only by planting a new tree of the same species at that place could the imbalance be rectified. In our attempt to restore balance, it is possible to get some of the old sites re-stocked with the appropriate trees. Although this may not appear to be very important, symbolically and traditionally, it can revitalise a whole area.

The 11th century planned towe of Trelleborg in Denmark was laid out according to the Holy City plan, using accurate measurements and precise geometry

Chapter 9
Human Settlement in the Landscape

"No one can carry out a plan better than the man who has conceived it; for no-one can interpret perfectly the thoughts of another" Domenico Fontana.

The builders of former times made their constructions to harmonise with the character of the site, but usually that is no longer the case, for the modern emphasis on literacy and printed matter is nowhere more apparent than when designers get to work. In most modern work, the fundamental basis is the map, not the terrain. Maps, however, do not reproduce the fine features of the terrain which must be taken into account in order to harmonise human habitations with the environment. Contour lines, generally at 5 metre intervals, do not show where slopes begin and end, nor do they record small but significant features which fall between the contours. Small variations in level, dips and valleys, flat areas, low knolls, locally dry or damp areas, local variations in rock and soil, and especially traditional places of power can only be appraised at the site itself. These physical features have come about as the result of the history of the site, the sum total of the geology, geophysical processes and human intervention unique to that place. Maps cannot show the hidden element in such places, the gravitational, magnetic, electrostatic, atmospheric and other qualities which are forever changing yet which determine the microclimate of a place, and thus its suitability for human purposes. Physical maps do not show these features, which are nevertheless essential factors in the achievement of harmony. These factors are not amenable to being mapped, for they are that part of the natural world which are subject to rhythm, for they are dynamic and not material. The map can only chart the material world, and because of this, activities which deal with only this aspect are doomed to be partially successful in their application. In everything dynamic, everything living, there is rhythm.

Every movement in the world is rhythmic in character, and earth harmony is concerned with fitting in with these subtle rhythmic and cyclic patterns. To understand rhythms is to understand the nature of harmony and discord, for rhythms in harmony express balance, proportion and integration with the universal order. If dwellings are built in the landscape without either regard or knowledge of these subtle variations, or even a concept that there is a universal order, then success will be a matter of chance, and a good deal less likely than failure. To get some idea of practical ways of dealing with this problem, we must look at the situation, layout and internal structure of traditional settlements.

The situation of a village is related to geographical, social and subtle factors concerned with the character of the place. Simple access to resources is fundamental: it is no use founding a village at a place where the agricultural base was sparse or non-existent. The immediate area had to have adequate arable- and meadowland, enough grazing for livestock, and woodland for fuel and building materials. Additionally, water is important, for without a good and regular supply, life, which was hard enough anyway, would become intolerable or untenable. Shelter also plays a major part. A southern aspect, considered harmonious in all the earth harmony traditions of the northern hemisphere, is necessary for light, and to mitigate the extremes of cold in northern climes. The slope of land is also important, for it needs to be sufficiently flat for building, and sloping enough for drainage. However, this factor is obviously subject to alteration, as steeply-sloping or low lying settlements are not unknown.

Examination of a village's layout and the factors leading to good or bad places within it must be undertaken with regard to the entire surroundings. We should not fall into the trap of examining only the grid or geometrical layout of the buildings and streets without taking every aspect of the whole village into account. A whole village includes the field system and local topography, including all modern structures which are here now. To examine a grid laid out in 1200 without taking the local motorway embankments into account is a futile act if one wishes to determine the present character of a site.

There is a fundamental distinction between unplanned and planned villages. Unplanned villages reflect the local pressures of transport, agriculture, and the placement of cottages and farms according to intuitive principles. They have a different character from planned settlements, for originally they were directly in contact with the local forces acting upon the site, which gave them their layout. Planned villages are generally laid out on a grid, which is identical in form with that underlying many towns, some significant examples of which are dealt with in the next chapter. Specific parts of the grid were allocated to specific functions. Unlike modern zoning of towns into various areas of use, which is done according to utilitarian principles, these were located according to rules which today would be called esoteric. The sacred geometry of temples, synagogues, churches and towns have certain places allocated to certain deities, planets, zodiacal qualities or saints, ideally using definite dimensions that relate symbolically to cosmic measure. The layout of any grid, whether it be a fair, village or town, reflects this cosmic order. The task of the locator who laid out such a town was to harmonise this cosmic grid with the existing landscape, making it appear to grow from the land rather than to stand upon it as an alien intrusion. Although relatively ignored today, these principles are as valid now as they ever were.

Sacred Space

'The place whereupon thou standest is holy ground.'
Exodus, iii, 5

The place where God has stopped is a vivid and poetic interpretation of a place of power, one of those places where we can recognise some special quality. In any natural landscape, there are places with outstanding qualities of peace and serenity which have been recognised since antiquity and which we can find today. At these places, images, temples and churches have been erected to express, contain and accumulate the powers of the site. Places of power have been recognised by many means: they have been found by accident, by revelation of a supernatural being in dreams, by the apparition of a sacred being, saint or deity, and by deliberate divination using animals or apparatus. However they have been found, today we can recognise two related forms of sacred place: that which remains in its natural form and that which is the locus for a building made by human ingenuity.

Natural places of power include the sites mentioned in chapter 1: rocks, springs, hills, isolated stones and caves. Regardless of continent or creed, these classes of place are sacred. The second type of sacred place is a natural place of power modified and enhanced by human action to express the powers inherent in the site and to link these with an eternal image of the cosmic order. Whichever tradition we choose to examine, we will find the same classes of place acting as places of power where human beings can gain access to higher states of consciousness and contact the eternal. A sacred place is a powerful area which has been set aside from the everyday world, hallowed by consecration and maintained by the observances of devout people. Sanctity is a state which transcends religions: that is why in countless places new religions have converted the shrines of the former faith. The sacred power present at such places, however, is accessible to those of goodwill of all faiths. Sacred places take many forms, from unadorned natural features to ornate complexes of shrines and temples. They are all characterised by a timeless atmosphere of prayer and contemplation, created by a combination of site and human activity. A true temple (and that term includes a church or other place of canonical worship) is a symbolic synthesis of cosmic principles, the character of the site and the emblems of the faith. On a basic level, this exists at stone circles, in the cruciform design of churches and the orientation of mosques. It is also present in architecture constructed according to the principles inherent in the natural world, that originality which consists of returning to the origin - nature - seen as a manifestation of God.

Underlying every human activity is the basic structure of matter and the laws of the universe by which things happen and interact. These laws have been interpreted and explained in many ways, from ancient mythology to modern science, but, whether we understand them or not, they are acting at all times and in all places upon everything. But whether we look upon things symbolically, in terms of myth, or in terms of scientific discoveries, the final reference point is within ourselves the consciousness of human beings. Of course, this anthropocentric view is inherent in all ancient views of the world, and every creation myth is seen in human terms. In the Norse creation myth, primeval space, ginnungagap, stretched out between ice in the north and fire in the south. Between the two, motion came into being and, from this, life in the form of the primeval giant called Ymir.

This ancient concept seems an archaic and poetic way of explaining the viewpoint which, in modern physics, sees matter as being 'frozen light'. The recent discoveries of organic material in Halley's Comet (cosmic ice) coming into contact with a star like the sun (fire) has been suggested as the possible origin of life on planets like ours so, in common with many ancient myths, the northern legend holds a deeper wisdom. The primeval giant Ymir is killed by the gods and, from his body, the world is built. In glaciated mountainous regions we can easily recognise the ice-polished rocks as the bones of Ymir. The archetypal human, personified as Ymir, is the literal foundation of architecture, built upon his plan, and, even though we do not take this tale literally, we can see in it the symbolism by which our perception of the world and our architecture is based upon our form and psyche as human beings.

The Navel of the World

In the womb our connection with our mother is through the umbilical cord and, after birth, the navel remains as a reminder of this life-giving connection through which we obtained our nourishment. Our gestation is a fundamental part of our life which all human beings share and so the transference of this symbolism to our place on the surface of the earth is particularly appropriate. The slaying of the primal giant and the creation of the world from his body places this navel at the centre of the world. Such central points exist in every tradition. They are called by their Greek name, omphalos, etymologically the same as the Latin umbilicus, meaning navel. This name takes on a greater significance when we remember that, in the oriental martial arts, the ki or vital energy of the earth is the same as the ki of the human body, centred in or around the navel; this connection, therefore, may have a link which goes deeper than the symbolic.

All over the world, regardless of their basic faiths, this omphalos principle can be found. For example, the Chickasaws of Mississippi called large mounds 'navels'. They thought that their land was at the centre of the world and so the mounds were equivalent to the navel at the centre of the human body. In Europe, the legends of Siegfried or St George depict the hero transfixing the evil dragon to the ground with sword or lance. Here, the energies of the earth are shown in physical form as a living creature which must be slain to free the land of its harmful influence. This dragon-slaying took place at a local or national centre omphalos at a significant time. This is the geomantic act which has the effect of fixing the qualities present at the point at that time, holding the character of the tulle (astrological) at the place. This is the basis of all foundation ritual, even today. The practice of driving stakes into the ground with the intention of blocking the underground streams associated with geopathic zones - called black streams by British and American dowsers - is a modern version of this traditional rite. In the modern manner, it is done with the minimum of ritual but, in earlier times, such an act would be to perform the geomantic act is an act of will, like slaying a fearsome giant or dragon. In the old Welsh group of myths, known as *The Mabinogion*, we are given a good example of the myth in the tale of 'Lludd and Llefelys'. Here, Britain is afflicted by a nationwide problem caused when two dragons fight at the centre of Britain - the Carfax crossroads at Oxford. When these are overcome by the King, a curse afflicting every hearth in the country is lifted. Somehow, by altering the conditions at the omphalos, by removal or by spiking the dragon to the ground, the character of the entire country is transformed as if random and harmful forces are harnessed and tamed. Sometimes, as in the legend of Apollo's conquest of the omphalos at Delphi, this destruction of the serpentine force at the central place has been taken to symbolise the overcoming of an older by a newer faith. At Delphi, the site sacred to the earth goddess Gaia was converted to the solar religion of Apollo by the god's destruction of the python, a classical dragon-slaying myth. Likewise, St George's geomantic act is usually understood as a Christian allegory of the suppression of paganism. The geomantic act, wherever it occurred, was seen as creating sacred space - even the abolition of harmful streams perceived beneath the ground is the creation of a form of sanctuary.

The Delphic omphalos is a dome-shaped stone carved with patterns that resemble skeins of wool. This carving is believed by some to represent the streams of serpent-like energy in the earth and their nodes, at one of which the omphalos was located. The shape of the stone is more important than the carving, however, as it is a form which existed at important cult-centres in ancient Egypt, Greece, Rome, Germany, Ireland and Britain. The famous egg-stone at Glastonbury is one such navel-stone. The existence of such a centre had a great importance in former times. It was the custom among the ancient Romans that no city, or even a military camp, was established and founded without a sacred umbilicus. This gave control over the city and founded it as an entity both in space and time. Traditionally, the staking of a place could be to defend a homestead against malevolent magic or to prevent the entry of harmful energies, seen in those times as spirits of the land. The navel is at the centre of the four quarters which divide the horizon according to the cardinal points. This fourfold division is fundamental to human consciousness and it recurs wherever we look, from the idea of the four elements and the tour types of frame in traditional timber-framed building to the customary division of society and the land. Earth harmony is concerned with the land and so we must look more closely at the concept of this fourfold division of the land. It is an idea which is found all over the world in the creation of sacred space, a place where immutable cosmic laws are manifested in the physical world.

The Design of Sacred Space

Sacred space is space which is orientated and subdivided according to a celestial model. Orientation is defined by the cardinal points, to which intersecting straight lines run at right angles to each other. The north-south line is known by its Latin name as the cardo, and the east-west as the decumanus. The sacred space defined by these is enclosed by a boundary, preferably circular or square. This space can be anything from a whole country down to a much smaller surface, such as an altar or a gameboard. This standard method of laying out towns in four quarters was used most notably by the Romans Their method was taken over from the Etruscans whose augurs carefully examined the form of the country, its hills, watercourses, trees and places of power before deciding upon the place to begin the layout. Other factors were also noted: the flight of birds, thunderbolts, cloud formation and other celestial phenomena In modern terms, viewing the flight patterns of birds gives clues to the local magnetic fields as birds have been shown to follow and be affected by them. Likewise, the local recurrence of lightning at certain places gives an indication of electrostatic fields, and cloud formation indicates prevailing winds and hence air-pressure effects. By taking these into account, the augur could harmonise all the environmental factors when laying out his town.

The Holy City

The augur's location was at the crossing of two straight roads, the point divined as the omphalos. Facing south, the observer had behind him the area north of the decumanus. This half of the space is known as the posterior part. In front, the southern half of the space was the anterior part. The holy-city plan is a recognition of this creation of sacred space, accounting for its uninterrupted continuity from ancient times into the Christian era. The augur's layout of an area naturally divided the visible horizon into four quarters. These four quarters of the visible world are still talked about when we speak of a town district as a 'quarter'. The term headquarters and the military rank of quartermaster come from the use of this layout of military camps. From this central point, two straight roads were laid out at right angles to the cardo, running north-south, and the decumanus, running east-west.

These two roads were the starting-point for the layout of the whole district controlled by the new town. The Romans' method of foundation extended into the surrounding area by laying out a grid of straight roads at fixed distances from one another, sometimes covering a large area of countryside. Unlike the grid that spans the United States, however, the Roman centuriation covered lowland areas which naturally formed units. There was no attempt made to link grids together over vast areas. At important places of

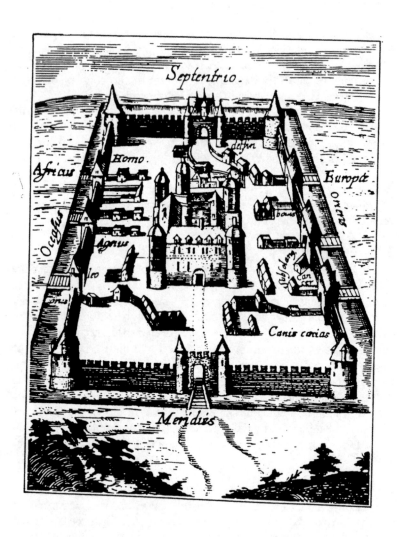

The Holy City, orientated foursquare and with its parts laid out relative to the four elements, the planets and the influences of the zodiac.

106

survey or natural power in this grid, the augurs erected shrines to the appropriate deities. In this traditional manner, the technically practical and the sacred were unified. Any oriented, formally laid-out city was automatically the correct place for the observation of the heavens, both for everyday time-telling by the sun and for more esoteric reasons, such as astrology. Ideally, the gateways, towers and important buildings were located to mark important sunrise positions, so that the whole city was an observatory. Within a town with this layout, certain places are therefore related automatically to certain functions, and each has its own specific character. If we live in such a town, we can determine easily these places and investigate whether they are good or bad for us as individuals for, in ancient times, it was believed that this archetypal layout gave humans the best chance of a harmonious coexistence with the cosmos.

The 'holy-city plan' is found all over the world. The Inca monarchs divided their Peruvian empire into four parts, called tahuatinsuyu, meaning 'the four quarters of the world'. The central point of these quarters was the city of Cuzco which means the navel of the world in the Inca tongue. This central city was laid out as a microcosmic image of the empire and the first king, Manco Capac, ordered that the chiefs of the tribes that he overcame should live in the city in houses located according to the positions of their homelands. One of the best known and most long-lived fourfold divisions is that of Ireland. Ancient Ireland reproduced the cosmic fourfold-plus-centre pattern in the layout of its provinces; Leinster, Munster, Connaught and Ulster. Each province had its own king and, at the centre, was the fifth province, Meath, over which the High King ruled from Tara, the sacred centre of Ireland. When the old Pagan system was overthrown by St Patrick, the fourfold division was retained in a modified form. Overlying the provinces (which still exist today, of course), was the ecclesiastical fourfold division, based upon cathedrals at Dublin, Cashel, Tuam and Armagh. The fourfold divisions of smaller islands follows the Irish pattern. Iceland, settled by Scandinavians in the ninth and tenth centuries, is divided into Ostfjorden, Sudland, Westfjorden and Nordland. Each quarter was subdivided into three 'thirdings', a division which existed in Yorkshire until 1974 as the three 'Ridings', and in East Anglia as Norfolk with east and west Suffolk. In Iceland, each of these twelve divisions of the island sent a given number of men to the annual parliament, called the Althing, convened at the sacred centre of the land. Here, under the direction of the Lawspeaker, a temporary town was erected, reproducing in its form the layout of the state with its four quarters, twelve magistrates, high priests, etc. People attending

Plan of the centre of the city of Oxford, laid out in Anglo-Saxon times according to the Etruscan Discipline and centred on the middle of Britain. This central point, marked by the Carfax crossroads, is recorded in the Welsh legendary text, Llys and Llefelys. The strong May Day traditions in the city continue the legend symbolised there.

the Althing resided in the places appropriate to the quarter of the island from which they came, and also from which station in life. In the Baltic, the smaller island of Bornholm is divided similarly. Coming down in scale, many towns and cities are divided in this way. Similar methods of town foundation and layout were practised in Europe until the eighteenth century.

In England, Huntingdon, founded by King Edward the Elder in 914, is a notable continuation of this tradition. The town was laid out on the old English royal road called Ermine Street. Around a small market-place, four quarters known as ferlings were laid out. Traditionally, Saxon towns were divided into four quarters; these sometimes coincided with parishes, quarters occupied by various trades or, at other times, were administrative districts only. These quarters were called Ferlings because they were one square furlong or ferlingate in area. Here, the unit of the furlong, one furrow's length in cultivated ground, integrates the town's dimensions with the layout of the surrounding countryside. The town of Brilon in Westphalia, Germany, whose plan is illustrated here, is a classic example, but it is far from unique and anyone investigating their own home town should look for indications of a fourfold division. Throughout this study it is apparent that a law of correspondences operates. The navel of the human is seen as parallel with the navel of the world, and the house as symbolic of the structure of the world. Likewise, the temple is seen as symbolic of the fabric of the universe and the body of God. The architectural theorist and mystic, W.R. Lethaby, wrote that the perfect temple should stand at the centre of the world, a microcosm of the universal fabric, its walls built foursquare with the walls of heaven. All over the world, sacred buildings can be found whose layout approaches this ideal. Laying out the lines to square with the world is a part of the rites at foundation ceremonies all over the world. The accurate squaring up of a building, like the mystical fabric of the earth, ensures its stability. The precise ritual of measuring and laying-out the site guaranteed an accurate layout, and the pious thoughts and energies generated thus were incorporated in the very foundation.

The Temple
Image of the Cosmos

A temple is the visible outer body of an invisible deity, the visible image of which pervades all nature. The temple is not just a place of devotion of the deity but is, in itself, an object of devotion. Like the human body, the temple is the outer visible shape of the shapeless. The various parts of the temple parallel the parts of the human body, with the same astrological and other correspondences which pertain to the body. To the believer, the temple is not just a collection of stones, bricks and wood, but is the visible representation of the deity, placed in a peculiarly appropriate location on the earth to harmonise with it.

The ancient canonical literature of all faiths provides us with detailed descriptions of perfect temples which have a remarkable conformity with one another. For example, the ancient Indian Hindu text known as the Silpasarini describes the perfect location and structure of the Hindu temple. The basis of all Hindu temples is the scheme of mystic diagrams, mandalas and yantras. These architectural yantras are not ground-plans for the temples but are the geometrical and locational essence on which the sacred precincts of the temple are constructed, a concept identical with that dealing with the layout of sacred space in pagan northern Europe and with the Church as the body of 'man the microcosm', manifested as Jesus Christ. These sacred diagrams are a crystallisation in geometrical form of a cosmic vision which is translated into material form in the temple. Many Hindu temples and early Indian towns were laid out according to the Vastu-Purusha Mandala which is a square of squares, either eight by eight or nine by nine. This grid of sixty-four or eighty-one squares exists in various forms from India to the West. In India, each part of the grid is assigned to different deities, the squares at the middle being assigned to the creator, Brahma. The sixty-four-square grid is familiar as the chessboard, whilst the eighty-one-square grid appears in a related form in the West as another board game, tablut. The earth harmony as a symbolic division of sacred space. Each square is assigned to a specific deity, the central nine sacred to the creator Brahma. The grid is used to determine the correct placement of images and symbols in the temple.

The grid, evidently, had sacred powers in the West as it was used as a protective design by folk artists on central European furniture until well into this century. By using the grid form, each and every one of these elements are implicit in any structure which is based upon the Vastu-Purusha Mandala. The grid represents various parts of the mythological giant who is slain to create the foundations of the temple, and also the twenty eight monthly positions of the moon as well as the solstitial and equinoctial points of the sun. The Hindu manuals of architecture provide thirty-two variations of these mandalas whose use depends on the various requirements of site and worship. Underlying Hindu temples are various different yantras which express the different qualities of the site and thus the form, dimensions, ornament and use of the temple. For example, the Yogini Yantra is installed in the twelfth-century Varahari Temple in Caurasi, Orissa, and the Surya temple at Konarka has solar yantras underlying the floor. Every feature of the temple, however small or insignificant it may appear, is related to some part of the underlying yantra. Whichever one is used, it is laid out ceremonially: at the appropriate location, a peg is placed in the ground, symbolising the central axis of the universe and called the Womb of the Yantra (Yantra Garbha). A circle is drawn around the peg and the eight directions are marked out on the ground. A specific deity is assigned to each of these points and, from these basic directions, the rest of the plan is laid out. This ceremony is basically the same throughout the world for, wherever humans interact with archetypal forces, archetypal forms will arise. By con forming to these essential archetypal forms, sacred buildings express the eternal harmonious unity of the cosmos.

The universal myth of the foundation of the world upon the body of the slain giant, and his connection with the grid pattern, has been mentioned above. In Hindu architecture, the ground-plan of the temple is based upon sixty-four squares, linked with the chessboard and the square from which the potent labyrinth symbol is derived. In the centre of this eight by eight square, the garbha (sanctuary) is placed, being four by four square (sixteen), each side being half the width of the temple itself. In the middle of the side, and equal to one quarter of the width of the sanctuary, is the door. The height of the door is prescribed as twice its width; only ten linear dimensions are permitted. The height of the image inside the sanctuary is related to door height. The image and its pedestal must be one eighth less than the door height, producing a fixed geometrical relationship between the size of the image and the ground-plan of the temple which, itself, symbolises the human body. The jamb, lintel and sill of the door to the sanctuary are in width and depth one quarter of the door's width. Jambs should never be made of a single piece but should be composed of three, five, seven or nine parallel perpendicular sections, each carved with symbolic protective sculpture. The top quarter of the door jamb carries the image of the door-keeper, a protective deity whose identity depends upon the deity in the sanctuary. The remaining part of the jamb bears protective elements including birds, vines, foliage and human couples.

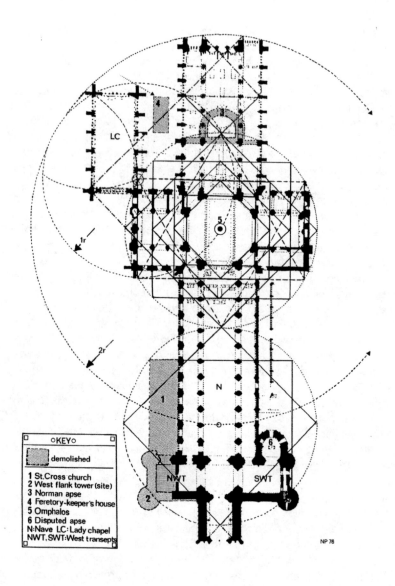

Ely Cathedral's sacred geometry is based upon ad triangulum principles (for details of this see Nigel Pennick's Sacred Geometry, Capall Bann, 1995)

Enclosures of Sanctity

All true sacred temples have various degrees of enclosure and sanctity, creating concentric areas of lessening holiness around the central holy of holies. Sometimes, this is truly concentric, as in natural or artificial holy mountains, where the shrine is at the centre and on top. This pattern can be seen in churches, but here the concentric pattern of sanctity has been made linear and the holiest parts are furthest away from the entrance.

The sanctuary at Beverley Minster in Yorkshire has this pattern in its most developed and overt form. In the Middle Ages, Beverley was one of the great sanctuaries of England, to which an accused person could flee and escape justice. Other such sanctuaries existed at Westminster and St Martin's le Grand in London, but that at Beverley had the most perfect and impressive layout. The shrine at Beverley was accorded its privileges in the year 937 by King Aethelstan in honour of St John of Beverley whose bones had been laid their 200 years earlier. As at the other northern sanctuaries of Hexham and Durham, the shrine of Beverley was so sacred that criminals who entered it were absolved of their offenses. By confessing their crimes there and doing penance, they were brought back into harmony within the natural order.

The town itself was a form of the holy-city plan, entered by four main roads. On these roads at the boundary of the town, 12 miles from the centre (the Outer Bounds), standing-stone crosses marked the transition from the secular world into sanctuary. Inside the town was an area of higher sanctity, closer to the Minster, the Second Bounds. Like the outer area, this inner one was marked by crosses. Inside this was the actual churchyard sanctuary, an area of higher sanctity still and, within this, the Minster church. This was divided into zones of increasing sanctity, beginning with the nave, then the chancel, finally the sanctuary itself by the High Altar. In the sanctuary was the frithstool, a stone seat on which the claimant of sanctuary had to sit in order to be freed from prosecution.

At Beverley was the perfect sevenfold levels of sanctuary, backed up by legal sanction. If the fleeing criminal was arrested in the outer bounds, a certain fine was levied on the person who arrested him or her. This fine doubled up each time a boundary was passed, until the profanity of dragging a claimant of sanctuary from the frithstool was punished by declaring the arrester Bootless, that is, an outlaw, liable to be killed by anyone.

To profane a sanctified omphalos in such a way would have an effect over the whole land, not just at the site itself, so the punishment for such sacrilege was death for, in medieval England, to kill an outlaw was considered an act of piety. Only with the death of the transgressor could the former state of grace be attained once again. Wherever we see them carried out, the factors of earth harmony are a balanced combination of unchanging universal principles modified and fitted in the best way possible to the existing landscape. Each example, therefore, has certain common elements, but sometimes these are overridden or cancelled out by other factors. There are few perfect examples, usually the result of no-expenses-spared regal command.

Thus, in Egypt, is the temple complex of Karnak. In China, the perfect example of Feng-Shui exists at the tombs of the Ming Emperors, the perfect geomantic site in every way (now sadly mutilated by a golf course!), whilst, in England, we have the perfectly harmonious cathedral at Salisbury and, in Cambridge, King's College Chapel. But at other places, where the manpower or money or appropriate site was not available, compromises had to be made. We may illustrate this by looking at monasteries. The monastery had a specific function: to maintain a community of monks so that they could perform sacred services in the main church of the monastery. Medieval monasteries have several basic components. These are the main church building with ancillary chapels, a cloister, facilities for cooking, halls for eating and a dormitory for sleeping. In addition, many monasteries had infirmaries and buildings for other purposes. Somewhere near, also, was a large barn or barns in which produce was stored and processed.

When we look at any one monastery, we can see that most of these features are present; but, when we compare one with another, we find that the precise layout and dimensions are never the same. Furthermore, the exact placement of each component with regard to the others may differ. The church will be orientated roughly towards the east, but the cloister may be on the north side, though it is more commonly located to the south. Certain elements may be absent altogether. The whole monastery will be laid out with regard to the terrain in which it is situated. The variation in monasteries precisely defines the nature of earth harmony. Monasteries were a class of settlement which existed to fulfil precise requirements and a prescribed type of architecture for the place of worship within the monastery. Despite the degree of variation from plan to plan, each site is recognisable as fulfilling the functions and each part of the monastery is recognisable as a refectory, infirmary, cloister or chapel. Their placement with regard to running water, hills and trackways takes into account the relationship between these factors and the requirements of the prescribed form and function of the settlement itself. The final design and layout is therefore the result of the accommodation of all these factors; this results in a unique structure, precisely tailored to its environment.

This analysis of a monastery can be extended to any human artifact placed on the earth's surface: the parameters of prescribed form and function may differ, yet it is only when the prescribed form is flexible enough to accommodate itself to the site that it is possible to attain a harmonious balance between it and its surroundings. When an inflexible form is imposed, inevitably it must clash with the environment and cause imbalance, with consequent effects upon its users and inhabitants. Although some of the best examples of this harmony at all levels are the houses of worship of bygone centuries, this tradition is being continued today in a perfectly modern way.

Unfortunately, many of the most sacred places of the world have become, primarily, tourist orientated. The authorities at several English cathedrals now levy admission charges and, despite protestations that the money is needed to assist in the horrendous running costs of a cathedral, it is seen by many as a negation of the essential sanctity of a great church. The charging of an entrance fee automatically transforms a cathedral from a living place of power into a museum, and limits its sacredness to the times when services are being held. Whilst it is recognised that cathedral administrators are in dire need of the money, there is a serious danger of desacrelising a holy place by charging admission.

The Church authorities themselves are admitting a twofold function of their sacred building; one as a consecrated place of holy power and another as a spectacle for tourists. This split has serious implications for any sacred place for, by definition, the tourists no longer regard the cathedral as holy. They have paid to get in and they are spectators, not participants. It is only through conscious participation m the present - literally, 'being present' at a place - that we can be in harmony with it. This element of participation has been lost in tourism and, because of that, tourists and site alike lose out.

In the case of cathedrals, if the admission charge was to pay for a candle which was then lit by the purchaser and placed among the thousands burning there, the tourist would be transformed into a participant and the sanctity of the site would impress itself upon the visitor. The performance of such a simple sacred act, of offense to nobody with any interest in cathedrals, would alter the consciousness of those who come now merely to visit the site as they would any other place on their busy itinerary.

Many modern places of worship lack the sacred element because they do not occupy an authentic place of power in the landscape. In addition, many of them have been designed according to the fashions of modern architecture whose basic ethos is universalism, consequently, a denial of place. Of course, modern architecture is not as timeless as it would like to claim, for modern sacred buildings reflect the architectural fashions of their time.

Of course, all sacred buildings have an element of this - otherwise, we would not have the diversity of church architecture, ranging from the Byzantine through the Romanesque to the Gothic, or the wonderful temples of India. All these 'styles' had something in common, however: they conformed to the underlying principles of sacred geometry and were erected upon places of power, determined by one of the several available techniques. In addition, the construction of these sacred buildings was done consciously as a sacred act by people who worked in knowledge and reverence. Their pious acts, conducted ritually, imbued the building with those qualities which we can recognise as sacred.

Today, this harmonious, integrated way of operating is largely absent. Similarly, the layout of the modern town contrasts markedly with its earlier predecessor, laid out according to precise principles as a ceremonial act of piety.

Chapter 10
Town Layout

There are two main factors that underlay the location of a town. Firstly, there is the position of the town in relation to its region, its relationship to the neighbouring rural district and its distance from nearby settlements. Secondly, there is the local site, the actual geolocation of the town itself. The reason for the location of a town stems, ultimately, from human consciousness, for all local and regional settings are the result of conscious decisions by people and do not result from 'randomness' or 'chance'.

Towns were and are founded at specific times at specific places for specific purposes. The requirements of the time at which they were founded, the traditions and customs of the contemporary society, are reflected in their placement and structure. Their present condition reflects the changes which have taken place since their foundation, and are as much a statement of contemporary belief as was the foundation.

It is rare to find an old town which has not grown or changed since its foundation so, to find out what sort of town we are looking at, we must examine the central part of the town. In Europe, these fall into two broad categories. The street-plans of the majority are irregular, the main roads radiating from the centre; the second type has streets forming a more or less regular grid. In the majority of larger towns of the second type, the grid has not been extended into later constructions and this complicates identification.

The two different layouts indicate a difference in origin. Those laid out on a rectilinear grid were surveyed as a unit, designed according to an organisational principle. The radiating-street town type began as a village and grew by accretion without an overall organised plan. This second type is the most common as most old towns had no formal planning, having grown as people built along the roadsides at the outskirts of existing settlements. Their streets follow former rambling tracks, contour lines or watercourses rather than a surveyed alignment. These towns are directly related to the landscape and, possibly, to invisible forces within it, for their relationship to contour and watercourse is immediate. The earliest parts of them are harmonious with the landscape on a direct level, unlike the rectilinear towns

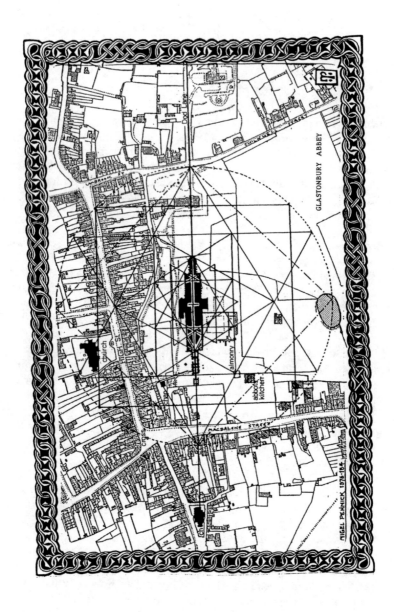

The sacred geometry of Glastonbury Abbey defines the layout of the town and the situation of the other holy places including the town churches.

118

which are an attempt to follow a perceived cosmic ideal, that of the divine order.

In the landscape, there are countless possible sites for any construction, bounded only by the constraints of land ownership, the prevailing social order, military considerations, economic factors and the capabilities of contemporary technology to cope with difficult situations. To understand the original nature of the landscape which moulded the existing town forms, we must examine the topography from every angle. Place-names often give an indication of the nature of the landscape upon which people built their settlements and, thus, of the conditions that still apply there today in many cases. Sometimes, they are the only indication of the original nature of a site. The landscape at the time of the foundation may have been very different from that which we see today. Apart from the physical structures of the town, and the transport systems it necessitated, the actual land forms may have been modified. Rivers and streams may have had greater flows than now, various watercourses may have been canalised, diverted or put underground. Marsh may have been drained, hollows filled and hills levelled, creating an altered urban landscape.

The importance of water as a primary factor, both for practical needs and as a subtle effect upon habitation, is evident from the many place-names containing the elements *brook, well, bourne, rey, for*d, or *ey*. The disposition of a settlement in the curve of a meander, or enclosed by diverted streams forming recognisable pattern-types, is in the sort of place recommended by geomantic practitioners. Monastic settlements often diverted streams to provide a water supply, to turn a mill or to carry away waste. At Fountains Abbey, the water runs beneath the Infirmaries, creating energies which aided healing. In planned towns, rivulets, ditches or water mains supplying fountains at certain places in the middle of the streets, provided water for the inhabitants and an artificial watercourse environment.

Many town names reflect topographical features: don, down or dune place-name elements suggest a hill or, perhaps, an ancient hill-fort as the key landscape elements; mere or more, a lake; or, a bank; and combe a valley. Some place names preserve the memory of former settlements, such as chester, caster, cester which refer to a former Roman city origin; places with street or strat refer to a Roman road near the settlement. Such places are not usually on the old Roman road, but just off it and at a lower level, for the

119

Roman roads were constructed along ridges whilst the villagers needed a water supply from the line of springs at the lower level. Other names commemorate founders, saints or legendary happenings: except in former colonial countries like Australia, Canada and the United States where names are often derived from the settlers' original homes, these names give an indication of the character of the place. Even in colonised lands, original indigenous names may still preserve the same information. By determining the original character of a place, we can gain a better understanding of its character today; this aids us in remedying any disharmonies or imbalances which might be present there. The ancient town of Glastonbury is held in almost as much regard today as it was in medieval times when it was a place of pilgrimage to the great Abbey which stood there.

Glastonbury's claim to fame as a Christian shrine rested upon the legends associated with Joseph of Arimathea. According to these legends, Glastonbury was the place where the first church anywhere - the Vetusta Ecclesia - was erected. This venerable building, destroyed in a fire in 1184, stood on the site of the now-ruined St Joseph's Chapel at the west end of the Abbey. The legends of the foundation of any place give us clues to the original perception of the nature of the place as seen by founders or later commentators. At Glastonbury, the nature of the site, a marshy, low-lying location is very similar to many of the important non-defended monastic places. In such a location, the verticality of the building compensates for the overwhelming flatness, as at Westminster or Salisbury.

Glastonbury Abbey has been the site of many investigations and the archaeology, sacred geometry and mystical elements have been well studied. The disposition of the key features in and near the town are well worth further study, however. Among these features are the local landscape, sacred sites, water courses and subterranean structures. The town itself lies in a valley between several hills, the main ones of which are Wearyall Hill, Chalice Hill and Tor Hill where there are, or were, important sacred sites. The late Chosen Chief of one of the Druid orders, Ross Nichols, called this setting The Bowl of Glaeston, 'an area of supernatural, visionary land'. To the northeast of Glastonbury stands Edmund Hill and, beyond Tor Hill, Stone Down Hill, the whole complex forming the legendary Isle of Avalon above the once-impenetrable swampy moorland. The roads coming to Glastonbury from the north and east run in a semicircle to the west of Tor Hill and Edmund Hill, joining the roads from the west and south at the end of Glastonbury High Street, to the south of which lies the Abbey. The

Abbey is protected from the northwest and north by the buildings of the town, and from the east and northeast by the hills. To the southwest, it is protected by Wearyall Hill but, to the south, it is open on a slight downward slope. Of the sacred hills, Wearyall Hill is the place where, according to legend, Joseph of Arimathea thrust his staff into the ground where it took leaf, becoming the Holy Thorn which flowered, out of season, each Christmas. The Legend of Crewkerne tells that Joseph and his twelve followers landed from Palestine at Bridgwater Bay and journeyed on foot to Glastonbury. Following a straight track eastwards across the Somerset countryside, the pilgrims rested at five-mile intervals. At each of these points one of them thrust a staff into the ground to mark the holy place and also the line. By Wearyall Hill, there was only one staff left- Joseph's. At the foot of Chalice Hill springs the chalybeate source known as the Chalice Well. Like most holy wells, Chalice Well never runs dry, even in drought years, producing a regular 25,000 gallons-a-day flow of radioactive mineral water with a high iron content that stains the channel red. The ancient well is lined with massive worked stones of great, though indefinite, antiquity, which form a polygonal chamber whose function is unknown.

According to legend, Joseph of Arimathea hid either the cup of the Last Supper, the Holy Grail, in the well, or the two 'cruets' containing the blood of Christ, giving the water its red coloration. From the well, the water flows in a westerly direction towards the Abbey site where it is reputed to be connected with the second well in the crypt of St Joseph's Chapel. Chalice Hill has a rounded summit, perhaps artificially modified, giving it a 'female' outline complementary to the 'male' outline of the Tor. Rising over 500 feet above the otherwise flat marshy lands of Glastonbury, Tor Hill is the dominant feature of the landscape. Known popularly as Glastonbury Tor, its name is a shortened version of Tor ('Tower') Hill, named after the tower of the former St Michael's church which stood at the summit. As an attractive place, it is seen by some as the holy mountain of Britain, a great magical centre of earth energies, linked to other holy sites by lines of subtle energy. The churches which have stood upon the Tor had the traditional dedication for churches on such high points, being holy to St Michael, slayer of dragons. Local lore asserts that, like the town and Abbey, the Tor is underlain by a network of tunnels, but the most obvious feature of the Tor is the array of seven distinct ridges or terraces which run right round the hill. These terraces, which are artificial, are indicated in an engraving of a drawing done by Dugdale in 1654; there is evidence from a tithe map of 1844 that some, at least, were used for cultivation. Most of the theories put

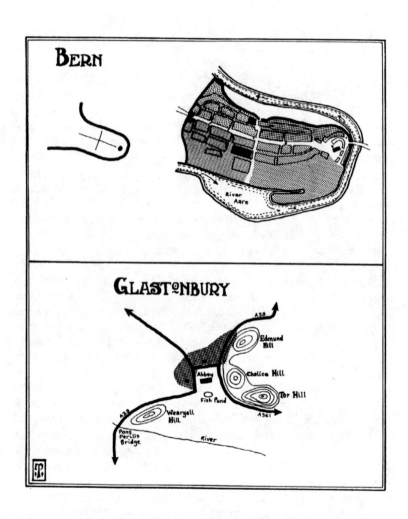

Comparative layouts of Glastonbury (England) and Bern (Switzerland)

122

forward to account for the terraces: sheepwalks, defence, etc., can be dismissed easily, and a more esoteric solution must be sought. There are two possibilities, not mutually exclusive: the labyrinth and the Calvary. Although there is no mention of a labyrinth in any of the vast documentary records of Glastonbury, in 1968 Geoffrey Russell noticed that the patterns on the Tor could be interpreted as a labyrinth. He saw that the terraces on the sides of the hill are arranged in such a configuration that they can he walked in the manner of the classical labyrinth. Subsequently, people began to walk or process around these paths, making the labyrinth pattern, and, on 7 February 1984, the 'Glastonbury Tor Labyrinth' received a sort of official recognition when the National Trust, which administers the Tor, erected notices which mention it. Whether or not it was laid out as a labyrinth in antiquity, it is a labyrinth now.

The character of a place can manifest in mysterious ways equally as well today as it did 1000 years ago. It is possible that the Tor was used as a Calvary, linked to the Abbey by a ceremonial pathway. Calvaries are physical representations on the ground of the Stations of the Cross, the fourteen stages of Christ's journey to his crucifixion. These Calvaries were laid out on a hill or mountain, culminating with a representation of the crucifixion at the summit. As in a labyrinth, the pilgrim progressed from the entrance to the goal, in this case, from base to summit, passing representations of the stages of the Passion. These Stations of the Cross are usually in the form of small shrines or chapels containing the appropriate image. Ideally, their siting should reflect the nature of the event portrayed. The ascent was not usually direct, rather being made purposefully difficult so that the pilgrim would experience some of the hardships of Christ in the ascent to Calvary. If the Tor was once a Calvary, then it complemented perfectly the Abbey, set in its valley. The entire landscape of the Abbey's neighbourhood could then be experienced in the light of Christian symbolism, incorporating all the physical features in a coherent overall pattern.

The Christian uses of the Tor certainly superseded a pagan presence which was remembered in the Tor Fair, held for many centuries on the second Monday in September every year and lasting anything up to a fortnight. The fair, which included horse, cattle and sheep sales, traditional games, gambling, drinking and merrymaking, was held on the western slopes of the Tor until 1850 when it was moved to a site closer to the town. Mythologically, the Tor was the Spiral Castle, abode of the Celtic lord of the Underworld and the Faerie Kingdom, Gwynn ap Nudd (Light, son of Darkness), a powerful elemental being, the genius loci. Those coming onto the hill without due reverence would be summoned to his presence by his servants who were dressed in red and blue, symbolising the unity of opposites. These supernatural beings were banished finally by a Christian hermit, St Collen, who sprayed them with holy water. As this legend dates from the seventh century, it appears that the Tor retained its pagan presence long after the original valley site was occupied by the church.

The dedication to St Michael, who pierces the Devil or a dragon with his lance, indicates a geomantic act on the Tor, parallelling that on Wearyall Hill, performed by Joseph of Arimathea with his staff. The conical form of Tor Hill, contrasted and juxtaposed with the rounded profile of Chalice Hill, is a landscape feature which can be found in several other important places; the verticality of Tor Hill has been reinforced by the church, whilst the subterranean cavity of the Chalice Well itself reinforces the character of that hill. On both sides of the Abbey, then, there are hills which have legendary traces of having been converted from the Old Religion to a newer faith and, apparently, in an eastwardly progressive fashion. The planting of the staff by Joseph was the first Christian act at Glastonbury, the founding of the Vetusta Ecclesia the second, then a possible Christianisation of Chalice Well and, finally, the conversion of the Tor by St Collen. This persistent movement eastwards is characteristic of many large churches and cathedrals, where progressive extensions of the east end took place at intervals.

This is especially noticeable at Canterbury Cathedral. In Irish house building tradition to this day, 'building to the west' - a westward extension - is considered extremely unlucky. The Abbey itself was laid out using a sacred geometry incorporating both the ancient systems in use in the Middle Ages - ad triangulum which uses the equilateral triangle, and ad quadratum, using the square. The pavement of the Abbey once contained a geometric floor, encoding the mysteries of its sacred geometry, of which the chronicler William of Malmesbury noted: *'In the pavement may be remarked on every side stones designedly interlaid in triangles and squares, and sealed with lead, under which if I believe some sacred mystery to be contained I do no injustice to religion.'* Like the Hindu yantras, the sacred geometry of the pavement expressed the eternal qualities of the site, built in physical form as abbey and town. These geometries are centred at the crossing point of the great church, beneath where the great tower once stood. It is possible that this point was a centre of veneration before the advent of Christianity for, in

1912, Frederick Bligh Bond, excavator of the Abbey ruins, discovered an egg stone which one of his colleagues believed to be the original 'cult-stone' or omphalos. A large boulder over three feet long, it has all the characteristics of a pre-Christian omphalos, completely in keeping with the universal tradition of converting sites of old religions into the shrines of the new. The tremendous sanctity of Glastonbury is obvious from the many Celtic saints who were buried there. King Arthur, too, is reputed to have been interred at Glastonbury and his remains rediscovered after the fire of 1184. The remains were transferred to a splendid new tomb in the nave of the rebuilt Abbey and a fragment of it, bearing the three crowns coat of arms attributed to Arthur, lies today in the Abbot's Kitchen. In Glastonbury, there are two ancient churches in addition to the Abbey, both of which remain in sacred use. To the west of the Abbey, and in line with the axis of the main building, is St Benedict's, whose position is determined geometrically with relation to the rest of the town. To the north of the Abbey is St John's, again sited with regard to the overall geometric layout. In addition to the two churches, there is the cross which, though not the original, stands on the site of an earlier one. The Abbey's axis, which runs from St Benedict's in the west, defines the alignment of Dod Lane to the east, an alignment which passes through Chalice Hill and which can be extended to Stonehenge, 3° 38' to the north of east from the central omphalos of the Abbey. Like Salisbury Cathedral, the Abbey thus has a geometrical relationship with Stonehenge.

As at Glastonbury, the construction of new settlements in medieval Europe was always accompanied by remedial action. When, in 948, Abbot Wulsin founded the town of St Albans, he diverted the course of the royal road Watling Street around the ruins of the Roman town of Verulamium, across the river and around the monastery. It continued past the monastery gate on the north side of the precinct, then back to its original alignment about a mile to the south. Because he had diverted the flow of one of the royal roads of Britain, he carried out remedial rebalancing of the disrupted situation. At the diversion points, two new churches, dedicated to St Michael and St Stephen, were erected. In medieval Europe, it was common practice to erect a stone, cross or church at a place where a road was diverted. These churches countered any harmful effects of the diversion and re-harmonised the area. Outside the Abbey gate, Wulsin laid out a triangular market-place with its broad base alongside the diverted royal road. Around this triangular market, a new town was settled. Plots on the two free sides of the market-place were offered to traders and settlers who were given free timber for house construction. At the far end of this triangular market-place, a third new church, St Peter's, completed the reordering of the landscape. This ancient understanding of appropriateness in the landscape was universal, linking the practical necessities of life with the cosmic order and managing the energies present within it. The foundation and subsequent construction of the city of Bern, capital of Switzerland, is an important example of this craft which lies at the interface between shamanry, the western martial arts and geomancy.

The martial tradition of pre Christian northern Europe involved the cults of the bear and the wolf; this implied more than just using these animals as totems or heraldic representations. In the ancient sagas we find numerous warriors with names derived from bear or wolf, of whom the great Saxon hero, Beowulf, is perhaps the most obvious. The exploits of these warriors resemble closely the feats of oriental exponents of the martial arts and further investigation of their practices has shown that, in ancient Europe, a form of martial arts, complete with its spiritual clement, was practised. As in the oriental martial arts with its trained channelling of ki, the western martial arts was concerned with the same energy that activates the body and the earth. This ancient tradition continued well into the Christian era, but eventually faded with changes in society and the advance of technology. The original part of the city of Bern is a classic example, at every level, of earth harmony. It was founded in the twelfth century after a knight, out hunting from the nearby castle, came across a bear. He was about to kill the animal when he realised that it was not an ordinary bear, but a sign that he should found a city. This uncharacteristic reaction of the knight to the creature indicates that he was a devotee of the bear cult.

Furthermore, the location of this event was close to the Celtic shrine of the bear-goddess Artio which, despite several centuries of official Christianity, must still have been the genius loci. An image of the goddess, bearing the inscription, Deae Artioni Licinia Sabinilla, was discovered there during the last century. It depicts her seated, holding a cornucopia. A large bear, backing on to a stylised tree, faces her in adoration.

Having been shown by a revelation of Artiona that a city dedicated to her should be built, the knight went through the appropriate bureaucratic procedures and received permission from the Emperor to proceed. Appointed Locator Civitatis, the knight, Cuno von Bubenberg, one of the Zähringer dynasty, proceeded to lay out the city in the quartered fashion.

The function of the Locator Civitatis was to determine the geolocation of the city, to set its standard measures, lay out its streets and building plots, and to recruit people of the necessary trades to live in it.

Bern was constructed as a combination of a dragon-form and the quartered square holy-city plan. It is located inside a 'hairpin bend' of the river Aare which flows round the site in a counter-clockwise direction. The river has both a strategic and a physical function, protecting the city from unwanted intrusions. At the eastern end, on the 'Dragon's Head', was a castle. Later, in less turbulent times, the castle was replaced by a church, outside which is a well. From this ran the central east-west street, intersected halfway along by the north-south cross street, making the four quarters. In the southwestern quarter, the cathedral was constructed, the common southern half location of cathedrals found in many European cities. Along the middle of the main streets ran water-carrying conduits. These were replaced later by fountains at important points, still a major feature of the historic core of the modern City.

Until centralised governments imposed standardised measure upon whole countries, each town or province had its own measure. This measure was tailored to the location, and so it varied from place to place. There were various standard measures within the local measure, based upon the local inch, nail, foot, ell and yard. It was customary for the standard measures of the city to be made in metal and fixed to the wall of the building that marked the central place. This seems to have been a refinement of the practice of having door posts of the standard measure, as at the palace of the Northumbrian kings at Yeavering (seventh century). At Bern, the measures were attached to the inside of the arch of the clocktower; at Vienna, they are on the west end of the cathedral. This practice was carried on into the nineteenth century when the standard measures of Britain were enshrined in the north wall of Trafalgar Square in London, close to the site of old Charing Cross, the central point of the metropolis. All ancient measure is derived from the interaction between the human body and place: although the foot is the basic measure, it is neither arbitrary, based on each individual's foot, nor standardised as a statistical average. It is the most appropriate measure for that piece of ground where it is used, derived by methods lost in antiquity.

When Bern was laid out, a foot equivalent in modern measure to 29.235 centimetres was used. Building plots were laid out with this foot in blocks that measured 60 by 100 feet. Freiburg-im-Breisgau, similarly founded by the Zähringers according to the holy-city plan, was laid out in blocks 50 by 100 local feet, each of which measured 32.4 centimetres. Clearly, the choice of these feet was not arbitrary, but neither was it standardised according to a central view of things. Appropriateness to the landscape was observed, giving measures and layout that, in later times, viewed from a distance with a centralist and universalist perspective, would appear quirky. But those who view it that way miss the basic point of earth harmony - appropriateness to place. Bern has all the elements of location, foundation, layout, measure and special place which we must study if we wish to find out about the character of that place. We are fortunate with Bern because the foundation legend and traditions are documented, as is its original plan which largely survives in the present-day inner city. It is classic because it combines a layout tailored to the qualities of the site with a design based upon a cosmic archetype - the holy-city plan. Rectilinear gridded towns are less related to the terrain for they have been designed according to principles independent of the landscape. Such towns fall into two main categories those with the Roman-style layout with two main streets crossing at right angles - the holy-city plan; and those which are just grids of more or less equal streets. The former type was the standard layout for 'planted' towns in the Roman period, located and laid out by augury, reflecting the divine order. Gloucester and Chichester are examples of this. In the perfect holy-city plan, the four quarters of the town were administrative districts or parishes. As a central point of order and civilisation amid the disorder and wildness of the outer world, the holy city symbolises the ordered cosmos brought out of chaos by the will.

In times before it was recognised generally that the earth is spherical, the world was perceived as a flat disc divided into four quarters, with a holy city at the centre. Pagans viewed Troy as the central city at the middle of the world, whilst Jews and Christians saw Jerusalem as that holy city. Each town laid out according to the quartered design was therefore a reflection of the entire world, and the stone, tree or cross at the centre was symbolic of the centre of the world. Effectively, the holy-city plan is sacred space which is orientated and subdivided according to a celestial model and laid out with sacred measure. The holy-city plan is a recognition of this creation of sacred space which accounts for its uninterrupted continuity from ancient times into the Christian era. In the western martial-arts tradition, the construction of the great military forts of Trelleborg, Aggersborg and Fyrkat in Denmark around the year 1000 used the quartered circle. The holy city was seen as containing the entire world within the compass of the city. Each quarter of the holy-city plan was assigned to a different quality, either a pagan deity, a Christian saint, or a trade. Thus at Nijmegen in the Netherlands, the quartered town was divided into the quarters of St John (northwest), St Anthony (northeast), Our Lady (southwest) and Broer (southeast). Rottweil-am-Neckar, another Zähringer city, had quarters (in the same order) of Holy Cross, St Lawrence, Sprenge, and St John. Bern's quarters were the Bakers' Quarter, the Smiths' Quarter, the Butchers' Quarter and the Tanners' Quarter. This symbolic division assigns the appropriate quarter of sacred space to its physical representatives on earth. In the case of Bern, these were workers with grain, metal, live animals and animal products. These qualities are still present in any city deliberately laid out like Bern. Whether we choose to recognise them or not is up to us. Any oriented, formally laid-out city like Bern was automatically the correct place for the observation of the heavens, both for everyday time-telling by the sun and for more esoteric reasons, such as astrology. Ideally, the gateways, towers and important buildings were located to mark important sunrise positions, so that the whole city was an observatory. Within a town with this layout, certain places are therefore related automatically to certain functions and each has its own specific character. If we live in such a town, we can determine easily these places and investigate whether they are good or bad for us as individuals.

Salisbury or New Sarum is one of the most important cities of the Middle Ages, for its foundation and layout demonstrates another of the universal principles of earth harmony. The city was built new to replace an older settlement, now called Old Sarum, that existed within the ramparts of a prehistoric hill-fort two miles to the north. The cathedral at Old Sarum was completed in 1091 but, only a few days after its consecration by Bishop Osmund, it was struck by lightning and seriously damaged. The cathedral, however, was located inside a castle and, gradually, relations between the clergy and the military garrison deteriorated. The final indignity happened when the clergy left en masse to visit another place and, on their return, found the gates of Old Sarum barred against them; they were forced to spend the night out in the fields. On hearing about this insult, the Bishop, Richard Poore, who was away at the time, vowed to build another cathedral, free from the influence of both military and royal power. The chronicler Richard de Blois, one of the Bishop's Canons, wrote:

'What has the house of the Lord to do with castles? It is the Ark of the Covenant in the Temple of Baalim. Let us in the name of God descend into

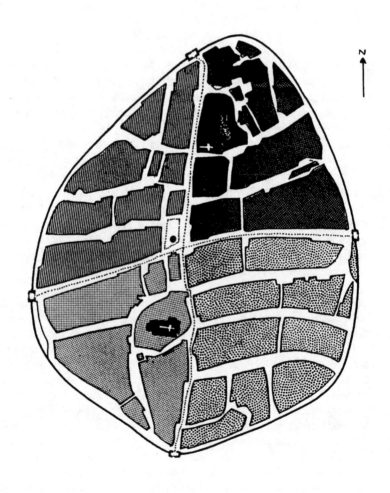

Brilon, Westphalia, Germany, laid out according to the Holy City plan, with four parishes divided by a crossroads.

the meads. There are rich meadows and fertile valleys abounding in the fruits of the earth, profusely watered by living streams. There is a set for the Virgin Patroness of our church to which the whole world cannot produce a parallel'. This sentiment is identical with the quest for the ideal site for a temple in Hindu Vastuvidya, as Bhattotpala wrote: *'A place where tanks full of sweet and transparent water, thronged with birds, abound .... where trees always blossom, where swans live in flocks, and where peacocks dance ..... there the Gods always remain and enjoy pleasure.'* Clearly, the geolocation of the existing cathedral was unsatisfactory for more reasons than the clergy's quarrels with the military. Bishop Poore's submission to the Pope for permission to build a new cathedral included the following: *'Being in a raised place, the continuous gusts of wind make such a noise that the clerks can hardly hear one another sing, and the place is so rheumatic by reason of the wind that their health often suffers.'* Other problems included structural damage to the cathedral by the windy weather, lack of trees and grass, and shortage of water. Again, there is a parallel in Vastuvidya *'The gods come near the places that have water and gardens in them, either natural or artificial'.* (Varahamihira: Brihat Samhita ch.55, v.3).

On Easter Monday, 1219, a wooden chapel was erected at Merrifield, the location chosen for the new cathedral. Merrifield, or Maerfield, was the location of the junction of the boundaries of three hundreds Underditch, Alderbury and Cawdon, and so was a central point. It would have been marked by a boundary marker known as a mere-stone. There, on St Vitalis the Martyr's Day, 28 April 1220, Bishop Richard Poore laid the foundation stone of the permanent cathedral. The Cathedral lies on a straight line that links the centre of the Stonehenge circle with the centre of Old Sarum and the ancient hill-fort of Clearbury Ring to the south of the present city. The distance from Stonehenge to Old Sarum is exactly six miles and from Old Sarum to the Cathedral is a further two miles. This landscape geometry, and the comments by Richard de Blois, show that several significant factors were taken into account when founding the new city. The geolocation of the new Cathedral has a specific legend which recalls the use of certain techniques by the locators of medieval sacred buildings. According to legend, the site was located by the fall of an arrow loosed by an archer who stood upon the southern rampart of Old Sarum. The use of the bow and arrow in divining a site is well known from the legend of Robin Hood who was contemporaneous with the foundation of New Sarum. On his death-bed he drew a last bow-shot and, where the arrow fell, he was buried. Similar legends exist elsewhere in European folk-tradition. At Old Sarum, however,

131

Sophisticated surveying instruments have existed in Europe since the days of ancient Greek culture. One cannot be a geomant if one does not know how to make a sundial.

132

the distance of two miles for a bow-shot seems to preclude a literal interpretation of the tale. The Cathedral's placement on a well-defined straight line, and the character of its surroundings, show that non-random factors were involved.

If any bow and arrow existed, then these must have had a different function. One ancient instrument used in navigation and surveying, the Jacob's Staff, looks something like a crossbow and locators using such an instrument might have been mistaken for crossbowmen. Equally, the bow has sometimes been used as a dowsing instrument and the precise location of the Cathedral might have required this technique. Dowsers have found that, beneath the crossing, is a powerful blind spring which, at times, attracts vast swarms of flying insects to congregate around the spire. On occasions, these swarms have been mistaken for smoke and the fire brigade has been summoned to the Cathedral! It is possible that the legendary arrow could refer to the use of a magnetic compass. Or, finally, the arrow might mean the line from Stonehenge upon which the Cathedral is located. Whatever the interpretation of this legend, it shows that something very special was done when a cathedral had to be relocated, and that the location of both the Cathedral and its associated city are far from random events.

The cathedral's location has been recognised as the ideal harmonious balance between the natural land and the works of humans. It has proved the inspiration for some of England's best artists; it is the city's focal point, being visible for many miles around, set symetrically among the Wiltshire hills. It is orientated due east-west and its sacred geometry is related to the line from Stonehenge which passes through the centre of the crossing with its tall spire and then through the octagonal chapter house. As with Winchester Cathedral and Westminster Abbey, the low-lying watery character of the place is augmented by the verticality of the building. This modification of the character of a place to bring balance is the epitome of Earth Harmony. Salisbury's street arrangement is based upon two overlapping grids that define the locations of the parish churches. One of the grids has the same orientation as the line from Stonehenge to the Cathedral, and important locations in the city, such as the market place, the City Cross, parish boundaries and the former watercourses are situated in an integrated relationship.

During the Middle Ages, many new towns were founded in Europe and many of them have patterns which show a high awareness of the landscape

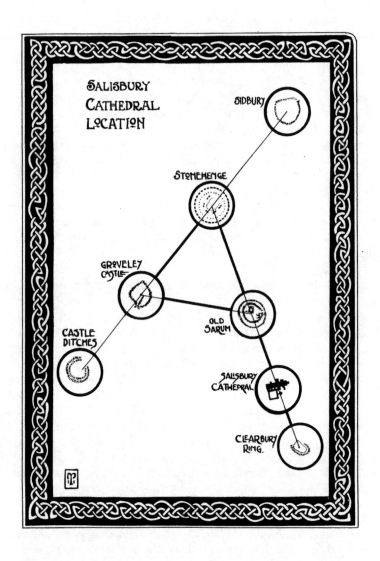

This system of alignments of earthworks, Stonehenge and Salisbury Cathedral, noted by landscape researchers at the beginning of the twentieth century, implies certain knowledge among the locators who situated the city of Salisbury in 1219.

134

and a regard for the perceived cosmic order. These new towns are of interest because they were founded on virgin soil and give us examples of the ideal settlement of the era. New fortified settlements, often erected in the face of the opposition of established towns, brought in new inhabitants who enjoyed privileges unknown outside the new towns. Wherever new towns were founded in medieval Europe, they often gave their inhabitants a better life than they had enjoyed formerly in their original settlements. Because of the increased freedom in these towns, several are called the linguistic equivalent of 'free town'. Fribourg in Switzerland and Freiburg-im-Breisgau, Germany, are two such founded cities. In these towns, an approximation to the contemporary idea of an ideal society was set up. This social order was seen to reflect the cosmic order and so it was natural that their design should reflect this, too. In such places, we find the quartered 'holy city' plan, usually accompanied by a gridded street plan.

This usage goes back to the 'Etruscan Discipline' of augury, as used by Roman engineers in Imperial times. In England, the Saxon port of Hamwic (now Southampton) was laid out in a gridded plan as early as the year 700 but, when we recall gridded street plans today, we think of the great North American cities with their unyielding rectilinear block systems. Because of this point of reference, a gridded plan like Salisbury or many other medieval grid-street plans appear to be the result of incompetence or an inability to carry out an adequate survey. Medieval surveyors were quite capable of making rigid grids, however, as witnessed in the bastides of France. The term bastide is applied to a group of towns in France and England founded in the twelfth and thirteenth century. These were founded and laid out by specially selected experts.

When Berwick-on-Tweed needed rebuilding after its destruction by the Scots, King Edward I, in a Parliament held at Bury St Edmunds in 1296, ordered the representatives of twenty-four English towns to 'elect men from among your wisest and ablest who best know how to devise, order and array a new town to the greatest profit of Ourselves and of merchants'. These towns were laid out according to principles which combined the practical with the mystic and the symbolic. In the Languedoc, these towns replaced the settlements annihilated in the bloody crusade against the Albigensians which depopulated the countryside, leaving it devastated. The new towns were laid out with precision, using rectilinear grids which, nevertheless, had relation to the terrain. Towns such as Sainte-Foy and Libourne, Gironde and Monpazier, Dordogne, have rigid grids demonstrating a high degree of

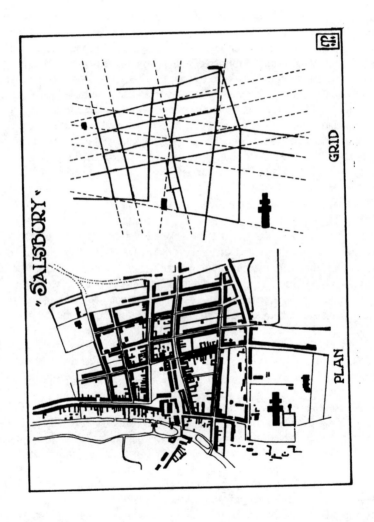

The street-plan of Salisbury and the underlying grids that define the streets and the other significant features.

136

constructional ability when gridded systems departed from right angles and rigid lines, this was part of the plan, as at Salisbury. If we live in a town planned originally in this way, we can locate both the places of power and the remedial structures which existed then. If they have been modified or destroyed, as is likely, then we can carry out our own remedial action in the places in which we live, restoring balance to our own environment.

Chapter 11
Holy Ground
Ancient and Modern

Throughout the world there are certain locations containing a number of places of power expressed as related sacred sites of varying kinds. The greatest concentration of these places are at the famous shrines and places of pilgrimage like Jerusalem, but many lesser locations have such a power that they have led to the recognition or creation of additional sacred places around themselves even into the modern era.

Water Sources and Watercourses

Springs are among the most interesting of sacred places, for they are living, vital sources of life's necessity, water, as vital today as it ever was. Their curative powers have been recognised by peoples of all cultures, and in Europe many still exist to-day in use for their original sacred function. Running water has always been associated with energy, perhaps because of its production of charged ions in the surrounding atmosphere, and also because the water in many springs contains minerals which have curative effects. The Celtic tradition venerated springs greatly, and today in Wales and Scotland, there are still holy wells with their associated bushes upon which rags are tied as offerings. The shrine of the goddess Minerva Sulis at Bath, which has curative hot springs, and in France, the sacred source of the River Seine, dedicated to the goddess Sequana, are particularly important sites. (For further details of Celtic spring-shrines, see Nigel Pennick's book *Celtic Sacred Landscapes*, London, 1996).

The former shrine of Sequana is north of Dijon on the Plateau de Langres in Burgundy. The spring is at the foot of a westward-facing cliff, and the water is carried away from it in a stone-lined channel running in a north-westerly direction. Begun around the year 50 c.e., this shrine consisted of the spring itself, a square Gaulish temple surrounded by an open porch. Down the westward-falling slope, over the other side of the stream was a marshy area in which the healing rituals of the goddess took place. At a later period, a series of additional buildings was put up on the higher ground to the south of the spring. A courtyard, entered by a ceremonial gateway with four pillars, contained the spring at its northern end. Access to the spring itself was gained by three steps down from the courtyard pavement. At the southern end was a building with seven rooms: four square ones, and three larger, rectangular rooms with a north-south axis. It is possible that the small rooms were accommodation for the priests and priestesses of Sequana. The shrine was abandoned, round about the year 300, either during internecine warfare or Christian depredations of Pagan sanctuaries, the most sacred paraphernalia of the shrine was buried in the base of the cliff behind the east wall, to the south-east of the spring. Here, in 1933, an exquisite bronze image of the goddess Sequana, personification of the source and river, came to light, giving us an insight into the nature of the presiding deity of this place. Her rediscovery and recognition came at a time when the old attitudes which destroyed the shrine had faded, and the Anima Loci could reappear.

Holy Places of Pilgrimage

In every land there are sacred places whose power continues to draw people to express those special qualities in concrete form. In the vicinity of Guildford, Surrey, in the south of England, where I was born, are a number of such significant sacred sites, ancient and modern which bear a subtle relationship to one another. Guildford is situated on the River Wey, a medieval crossing-point of the Pilgrim's way, the ancient ridgeway which led pilgrims to the shrine of St Thomas á Becket at Canterbury. According to local tradition, the town is located on the site of Astolat, important in Arthurian legend.

Just outside the town, on opposite sides of the river are two sacred hills, dedicated to the female saints Catherine and Martha. Like the many St George's and St Michael's hills, St Martha's is a high point which commemorates a dragonslaying saint. It may once have had a turf labyrinth in addition to the church, a parallel with that at St Catherine's Hill at Winchester, which still exists. Complexes of chapel/shrine, labyrinth and other structures existed at several places of pilgrimage, and the labyrinth itself was a symbol of the Christian pilgrimage to Jerusalem. To tread the labyrinth, or perhaps to traverse it in a kneeling pose, was considered the spiritual equivalent of accomplishing the pilgrimage to the sacred place.

Not far away, at Compton, is a most unusual Victorian building in the 'Arts and Crafts' style which incorporates the significant elements required to produce a harmonious whole. At the end of the last century, Mary Tyler Watts designed this remarkable memorial chapel which is a part of a

Guildford Cathedral, designed by Sir Edward Maufe and built according to geomantic principles between 1936 and 1961.

complex which harmonises with the landscape. The Watts Mortuary Chapel has the form of a Greek Cross intersecting a circle, the symbolic form known as the Celtic Cross, which Jung described as the archetype of wholeness, and which is, of course, the Holy City Plan. Here, it symbolises the circle of eternity merged with the cross of faith. In her small book *The Word in The Pattern*, published under her 'married name' of Mrs George Frederick Watts, she described the symbolism which permeates the building. The pillars flanking the doorway bear the name "I AM"; every buttress in the chapel is a tree of life; and among the many other symbols covering the highly-decorated surfaces is the labyrinth symbol, an allusion to St Martha's and the pilgrimage route.

Holy places are living entities which continue to create fresh expressions of their sanctity. The cathedral at Guildford is one of the most remarkable examples of modern sacred geolocation. In 1932, five years after the formation of the diocese of Guildford by dividing the area formerly under the control of Winchester, an open architectural competition was held for the design of a new cathedral. One hundred and eighty-three architects entered the contest, and Edward Maufe's design won. In 1933, the Earl of Onslow donated a classic location for the new cathedral - the summit of Stag Hill, the highest point in the neighbourhood of Guildford. To mark the site, a cross made from teak taken from the ship HMS Ganges was erected, and the ground-plan was perambulated by the clergy in the age-old traditional manner. The foundations were made by driving piles into the ground, 778 in all. Thus the cathedral is founded on 778 points. In the western esoteric tradition, Christian and non-Christian, there is a science or art known as Gematria. The characters of the Hebrew, Greek, Roman and Runic alphabets all have numerical values which means that any name or word adds up to a certain number. Various words may add up to the same number, creating an esoteric correspondence between them, which then may be expressed in any geometric, artistic or literary form.

The name of the Anima Loci, or the patron saint or quality of a church, may be expressed in the dimensions of the buildings, the number of windows, pillars, or in its underlying sacred geometry. In synagogues, sometimes the date is expressed over the entrance in a Biblical inscription whose words add up to the year number. At Guildford, the number 778 symbolises the unity of God (1) added to the number of the Greek word ETAYPOE - The Cross, whose number in Gematria is 777. This numerological tradition is completely in keeping with the Christian esoteric tradition. This Cross connection was made overt by the adoption of a logo of the cruciform ground-plan of the cathedral which from then on represented the cathedral and all of its associated activities.

In 1936, full ritual was used again in the laying of the foundation stone by the Archbishop of Canterbury. The foundation stone is made from stone extracted from the same quarry from which the Temple of Solomon at Jerusalem was mined, sandwiched between stones taken from Winchester and Canterbury Cathedrals, between which Guildford stands. In 1937, the last pile was driven with the assistance of Queen Mary, and the consecration of the cathedral was planned for 1941 but the advent of World War II brought work to a halt. Work resumed in 1948, and the final consecration took place on May 17, 1961, exactly twenty years after the planned date. The geolocation, design and foundation of the cathedral is a classical example of a sacred building built according to harmonious principles. Unlike some other twentieth century Anglican cathedrals, it is orientated correctly, east-west, with the altar in the east end. Internally and externally, there are key symbols and carvings which indicate the esoteric purpose of various parts of the structure. The rose window above the high altar depicts the Dove and the Gifts of the Holy Spirit, to which the cathedral is dedicated. At the crossing, the omphalos of the church is the highest point of Stag Hill. This is marked by a small metal plaque of a stag set into the floor. Before it was Christianised in the 1930s, Stag Hill was a place of power of the Celtic Lord of the Forest, the horned deity known by the epithet Cernunnos, and fittingly the whole district was a Royal Chase for the King's hunting in the Middle Ages. On the cathedral tower, this is emphasised by the south-facing statue of St Hubert, looking out over the Royal Chase of which he is patron saint, a version of the Anima Loci.

In addition to St Hubert, the tower bears three other saintly guardians of the four directions. The east is guarded by St Blaise, patron of the Guildford woolmen of the Middle Ages; the west, facing Canterbury, has St Augustine, founder of the Archbishopric there; and to the north is St Swithin, now famed for his 40-day rain curse, but historically the most loved prelate of Winchester. This modern rendition of the powers of the four directions is most appropriate for a hilltop site. The underlying sacred geometry of Guildford Cathedral is based upon the equilateral triangle, a system known as Ad Triangulum. The Vesica Piscis associated with the Great Mother Goddess and Our Lady, and Solomon's Seal, the symbol of God the Father and the Quintessence are part of this geometrical system.

This geometry is developed from the central point where the stag is set in the floor, directly beneath the gilded angel that tops the tower. Every feature of the cathedral is defined by the geometrical figures and their intersections, which relate mystically to the Divine Harmony inherent in the Universe. This harmonious relationship with the fabric of the world is emphasised again in the length of the building - 365 feet, the same number as the days in the year, making the church symbolic of God's year and hence identified with the whole of progressive creation. By using the correct principles, Guildford Cathedral, built in the twentieth century, an age not known for its esoteric sense of Earth Harmony, nevertheless accomplishes spiritual harmonisation at all of its many levels as well as it would if it had been built in 1332.

Sacred Analogical Forms

Throughout Earth Harmony runs the principle of analogous forms. It is through analogy that we manage our everyday lives, the recognition of familiar and less familiar things, our actions and beliefs. By comparing things, consciously or unconsciously, we draw parallels which enable us to survive in the world. Our relationship to the deeper realities of the world and the cosmos are best understood through analogy, and the expression of the character of sacred places is by means of analogical forms. The best known of these are found in European sacred geometry, but less basic structures also are used. The reproduction of a real or conceptual sacred place in concrete form is an important aspect of Earth Harmony. The analogical practice which is the epitome of Earth Harmony, is the modification of part of the landscape to reproduce a sacred conceptual landscape where a cosmic ideal is manifested on earth in physical form. Natural features of the landscape recognised as being close to this conceptual form can be used in producing major symbolic shrines and holy places.

In the Hindu tradition, mountains have been modified to conform with the pattern of the sacred central cosmic mountain, Meru. In the Renaissance times, European Christians modified mountains to resemble Calvary. Traditionally, Mount Meru is represented as a four-sided conical form, and the holy mountain of Deva-Kuta (The Peak of the Gods) in Sri Lanka is one such mountain, modified to resemble the cosmic mountain, with four streams descending from its sides to correspond with the four rivers of paradise. In India, it was a practice of monarchs to raise artificial mounds in the form of Meru, and the Gods were called down by rituals held at auspicious times to come and dwell upon them, radiating out their beneficial energies to the surrounding countryside. They are called Meru-Sringas, The Peaks of Meru. Like these artificial Merus, towns laid out as analogues of the Holy City, and labyrinths are forms which still retain their former power, when done correctly in the appropriate place. If we wish to create one of these analogous forms for ourselves, then a traditional unicursal labyrinth is the most readily constructed and most versatile. The labyrinth is a universal symbol: it is known from most cultures of the world except China and Japan. The labyrinth is a mythic fundamental expressed in concrete form, giving the feeling of an all-embracing unity. It is a reflection of the landscape of the soul, a vessel of the divine, forming a bridge to the supernatural. As a symbol it is unique because it can be of any size from a motif on a coin to one large enough to walk through. It represents difficult entry, and as a pathway of the pilgrim, soul or spirit to transformation. Unlike the related puzzle mazes, usually made of hedges, in which one can get lost, the unicursal labyrinth has a single pathway to the centre. Only this labyrinth has the protective, initiatory and locational uses. Its use in European geomancy is as a protector beside or over doorways. On a larger scale, the labyrinth has been built in stone, turf, or laid out in mosaic on pavements, as in the most famous examples in French cathedrals.

There are five basic types of unicursal labyrinth. The most widespread is the classical labyrinth, with a single, relatively simple, pathway to the centre characterised by intricate turns. Simpler than this, but less common, is the labyrinth which has one-way loops leading to the centre, and related to this is a type, known from Scandinavia and Germany, where the path does not end at the centre, but returns to the entrance. More complex forms are the Roman labyrinth, common from many villa sites, which is divided into four quarters, each of which is walked in turn. Finally, the most complex form is the Christian labyrinth, derived from the Roman form, but with a most elegant geometry. This is the form for most of the pavement labyrinths in French cathedrals, the best known of which is that at Chartres.

The character of a site is altered by a labyrinth: a formerly plain area becomes a focus of human interest, and energies are generated there. Wherever one is built, there is an immediate change in human perception of the place. In 1986, at the Ojai Foundation in southern California, I laid out and directed the building of the first stone labyrinth in North America. Its geolocation was chosen to regenerate a derelict site covered with debris, and which was appropriate with regard to the form of local hills and mountains.

The form chosen was the classical labyrinth, appropriate to the area from its traditional use in smaller forms by native Americans. The construction caused the immediate regeneration of this abandoned area, which took on a new character because of the labyrinth. Here, the geolocation, combined with the focussing of consciousness upon the task in hand, altered the character of a site which previously had been negative. Since then, following the Ojai example, many labyrinths have been built in North America.

It is possible to create a new atmosphere at any place by constructing a labyrinth. The alteration of the atmosphere occurs simultaneously at many levels. The work of construction focuses consciousness upon the area, and adjusts attitudes towards a place that might have been considered negatively in the past. It brings people to a place where human activity may have been absent, and as nobody can resist walking, running or dancing round a labyrinth, creates movement at a site. The laying-out of a classical labyrinth is relatively simple: it has an elegant and sophisticated geometry which enables us to construct the seemingly-complex form in a short time. Laying out a labyrinth is a piece of practical Earth Harmony which will produce a spiritual as well as a practical result. Labyrinth construction is an archetypal ceremonial act, creating ceremonial sacred space and a place of power. The most appropriate forms for such spiritual precision are the geometrically-perfect forms of labyrinth: the classical and the Christian labyrinths. The former pattern is easier to lay out, for it has within it a sophisticated and elegant geometry described below. The Christian labyrinth is much more modern than the Classical form, having been devised some time after the year 1000. One of the earliest representations is in a manuscript of the *Etymologium* of Isidore of Seville, written in 1072 and now in the Bibliotheque Nationale at Paris. It is a door guardian figure at Lucca Cathedral, Italy, and forms the basic pattern for many of the ancient turf mazes of England.

The form of the Christian labyrinth is very subtle, for if straightened out, its symmetry is apparent immediately. The centre is reached by a symmetrical pathway. Firstly, there are 17 moves; then an asymmmetric move, and finally another 17 moves, a mirror image of the first. Moving or dancing through such a pattern, especially if it overlies a site of perceptible energies, has a psychological effect on the participant, and, if carried out with appropriate ritual, can be a powerful religious experience. In Scandinavia and France the general orientation of ancient labyrinths is with the entrance towards the western quarter of the sky. If we use this orientation, the north-south axis is the first to be drawn. In the Northern European Tradition, the north-south (meridional) axis is the primary direction of sanctity. The starting-point, from which the whole labyrinth is derived is at the middle of this axis, which measures 30 units in length. Apart from the axis, the other important figure in labyrinth design is a pattern composed of a cross, corners and dots. This pattern is linked in geometric ways with the shield-knot and other ancient sacred symbols of protection, but here it is the geometric division of the square which forms it that makes it significant. This square lies to the west of the main axis, with its eastern side part of the axis itself. Here, the nine points in the side of the square coincide with points 11 to 19 on the main axis, which makes the original central point, 16, off centre with regard to the 9 points of the square.This square, which measures 8 units per side and is the familiar chessboard, one of the sacred grids underlying Hindu temples. At the four corners, pegs are put in the ground. These points become the four 'loose ends' of the final labyrinth, where a person threading the maze turns back. They are the centres from which radii are taken to create the curves of the appropriate sectors.

The design of the classical labyrinth is a system of stunning elegance, which renders its laying-out with the minimum of tools a simple act. All that is needed is a rope with sixteen regularly-spaced knots, which define 15 units, and five pegs to put in the ground. Significantly, fifteen is the number of Saxon Feet in the Rod, a unit of land-measure built into the countryside of England, Australia, Canada, New Zealand and the United States. After the original location of the first peg, then the square can be laid out from this. Once the four corner peg positions are determined, then the 15-unit cord is attached to the original peg, and the eastern arcs of the labyrinth are defined by marking out semicircles. Once this is done, the knotted cord is not removed from the original peg, but pulled round past the southernmost peg on the axis, to lay out the southwestern sector. The turns at the southern side of the entrance are made by laying the cord along the side of the square from the previous peg to the southwestern one, from which those gyres are measured out.The cord reaches to the middle of the west side of the square, defining the southern side of the entrance. It can reach no further.

The northwest sector of the labyrinth is laid out similarly with the cord centred at the original peg. The northwest curves are centred on the northern peg of the axis, which is five units from the original peg. The curve near the entrance is drawn around the northwest peg as with the opposite entrance.

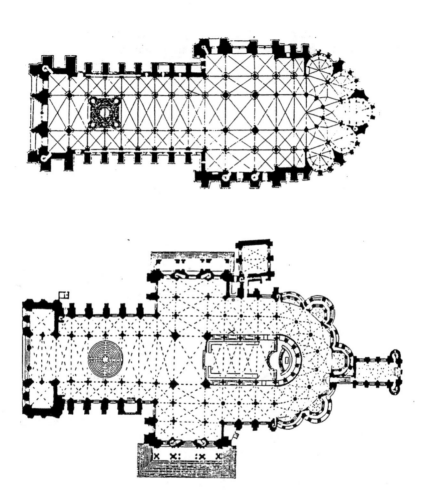

The location of the medieval French cathedral pavement labyrinths, in the western end of the nave; (top) Rheims), (bottom) Chatres.

The full reach of the cord from the original peg thus defines the other side of the entrance. Once the pattern of the labyrinth is laid out, the paths can be defined by large stones placed between them, or by digging trenches between them making a turf labyrinth like the eleven ancient ones in England and Germany. Whatever the final labyrinth is made of, the original laying out of a grid upon the ground is the traditional act of foundation, linking the labyrinth with the temple ground-plans of India and the traditional board games of northern Europe. By laying out a labyrinth on the ground to-day, we are not only building an interesting and powerful construction, but also we are tapping a vast store of symbolic meaning which is connected at the deepest level with the cosmic order.

In recent years, a new understanding of labyrinths has arisen. Fieldwork carried out since 1980 by members of the Caerdroia Project has revealed the sites of many lost or destroyed turf mazes in Europe, and the practical construction of new labyrinths has begun again. Some of these new labyrinths have origins as mystical as any medieval site, and deliberate symbolism built into their design. One of these, at Greys Court, Henley, Oxfordshire has a notable new labyrinth built in 1981 as the result of a dream described by the then Archbishop of Canterbury in his enthronement sermon given on March 25, 1980. In this sermon, Dr Runcie told that he had dreamed of a maze in which there were people close to the centre wishing but unable to speak to those who had not entered it. Inspired by this metaphorical dream of the church, Lady Brunner decided to construct a labyrinth in the grounds her home, Greys Court. A new maze, devised and laid out by Adrian Fisher and Randoll Coate, was constructed. Its design uses Christian symbolism, being a simplification and modification of the traditional Christian labyrinth. The maze measures 85 feet across, with a total path-length of a quarter of a mile. Its seven rings represent the seven days of the creation; the diameter of the centre is nine times the distance between each path, representing the ninth hour of Christ's agony, and the overall design symbolises the crown of thorns. Thus it is a modern form of the penitential mazes known to have existed in medieval times. After its construction in early 1981, it was blessed by the archbishop of Canterbury, whose dream it represented. It exists today as another example of a symbolic reality in the landscape whose origin is outside normal channels of experience.

Analogical structures can take other forms, being reflections of local landscapes. The gardens of Brazilian artist Roberto Burle Marx were built to reflect the locality. Of his roof garden at Reseguros, he remarked, "*Looking across the Guancha Bay to the baroque forms of the mountains in the State of Rio, I reproduced analogical forms on the ground.*" Although done with the eye and intentions of an artist, Marx's construction expresses one aspect of contemporary Earth Harmony. The creation of new places of power involves a connection with age-old principles on appropriate sites expressed in a modern manner. They may range from symbolic gardens to the shrines of all faiths, and to symbols which transcend factions, denominations and religions, but their integration of eternal principles with human needs related to the site's character produces that quality we recognise at the greatest of ancient sites.

Chapter 12
Living Traditions

"Commande the roofe, great Genius, and from thence
Into this house powre down thy influence,
That through each room a golden pipe may run
Of living water by thy benizon;
Fulfill the larders, and with they strength'ning bread
Be evermore those bynns replenished.
Next like a Bishop consecrate my ground,
That luckie fairies here may dance their round;
And after that lay down some silver pence,
The master's charge and care to recompence;
Charm then the chambers, make the beds for ease,
More than for peevish pining sicknesses;
Fix the foundations fast and let the roofe
Grow old with time but yet keep weatherproof" -

Beaumanor, from Robert Herrick's, *Hesperides*.

"Make me your Dore, then, South; your broad Side West:
And on the East-Side of your Shop, aloft,
write Mathlai, Tarmiel and Baraborat;
Upon the North-Part, Rael, Velel, Thiel,
.....and beneath your Threshhold, bury me a Load-Stone" -

Ben Jonson, *The Alchemist*.

For a person to feel happy or contented in a place requires more than just having material comfort. There must be a sense of completeness and security if material comfort is to be enjoyed. The attitude of people to their home is an all-important yet underestimated factor in this. Security for the residents comes only with a positive attitude to their dwelling-place, and this is engendered by participation in ceremonies of foundation and entry. Through shared common experiences at a certain location, ceremonies create a sense of belonging which is difficult to produce by any other means. Ceremonies are symbols which create positive attitudes in the minds of the future users of the house. Symbolic ceremonies reveal some of the underlying realities of the world that are not commonly apparent in everyday experience. They relate to the underlying pattern of the world to reveal a comprehension of the universal. A conscious, or even subconscious knowledge that things have been "done right" produces peace of mind, and a harmonious relationship between that person and the environment which might otherwise be absent.

Earth Harmony in its widest interpretation involves a harmonious relationship between the Earth, human beings, their artifacts and actions and celestial influences. Human consciousness is the mediator in the equation, so if that consciousness is incomplete or disrupted in some way, then there is no true harmony. It is necessary for us to have an awareness of the subtle differences between different places in order to come into harmony with them. The means of dealing with these differences remain with us in the forms and ornament of traditional buildings. Since a general loss of this subtle awareness, however, ornament on a building has been seen at best as "explanatory articulation", components that indicate to the beholder the structure of the building it decorates. According to this theory, this is the reason for placing pilasters or false columns along a plain wall, or masks, lions' heads, florets etc. along a string course on a Gothic building. This view assumes implicitly that no place within a building has any different qualities from any other part, except those created by the architect. The 'explanatory articulation' theory, which is dominant today, excludes the possibility that the forms and location of ornament might be related to various subtle qualities present at the site.

If we look into the use of ornament in various traditions, however, we will soon find that the modern viewpoint is completely at odds with the traditional one. Here, ornament is used as a means of instilling the object it adorns with some quality which we might call 'sacred' or even 'magical'; that is, with an intrinsic energy beyond the aesthetic. The dragons on the end of a roof ridge on Norse temples and churches; the 'rosettes' on a Gothic sacred building; stone lions guarding a gateway; these have a primary function to protect the building against harmful energies and psychic intrusions. Such ornament might have the effect of altering magnetic fields around a building, as in the use of iron chains in European Pagan temples, or the iron 'tie beams' in houses. They might affect the flow of air around a building, as with roof ornament, which also could have the effect of changing the building's electric charge. This could reduce the likelihood of lightning strikes, and subtly control the mood or consciousness of the inhabitants by direct interaction with their brains. The many subtle fields which surround us in the environment are only now being investigated. It is likely that traditional building dealt with many of these forces, even though the explanation of what was being done might have involved fanciful theories or erroneous beliefs. To be effective, ornament was made according to certain precise rules, and installed with ceremonial rituals at the appropriate place at the appropriate astrological moment. This precise and conscious preparation ensured that these objects would have protective powers, and impart their symbolic message to the beholder.

The principle of protection may be viewed as the ceremonial installation of a charged object at the appropriate place in the appropriate manner with the intention of blocking, deflecting or dissipating harmful energies. If we look upon these energies from the spiritist viewpoint, then the entities are bound or expelled by the magical powers of the 'ornament'. If we think of them as energies at the interface between the physical and the psychic, then the fields generated in the ornament by conscious manufacture and ceremonial 'charging' distort or deflect the harmful fields present. Lethbridge's interpretation of dryad, etc. fields creating impressions within the receptive human is compatible with this view of ornament as deflector. The German dowser Karl Sauerland believes that certain types of dragons, fluted or spiral columns and various kinds of leaf ornament all indicate their own type of energy, some beneficial, such as 'growth lines'. These energies can be detected in woodland and their effects manifested in twisted, distorted, bifurcated or fused tree trunks. Its is possible that the forms of some of this ornament is derived from these natural forms.

There are two types of ornament we can see in buildings: the built-in type which is an integral part of the building, such as foliage on stone carvings, or pargetting work; and that which is added, such as horseshoes over the door etc. The former type is installed with due ceremony as part of the builders' rites at the appropriate time during construction. It is a direct response to the location, combined with traditional observances. The latter type is more obviously protective in intention, for its is added willingly by the inhabitants after - sometimes long after - the building is finished. This type of protection may be put in as a response to something noticed or felt, or at the suggestion of a practitioner of harmonisation. Although they are no longer enacted as a matter of course, builders' rites and ceremonies still have

St Edmund, tutelary saint of East Anglia and the town of Bury St Edmunds in Suffolk, is an example of the spirit of the place manifested through an apotheosized human being.

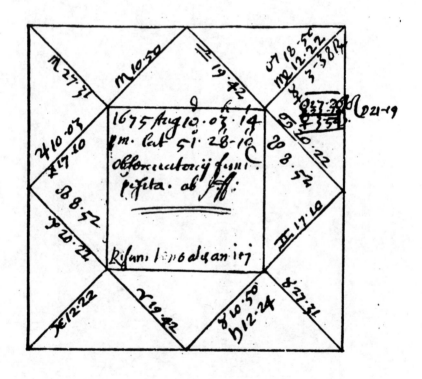

The horoscope for the electional astrology for the foundation of the Royal Observatory at Greenwich, set up in 1675, drawn up by the Astronomer Royal, John Flamsteed.

meaning to those who take part in them. If a community is to have any identity, important events in its life ought to be celebrated. By involving the users and the community at large in the building process, builders' rites and ceremonies help to create a bond between the people and the place. These ceremonies reflect the idea that to construct a house or other structure is to build a new world, and in order for it to harmonise with the existing world, its gestation should be acknowledged by the community. Builders' rites and ceremonies are conducted at the times of selecting the site, laying the foundation stone, fixing the first doorframe, 'topping-out' the roof, and finally entering the building for use. In sacred buildings, ceremonies of consecration and installing the image of the deity must be added to this list. Builders' rites and ceremonies exist everywhere, transcending the boundaries of culture and religion. It is only in industrialised societies where they have declined, and even here foundation and topping-out is usually celebrated. After the location, laying the foundation stone is the most important act in the creation of a new house.

All over the world, the laying of the foundation stone is recognised as the birth of the building. Conceptually, the foundation stone is a local replica of the omphalos, the stone which is the centre of the world, fixing the serpentine earth spirit at that place. In ancient sacred usage, the erection of a stone, and the building above it, protected an active place of power from misuse by evil, foolhardy or ignorant people. The foundation-stone of a new building likewise seals off the active site from the world, protecting is special character from alteration. The foundation of any building can be thought of as the inception of a new world, and so traditionally the rite was performed only after meticulous calculation of the astrologically auspicious hour. Before that hour, everything was prepared so that the ceremony could proceed smoothly and on time. Often, with important buildings, a procession of the participants would make its way to the place where the foundation was to be laid. When the stone was laid, appropriate prayers or orations would be offered to the gods. The coming together of the place, the time and the participants in the ceremony formed a permanent bond between heaven, earth and man at that location, influencing the subsequent events which could take place there. All of the major events in the construction of a house have their traditional observances, which are remarkably similar regardless of national origin.

The commencement or completion of each part of the building from the walls to the roof can be accompanied by ceremonies, sacrifices and celebration, marking a stage in the gestation of the final building. Furthermore, in traditional architecture, each important part of the building is designed and ornamented in ways which add protection and prevent harm. Often, in addition to the laying of the foundation-stone, the precise time of beginning or completing each stage is considered to be of great importance. The precise time of a foundation is important astrologically, whether done deliberately, or by 'chance'. All over the world, there are local traditions of astrology where a special time on which to begin an important undertaking is 'elected'. By so doing, the undertaking is given a birth time and a horoscope, which, like the horoscope of a human being, can affect or guide its future existence. Unlike a human, who is at the mercy of her or his birth time, the horoscope of a building can be selected, and each of the traditions has well-defined rules to ensure the best possible horoscope. Ideally, auspicious planetary aspects should be selected for the laying of the foundation stone, digging the well, building the walls, erecting and completing the roof, and finally the first entry into the completed building.

Western electional astrology, though little noticed to-day, has an equally long history, dating back at least to ancient Babylon. In medieval and Renaissance Europe, there are many documented instances of electional astrology being used to found buildings, such as the palace monastery of the Escorial near Madrid and the English Royal Observatory at Greenwich (1675) whose foundation stone was laid at the precise moment elected as the most auspicious by the Astronomer Royal, John Flamsteed. The diaries of the seventeenth century businessman Samuel Jeake show that he elected the date for the foundation of his storehouse at Mermaid Street in Rye, Sussex. Jeake laid the foundation stone at noon on June 13, 1689, the moment at which the planet mercury, signifying commerce, was in the same position that it occupied when he was born. The moon was in the twelfth house at that moment, propitious for storage, and other planets occupied appropriate positions. The horoscope of the owner was taken into account when electing the time for foundation. To record the elected time, the building's horoscope was engraved upon a stone and set into the front wall, where it remains today. Until the seventeenth century, there was nothing unusual about this. Whilst the electional astrology of buildings is little used today, the principles remain as valid as they ever were, and it is not inconceivable that at some time it may again become popular.

All over the world we find the legend that the foundation stone pierces the head of an earth-serpent or dragon, which symbolises the energies in the earth. In traditional Indian house building, this is still an integral part of the rite of foundation. At the appropriate time, an astrologer shows what spot in the foundation is exactly above the head of the snake that supports the world. The mason building the house fashions a little peg from the wood of the Khadiva tree, and uses a coconut to drive the peg into the ground at this particular spot, in such a way as to peg the head of the snake securely down. A foundation-stone (padma-sîla), with an eight-petalled lotus (the 'God's Nail' of European tradition) carved upon it is set in mortar above the peg, fixing the serpent for ever.

The exact time of the foundation of a new building is always considered to be the time that the foundation stone is laid. This act is the first permanent incursion into the ground of the new building, and traditionally it is accompanied by some form of sacrifice. Traditional building methods always include the placing of certain non-structural items beneath or in the fabric. These may be the remains of people or animals, ritually-made or consecrated artifacts, sacred relics, coins, tablets bearing prayers or the horoscope of the building, documents, vessels or pieces of clothing. The generic name for this motley collection of things is foundation deposits or foundation sacrifices. This is only partial description or explanation of their presence in a building, The usual explanation is that people practising foundation sacrifice considered it necessary to put animals or humans into the foundations of a building as a sacrificial offering to the Earth. The foundation sacrifices commemorate the slaying of the earth serpent to provide the building with spirit, and obtain authorisation from the nonmaterial world for the building to remain there. The idea is that if authorisation for the building is not gained from the Earth Mother or spirits of the Earth in this way, then the building's stability would be suspect, and the inhabitants or users would suffer ill effects, because the forces acting there would seek revenge against the unauthorised building. It was believed that the spirit of the place required the blood and body of a living creature as payment for the sacriligeous act of breaking the ground. By offering the life of an animal (or a human being), the spirit of the place would be placated and allow the building to be erected without trouble. If the Earth Mother or the spirit of place were not placated in this way, then the stability of the building would be uncertain, and the inhabitants or users would suffer ill effects from the failure to comply with the prescribed rites.

Another reason for sacrificial foundation was the belief that the spirit of the person or animal sacrificed would act as a guardian to the new building, and ward off evil spirits which might attempt to cause trouble. The many sacrificial remains, human and animal, which have been discovered beneath buildings, attest to the power of this belief. This is the traditional interpretation, based on the spirit view of earth energies current in former times. However, foundation sacrifices can also be examined in terms of modern discoveries and interpretations of geolocation, possible earth energies and psychological well-being. As with many ancient practices and 'superstitions', it is certain that they served a useful function, even though those using them explained that function incorrectly or in terms which are now unacceptable to modern knowledge. If we are to harmonise with our environment, then it is necessary to understand the essence of these practices without necessarily copying their outward forms. Foundation ceremonies are still common for important public buildings, when some dignitary will lay the foundation stone. It is customary in Britain to embed coins, documents or 'time capsules' beneath the foundation stone, which may be seen as payment for the earth spirit, the lineal descendants of the sacrificed animal.

In the Christian tradition, it was considered essential at one time that some relics should be buried at certain places in the church fabric in order that the sanctity should protect or be transferred to the building. The bones of saints, or fragments of artifacts believed to have association with Christ or his disciples, were placed with due ceremony at appropriate locations in the church. They were deposited in foundation stone footings, the capitals of pillars, inside altars or on top of spires. The basilica of St Peter's in Rome, built on the site of a Pagan cemetery, was designed to incorporate the reputed tomb of St Peter, founder of the Western Christian church. The sacred geometry of the church was centred upon the tomb. When the present basilica replaced the Imperial period church, Pope Clement VIII incorporated several further relics into the fabric. The cross on top of the dome of St Peter's contains two leaden caskets. Inside these caskets are reputed fragments of the True Cross and relics of St Andrew, St James the Great, and the early popes Callixtus, Clement and Sixtus. In addition to these human fragments are seven Agnus Dei, ritually-prepared medallions made from the wax of Easter candles, containing dust from the bones of martyrs.

The eastern counties of England furnish us with a protective device, used in foundation, and one which has a recorded magical function and theory behind it - the witches bottle. Many museums in the eastern counties have these bottles or jars on display, and they fall into two broad categories; the jug-like stoneware witch bottle commonly called a Bellarmine, and smaller, glass, bottles known as Cambridgeshire Witch Bottles. The larger bottles known as Bellarmines are best known. These are squat, round-bellied stoneware jugs, ranging from five to nine inches high. They are salt-glazed with a rich brown or grey finish. The name comes from the supposed likeness of the churchman in the fierce bearded face which adorns the front. Below this face is a coat-of-arms or an eight-branched solar symbol. Sometimes there are also small star-like symbols elsewhere on the bottle. Although they are named after Cardinal Bellarmine (1542-1621), inquisitor and persecutor of Protestantism in the Low Countries at the time of the counter-reformation, their manufacture pre-dated the Cardinal by at least a generation. Various theories have been forwarded to identify the face, including the claim that it is the Celtic god Esus. Whoever it is, the face has the fearsome mien of protective beings seen on buildings.

Bellarmine jugs are usually contemporary with the buildings in which they are found. First produced in the German Rhineland in about 1500, their manufacture spread through the Low Countries to England, and production ceased around the beginning of the eighteenth century. These bottles were used as a means of warding off the unwelcome attention of magicians and witches: containing urine, nails, pins and sometimes bones, until the nineteenth century they were installed in buildings. Cunning Murrell, the famous wizard or cunning man of Hadleigh in Essex was amongst those practising the craft as late as 1860. Often, Witch Bottles were buried beneath hearths in order to protect the navel of the house from harm. Others have turned up under doorsteps or even in back gardens. Although, fortunately, the custom has almost died out now, the sacrifice of animals under or in buildings was formerly almost universal. Of the many animals which have suffered in this way, the most commonly found are horses, oxen and cats. The horse was one of the most important sacred animals in the Elder Faith of northern Europe, and so it is to be expected that horses would be buried as foundation sacrifices. The horse has a general connection with solar heroes, and more specifically with the Celtic goddess Epona and the Germanic/Norse god Odin. Horse skulls play a large part in the shamanry of the north, still recalled in the Hobby Horse of the Morris Dancers. Horse skulls were used in votive offerings to the gods, and in various forms of protective and aggressive magic. Their use in foundation was very widespread as a means of protection, and many skulls have come to light during demolition or reconstruction of old buildings. The practice continued well into the twentieth century, and may still take place in remote communities. In 1895 in Cambridgeshire, at Black Horse Drove, the head of a horse was buried in the foundations of a Methodist chapel, and as late as 1913 a carthorse was buried beneath the terrace foundations of Arsenal's football stadium at Highbury in north London.

In addition to their function in foundations, horse skulls were often used to enhance the acoustic properties of a place. When the Bristol Street Meeting House in Edinburgh was demolished in 1883, eight horse skulls were found embedded in the pulpit At Llandaff Cathedral, horse skulls were incorporated into the choir stalls at the east end of the south aisle. Irish folklore asserts that horse skulls laid under the flagstones of a house improve the sound when the occupants dance. Horse skulls were buried also under the middlestead, the central threshing floor of a barn. The construction of barns with threshing floors was a great craft, and the builders took great pains to construct floors which would make the flails sing. Sometimes they were strung with wire, and to improve the acoustics of the clay floor, a horse skull was buried under each corner. 'Acoustic Jars' are related to skulls and witches' bottles, for they are of the material of the former and replaced or substituted the latter. Whilst they are usually specialised artifacts, usually found only in churches, their manufacture and setting was part of the same tradition that includes witch bottles and skull burials. The practise of using acoustic jars goes back at least to Roman times, for they are mentioned by Vitruvius, and exist in the Coliseum at Rome.

The function of acoustic jars was to improve or amplify the sounds of theatrical oratory, chant and music. In medieval times, specially-made jars were installed at many churches all over Europe. In England, these acoustic jars were built into the chancel wall of many churches, most notably at Sandwich and Leeds, in Kent; East Harling and Norwich, Norfolk. At Fountains Abbey, acoustic jars, lying on their sides, were incorporated in the choir screen. Although medieval in date, these jars are of an archaic design, retaining Celtic characteristics.

The knowledge of harmonics was part of architecture in former times, for the integration of a building at all levels, into the cosmic continuum, was the aim. The many explanations of the Divine harmony and its relation to sacred geometry incorporate acoustics as integral with that geometry. Sound is, of course, a means of generating a charge, both physical and psychic, at a place. The subtle enhancement of such vibrations by jars made and placed according to canonical dimensions would aid the harmonisation of the structure with the universe.

Some of the strangest objects found when old houses are renovated or demolished are mummified cats. These are the remains of animals immured alive as protection, usually in the roof. Many mummified cats have been discovered, often with their feet tied together or with other indications that they were alive when deposited in their last resting-places. Various folklore is attached to mummified cats, especially the ill fortune said to follow those who remove them from their resting-place, but little exists to inform us of the precise function they play. In Devon, local tradition tells that they were crucified and placed in the roof as a charm against 'witchcraft'. Strangely, however, the only two records we have of the burial of cats as sacrifices are both from the trials of alleged witches, when the act of burial was considered to be the performance of witchcraft. In 1971, a mummified cat was discovered when an old watermill at Sudbury in Suffolk was being converted into an hotel. The mummified cat was discovered immured in the roof, and it was removed. Following its removal, a series of strange accidents occurred, including two inexplicable fires at places to which the cat had been taken. Finally, the proprietors of the rebuilding decided to re-bury the cat, and a local vicar conducted a funeral ceremony for the cat, which was reburied with a note from the management apologising for having disturbed its rest.

Cats were not the only domestic animals to be used in house protection. In 1984, during the conversion of some stables behind the Carlton public house in Leigh Broadway, Leigh-on-Sea, Essex, a mummified whippet was discovered buried in front of the hearth in the tackroom. This dated from 1898, when the stables were built. After the customary spate of accidents, it was decided to re-bury the dog at a place as close as possible to the original grave. The new grave was framed with wood, and lined with red velvet. The dog was reburied in it, along with a piece of yew wood and a sprig of thyme, and a note apologising to the dog stating: "*We apologise for disturbing you and hope you will continue to act as guardian to the Carlton....*".

The popular idea that the burial of an animal somewhere in a house was "to ward off witchcraft" is only a partial explanation of the practice. This interpretation comes from the period when any and every ill occurrence was

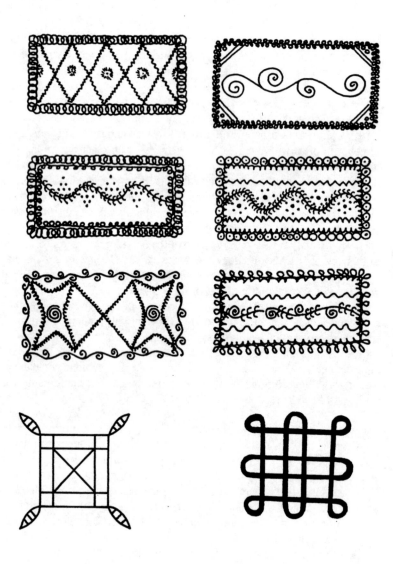

Chalked step patterns used in Scotland to protect the household against the entry of bad luck and evil.

ascribed to witchcraft, with the assumption that a specific malevolent individual - a witch - was the primary cause of that event. In such a world-view, any accident, illness or misfortune could not occur by chance. The very concept of randomness had not been invented then, so every event was seen as a result of an individual, conscious, action. So although the placement of the animal probably had the function of blocking or absorbing energies present at the site, these energies were interpreted as being sent by witches to do harm. The idea that energies could occur naturally or be generated by the layout of the area was not compatible with the world-view then current, and so the animal was believed to be a protection against witch rather than energy. The modern interpretation that energies are being blocked or absorbed leads us to the search for substitutes for the hapless animals - means of accomplishing the same protection without the cruelty of the old methods.

The Door

Openings in anything, whether the human body or a house, are vulnerable places where unwanted things may gain entry. So as the main entrance of the house, the front door needs protecting. The front door is the first part of the house with which a visitor has contact, and so the impression given there sets the tone for the whole building. Entrances can be designed to welcome, to impress or even to deter the visitor. Whilst doors exist to exclude the unwelcome, a sense of welcome is given when an impenetrable door is opened and the visitor is admitted. The door's function is to admit the wanted whilst excluding the unwanted. In human terms, this is done by the normal defensive methods: a solid door with appropriate locks, bolts and security devices. But in the traditional view of things, human intruders are only one of the problems. Assailants from the non-material world, whether interpreted as bad luck, demons, or harmful energies, must be excluded as well.

This process of protection begins when the house is being built. There are two types of traditional building; those built up from the ground piece by piece, using logs, stones or bricks; and those constructed of a prefabricated timber frame made elsewhere. Laying out the first type requires the door spaces to be left open when the walls are built. These entrances are protected by the doorstone or step. Where they existed, doorstones often had names, giving them an individual quality. As names are given ceremonially, these stones went through a form of baptism or naming which bestowed

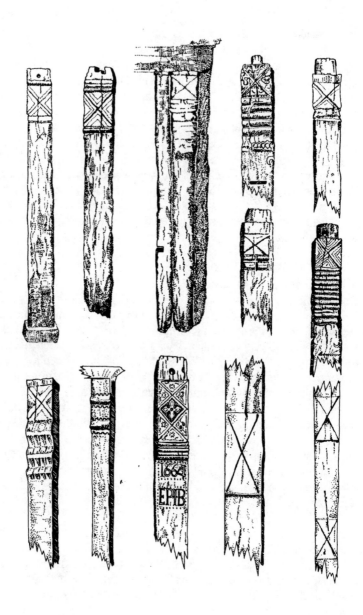

Witch Posts from England and Germany.

protective powers upon them. Beneath them, it was customary to place objects which served to protect the house. These threshhold protectors range from animal sacrifices to metallic or magnetic objects. It was believed that evil people and harmful forces were disempowered by magnetism or iron, a magnetic material, so iron knives or open scissors were buried under thresholds. The naturally-occurring magnet known as a lodestone was considered particularly effective. This practice is mentioned by Ben Jonson in his play *The Alchemist*. In addition to metal objects, witch bottles were used to ward off unwanted people or powers. Whatever was put beneath the threshhold, it was put there with appropriate ritual which served both to empower the object and to remind the participators in the ceremony that the object was present.

The function of the doorstep as an exclusion of unwanted intrusions meant that it had to be tended and kept in good order. Until World War II, which put an end to the practice, people in various parts of Britain would decorate their door steps with patterns executed in coloured chalks, flour or sand. Known as Step Charms or Devil's Patterns, there were several well-defined designs, each appropriate for certain positions and times of year. An important element in them was the 'tangled thread', an intricate wavy line which has protective powers wherever it is used. A last survivor of the practice is enacted in Knutsford, Cheshire, each year, when patterns are made in sand in the street to celebrate the ancient Maying ceremonies. Although the practice of decorating steps has almost died out in native use, it has been brought back to Britain from the Indian sub-continent. The Hindu custom of decorating doorsteps at certain times of year with patterns known as Kolams is practised now in many parts of Britain. The word Kolam, has several meanings which give us some insight into the perceived function of a door step pattern. It can mean line, current, watercourse, ornament, figure, mask, display, bird, areca nut, loofah and the planet Saturn. These various attributions reflect a continuously moving line, corresponding with the British 'tangled thread' design. Indian threshhold designs connected with the Moon, Saturn and the Pleiades indicate an astronomical element. This connection is a reminder of the ancient use of the door step, when the householder would stand upon it to view the sun. By viewing its position over landmarks on the horizon, the observer could tell the time of day, and the season of the year. It is probable that the traditional step patterns symbolise the apparent astronomical motions, linking the entrance of the house with the landscape and the cosmos. Documentary evidence from many cultures shows that the oriented gateways and doors of

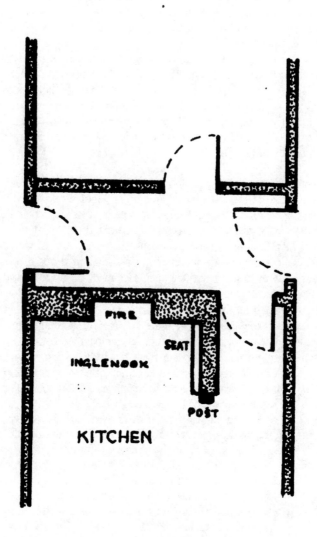

The customary placement of the Witch Post in the Yorkshire house.

many ancient buildings were used for observing the sun. This had the dual function of marking time of day and year and also the element of worship. Observation of the rising sun through such a gateway is epitomised at Stonehenge, where midsummer sunrise can be viewed from the centre of the circle. The sun rises over the outlying Heelstone, and is framed by the gateway of the trilithons. The power of this image today is obvious from the many photographs, posters and other graphic artwork that it inspires each year.

Objects near or around the door may also have a protective function. Various plants including trees have been used customarily to aid the protection of the area around the door. Even the symbols on bootscrapers have a protective function, but it is the door itself and its surrounds which carry the most important protection. The visible parts of the door, especially the knocker, locks and hinges, which express its strength, are reinforced symbolically by protective designs. Hinges may be made with cocks' heads or in the forms of the tree of life or dragons. Door knockers are held in the mouth of demonic beings, lions' or humans' heads, and locks may be engraved with emblems derived from Runes or Qabalistic symbols. Certain colours are deemed protective. In the southern states of the U.S.A., dark blue wards off the unwelcome ministrations of 'root doctors'. The division of farm or barn doors into four triangular panels painted green and white or blue and white alternately - the Dag symbol - is customary in parts of Germany, and we can find our appropriate local custom by examining old buildings in our own locality.

Much of the ornament associated with doors, ancient and modern, has solar symbolism. Windows above the door often have a semicircular form, with the window panes arranged in the pattern of the rising sun. This pattern was popular in British suburban housing of the nineteen-twenties and 'thirties, where it was made in coloured leaded glass. The pattern appears also on garden gates and garage doors of the period, and in comparable buildings in continental Europe. The connection between the door and the sun goes back to the earliest cosmologies. There, the rising and setting points of the sun were seen as gateways in the sky through which the sun entered and left the world each day. There were two gates: the Gate of the East, for the rising sun, and the Gate of the West, for the setting sun. Through the first, the sun entered the temple of the world, and through the latter it left, to return by way of the "dark path of the underworld". Although this cosmology is known to be based upon incomplete knowledge of the status of the Earth as

167

a spherical planet in orbit around a star, it is a description of the phenomenon as observed. That phenomenon is ingrained biologically in our being, and hence is part of us at the deepest levels. In harmonising with the cosmos, traditional building reproduces that cosmos symbolically in the structures of the building. The orientation of the four walls to the four quarters of the heavens, automatically relates the parts of the house to sunrise and sunset. The solar emblem on or over the door symbolises the triumph of light over darkness. The antiquity of this tradition is shown by an ancient Egyptian inscription at Edfu, which tells of the victory of the solar hero Horus over Set, lord of darkness. After this victory, Thoth, god of writing and wisdom, ordered that the solar emblem should be engraved over every door in Egypt. The stained glass of 1930s suburbia is a continuation of this tradition! But although it is very common, the solar emblem is not the only window protection we can find. Rectangles divided to produce the Runic forms of Ing or Gar act as protective invocations of the gods of entry and transition, or law and stability, and protect the house.

Traditionally, doorposts carry protective emblems, objects and inscriptions. The two door jambs are ascribed the qualities of day and night, male and female. Today, this can be seen best on churches, where male and female heads are incorporated in door frames or at the base of mouldings around windows. Looking towards the door from the outside, the man is to the right and the woman to the left, the man symbolising day and the woman night. Only by the unity of the two can the door frame stand. Another important protection for the doorframe is the Dag-rune sign, which may be painted, incised or engraved in the post. This symbol is used also on the so-called 'witch posts'. The use of iron appears again here, with the custom of hammering iron nails or pins into the doorframe to ward off evil. A modern device used in the United States is a small metal representation of a cock's head nailed or screwed to the door frame.

Protection of the frame can take more sophisticated forms. Orthodox Jews use a special scroll-holder called a Mezuzah, which is attached to the door jamb. This contains a protective scroll bearing scriptural texts including the following from *The Book of Deuteronomy* (Chapter VI, v. 4 - 9):" *Hear, O Israel: The Lord our God is One Lord: And thou shalt love the Lord thy God with all thine heart, and with all thy soul, and all thy might. And these words which I command thee this day, shall be in thine heart: And thou shalt teach them diligently unto thy children, and shall talk of them when thou sittest in thine house, and when thou walkest by the way, and when*

thou lyest down, and when thou risest up. And thou shalt bind them for a
sign upon thine hand, and they shall be as frontlets between thine eyes. And
thou shalt write them upon the posts of thy house, and on thy gates."

Another protective device of great antiquity associated with entrances is the
labyrinth. The unicursal labyrinth has been used from Europe to India as a
means of warding off evil spirits who are supposed to be 'amazed' by
attempting to follow the twists and turns, and fail to enter the house.
Complex signs like labyrinths contain an element of confusion about them,
a seemingly indeterminate structure which would puzzle those who had not
seen them before. The labyrinths carved on stone walls in front of houses of
the Nilagiris in south India are called Kota, 'the fort'. This is a description of
their defensive function. Sometimes, these labyrinth patterns were intended
to be followed with the finger. The Christian labyrinth carved in the stone
beside the entrance of Lucca Cathedral in Italy was used in this way. It is
possible that this act was considered to be a way of reconsecrating or
recharging the labyrinth, though small protective labyrinths also exist out of
reach above the door. One of the few European survivors can be seen still
over the door of a shop in Zürich's Augustiniengasse, and several exist as
wall-paintings in Scandinavian churches. Small labyrinths engraved on
stone slabs known as 'moon stones' or 'sun stones' were used formerly by
witches in various Celtic parts of Britain. They were used in a form of
meditation, where the path of the labyrinth was followed again and again
with the finger until a trance-like state resulted. 'Sun stones' were carved on
light-coloured stone and used during daylight hours, whilst 'moon stones'
were carved on dark stone by moonlight. These were never allowed to be
unwrapped in daylight, and were used only at night. It is likely that this
secret tradition, recently revealed for the first time, has a close connection
with the use of labyrinths as protectors of the threshhold.

Timber-framed buildings are especially fertile ground for protective signs,
as it was possible to do elaborate carvings around doorways. The German
and Pennsylvania Dutch Hex symbols, inscriptions invoking luck, blessings,
the intercession of saints or God, are among the almost limitless variety of
protection we can find. Many of these signs are of pre-Christian origin,
invoking the Pagan deities' to protect the house against harm, or to ward off
lightning or other specific ills. Often, they are painted in colours which have
a symbolic nature in themselves. As well as protecting the door jambs, it
was often considered necessary to protect the lintel above the door. In many
parts of Europe and North America, iron nails, often horseshoe nails, were

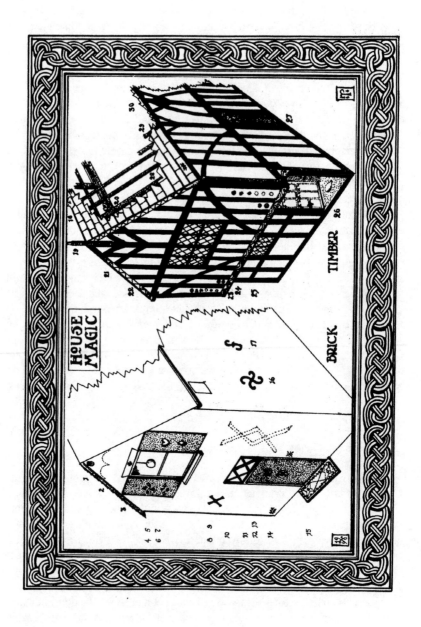

HOUSE MAGIC

BRICK

TIMBER

hammered into the lintel of the kitchen door, or a coin was nailed up there. This was another use of iron as a protection, and the creation of some sort of energy by the activity of hammering The best known lintel protector, however, is the familiar horseshoe, popularly known as a charm against evil witchcraft and a luck-bringer. The horseshoe is made of the protective metal iron, and echoes the form of the crescent moon, being symbolic of growth. Preferably, the horseshoe should be found on the highway, having been lost from a horse's foot, but to-day there is little chance of getting one this way. Like coins, sometimes horseshoes were nailed to a ship's mast to avert evil. Nelson's flagship, Victory, had one.

According to custom, horseshoes should be nailed with the points upwards, "to keep in good luck", as an inverted one "spills the luck"! This usage shows that the horseshoe is considered to be some sort of container, like a cup. The horseshoe is an enclosed form, holding in energies like the horseshoe magnet. Similar enclosing forms in the landscape such as Horseshoe Cloister in Windsor Castle, which encloses the west end of St George's Chapel, are considered to be accumulators of önd. The erection of a horseshoe should be a ceremonial act. If more than one horseshoe is used, 3 or 7 should be put up, as even numbers are considered to negate the horseshoes' power. At least one traditional rhyme for use when nailing them up has survived:

"Father, Son and Holy Ghost,
nail the Devil to the post.

Opposite: Traditional House Protection. 1. stone head under gable; 2. plasterwork 'goddess eyebrows'; 3. cross over window, witch ball in window; 4-7. shutter patterns: 4. Celtic rose, 5. Heart, 6. four elements, 7. Ing-rune; 8. cross wall-anchor; 9. Ing-rune in brickwork; 10. Ing-rune window over door; 11. horseshoe on door; 12. lion-head knocker; 13. warding-sign next to door; 14. warding sign in brickwork against lightning; 15. tangled thread doorstep pattern; 16. fylfot wall-anchor; 17. pot-hook wall-anchor; 18. roof-ridge head; 19. hipknob; 20. mummified cat in roof-space; 21. tree-of-life timbering; 22. wolfstooth barge-boards; 23. bressummer with tangled thread pattern; 24. Ing-rune leaded lights; 25. nails driven into corner post; 26. witch-bottle beneath threshhold; 27. dragon image on dragon post or bracket; 28. protective sigils on roof tiles. 29. Mann timber framing (German Fränkischen Fachwerkbau); 30. 'Wilder Mann' timber framing (German Alemannischen Fachwerkbau).

171

Thrice I smite with holy crock,
With this mell I thrice do knock.
One for God,
One for Wod,
And one for Luck.

Sometimes, the renovation of an old house will reveal a custom-made slot cut into the lintel to hold a protective object, such as a bottle. One of the characteristic types of lintel bottles is the so-called 'Cambridgeshire Witch Bottle'. This is a type which is known also from Germany, being made of greenish or bluish glass, often with an iridescent patina. They are long and narrow, and contain strands of hair or threads of various colours, with red predominant. The many threads recall the 'tangled thread' motif of doorstep patterns as well as the labyrinth - the classic way of fooling evil spirits! A bottle-placing, dating from 1904 and using a lemonade bottle, was reported from Bromley, Kent, in 1985.

Windows

Like the doorway, a window is an opening through which anyone or anything may enter or leave, and many of the protective devices used in doors were also considered appropriate for windows. In early times, windows had no glass, but were closed when necessary by shutters. However, unlike doors this meant that they were often completely open to the external environment. This subtle difference in function required a different sort of protection than doors, which were only opened to allow passage, and then closed again. Again, the windows of sacred buildings are treated differently from those of the secular. Unlike houses, ancient Jewish synagogues were designed with their window openings narrower on the inside than on the outside, in order to project and funnel the holy power outside the shrine so that a zone of sanctity would be generated around it. This is the reverse from castle-design, where the windows are large on the inside and small outside, to permit the maximum angle of fire for the defenders whilst presenting a minimum target for attackers' projectiles.

In ordinary dwellings, however, neither the sacrally projective nor the strategically protective are uppermost in design requirements. Here, the concern is primarily of protecting the house and its inhabitants against "bad luck" 'evil spirits', or other harmful energies of earth and air. Emblems and sigils over the windows were the most popular. These are many and varied.

172

They range from the sign that looks like a letter 'X' with dots in the four spaces to the parallel wavy lines that are supposed to ward off lightning and the crosses popular in Victorian buildings. Beside the windows, intended for closing them at night are the shutters, which often have cut-out patterns such as the heart (symbol of the Great Mother Goddess), four comma shapes arranged in a circle (the so-called Farmer's Fylfot or Celtic Rose), diamond-shaped apertures (the Ing-rune), or various other arrangements of drilled holes. In addition to these signs, many Continental shutters are painted with the Dag-rune. Even the custom of painting the windowframes white originally had the intention of warding off harm.

Because glass lets light through, it may also admit harmful intrusions, so at one time, 'witch balls' were hung in windows to prevent this harm. 'Witch balls' are large silvered glass spheres, oversize versions of the familiar Christmas tree ornaments, which can be seen sometimes hanging in the windows of old houses. As reflectors, they were hung in windows to deflect everything from the evil eye to ariel demons and lightning, although some people believe that mirrors actually attract lightning. Sometimes mirrors are hung in windows instead of 'witch balls', and Chinese geomancy has given us a whole technique of deflecting harmful forces by the use of mirrors. The diamond-shaped leaded lights of old houses are another protective device. Their shape, often which is echoed in cut-outs in shutters, or in brickwork patterns, is the protective Ing-rune. The coloured glass in Victorian windows is another defensive device, bearing painted or cut-out symbols of eight-pointed stars derived from earlier protective symbols. Finally, inside the window, the traditional form of the bobbin on the end of the blind-cord, is held to be prophylactic against lightning. and thunderbolts.

Walls

Every part of a building can be protected in some way against evil spirits, harmful energies, bad luck or whatever we call those causes which bring misfortune. As the major elements of a house which exclude the outside world, the external walls often contain materials believed to have protective powers. Since antiquity, blood has been considered the source of the life energy, and it was often mixed with the mortar of walls, to give it material and spiritual strength. When the walls of Portsmouth Dockyard were rebuilt in the eighteenth century, for example, the blood of bulls was mixed with the mortar. Another way of protecting the mortar was the practice known as Garneting, carried out in West Sussex, Buckinghamshire and elsewhere.

This involved pressing small pieces of ironstone into the mortar of the walls in order to protect houses against harm. This relied on the protective and magnetic powers of iron, as did the use of wall anchors. When brick was superseding wood as a major constructional material, builders used iron tie-bars to hold the walls together. At the end of these tie-bars are wall anchors, which take the form of circular plates, or, more commonly 'S', 'X' and swastika shapes which were claimed to protect against lightning. Less common, but still obviously protective, are wall anchors in the shapes of lions' heads and the Celtic Cross or Sunwheel.

On the surface of walls, we can find images of angels, saints and deities whose protective function requires no comment. Inscribed in cement or plaster, pargetted emblems and symbols are more prominent than the wavy lines scribed in cement to protect against lightning, or the horse or lions' heads beneath the gutter. The image of the solar disc and the sun wheel are encountered frequently on buildings in pargetting stamps and wall anchors. Sometimes a wheel from a cart or other vehicle can be seen fixed to a wall, or on either side of a door. This is especially popular in parts of Germany. The wheel of the chariot of the sun is a well-known image in Hindu sacred architecture, and of course has parallels in the European tradition in connection with Persephone, St Catherine and the East Anglian giant-killer Tom Hickathrift. At Konarka, Orissa, India, the Sun Temple is a building with large chariot wheels carved along the outside of the walls, in imitation of the chariot of the sun. In Hindu temples, these wheels symbolise the signs of the zodiac, through which the sun passes in the course of the year, a symbolism applicable on less grand structures, and intimately related to electional astrology.

Internal Features

Inside the house, certain parts seem to be more vulnerable than others. As the repository of fire within the house, the hearth was thought of as its heart. Various kinds of protection were used in old houses. These ranged from things built into the hearth or chimneybreast during construction, including witch bottles, animal sacrifices or single shoes, to external protectors like firedogs and hearth implements bearing protective symbols. The cross-beam of the fireplace was often made of a wood believed to have protective powers, like Rowan. Large old fireplaces are known as Inglenooks, the word coming from the ascription of fire to the god Ing, whose protective symbol is used elsewhere in houses.

174

14c LINCOLN
ROOF TILE.

Hip·end pattern
Norfolk reed Thatch

Protective roof structures: (left) 14th century head roof ridge tile from
Lincoln; (right) hip-end in Norfolk reed thatch.

175

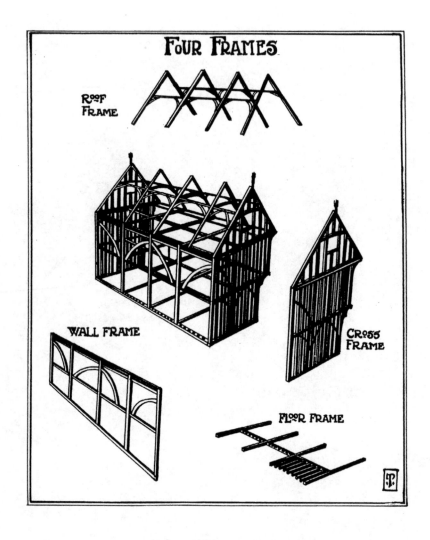

The four frames of traditional English timber-framed building construction.

The so-called Witch-posts are encountered in association with the inglenook. The technical name for these is a Speer-post or Heck-post, and their function is to form to end post of a wooden partition. Folklore insists that they should be made of Rowan, but every one so far examined has proved to be made of oak, the same wood as the rest of the timber-framed buildings in which they were installed. The posts were carved with a protective symbol, not the Christian cross, but one of Runic origin, the gyfu ('X' shaped), or the Ing-rune. Sometimes this was 'God's Nail', an Ing with an eight-petalled flower inside it, or occasionally a heart. These are the typical protective signs for posts, and are encountered all over northern and central Europe in such diverse locations as the entrances of barns and cemeteries.

Although the English examples are called 'witch posts', this name appears to be of recent origin. probably dating from the presentation of a post from Egton, Yorks. to the Whitby Museum in 1936. However it was believed that the posts were a protection against harmful witchcraft, and to increase the efficacy, some people placed a crooked sixpence in a hole made in the post. The grooves upon the 'witch post' were used to hold and charge other protective objects, such as knitting needles, which were used in butter churns when the butter would not solidify - a mishap attributed to witchcraft and neutralised by the needle. This practice appears to be connected with the custom of hammering nails into the doorframes and main posts of a house. These can be found still in the main posts of old buildings, notably the corner post of the Cross Keys Inn in Saffron Walden, Essex, which, like the Old Manor House at Knaresborough, is said to have been built on a living tree. The 'witch post' is acting here as the cosmic axis, the tree standing at the centre of the world.

In the Indian tradition, the ancient text called the *Paraskara Grhyasutra* states that when building a house, the corner post was erected with a speech beginning "*Here I set up the navel of the world*". This stood above the foundation-stone which bore the eight-petalled lotus, the 'God's Nail' carved on European posts. The custom of using a living tree in a building is recorded in the Norse *Volsunga Saga*, where we read that "*King Volsung built a noble hall in such a way that a large oak-tree stood within, and the limbs of the tree blossomed fair out over the roof of the hall, while below stood the trunk within it, and the said trunk did men call Branstock*". In the story, the Branstock did not hold nails, but a sword. By using a living tree, the roots, anchored naturally in the earth, became the foundation of the building, creating a true 'organic architecture'. Norse sagas also tell us of the 'high seat pillars' of the lord's seat which were carved with 'God's Nail' and set up with great ceremony when a new hall was built. These posts were held in such reverence that the first settlers of Iceland took their high seat pillars with them from Norway. The 'witch post' is obviously a descendent of this custom. The existence of such a post was a valuable comfort to people in an age of uncertainty. Like a national flag, which is a close relation, it was revered and defended as symbolic of the continuance of the homestead and family, a symbol of stability and protection.

The 'witch post' defended the hearth and the seat next to the hearth from unwelcome intrusions, and protective symbols can be found on many fixed seats in old buildings. At Craigmillar Castle, in Scotland, there is a labyrinth carved on the stone bench on east side of south window of the hall. Many monastery and cathedral cloister seats have carvings of the board game known as Nine Men's Morris. This pattern is an image of the cosmos with a protective function, as well as being a board game. It is carved on the roof-slabs of the temple at Kurna in Egypt (c1400 -1350 BC), and also in temples in India and Sri Lanka, where it is not playable and must have only the protective function.

Traditional furniture was carved with various protective devices, including labyrinths, swastikas, gridded patterns and representations of protective creatures. In addition to symbolic furniture, the traditional house sometimes contained glass wands, shaped like a walking stick. These were filled with hairline colour with the function of protecting the room at night. They were hung up, often in the inglenook, as protection against spirits, disease and infection. The hair lines were explained by the tradition that the demon was forced to count the lines, causing disease to fly to the stick. In the morning, the rod was wiped with a cloth to remove the demons. As this wiping would charge up the rod with static electricity, the glass rod would attract and collect airborne dust, bacteria and pollen, reducing the effects of hay fever and perhaps lessening the incidence of other illnesses.

As links between the lower and the upper floors of a house, the stairs are a point of transition which requires protection. Stairs seem to be places where a more than average number of ghosts or apparitions are witnessed, and even if this is just folklore, then additional protection would have been used to counter them. Protection of the stairs takes several forms. Their orientation in relation to the rest of the building was once considered important: to go upstairs towards the north was considered auspicious, linking the stairs with the cosmic axis concept. Patterns on the banisters are protective, and beneath the bottom step it was customary to deposit a small amount of grain as a foundation offering.

The Roof

Protection of the roof, both inside and out, required a number of different parts to be dealt with. Inside the roof, various offerings were inserted. Twigs of rowan, ash or palm (pussy willow), tied with red cord, have been found beneath the crown of the roof in old houses, and more unpleasant offerings like cats, now mummified, horse bones and dolls made from rags sometimes turn up during renovation. Outside, thatched roofs bear Ing signs and fertility patterns to ward off evil spirits. On haystacks, it was customary to make a straw cock to adorn the gable end. On houses with ceramic roof tiles, the ridge sometimes contains tiles with horsemen, other animals or human heads. At the end of the ridge, knobs or dragons were used sometimes, an echo of the carved hipknobs of timber-framed buildings. Hipknobs are uncommon today, but they were fertile ground for the woodcarver. The Ing sign, serpents, saints, heraldic signs and horse heads (known in Kent as Hengist and Horsa) provide protection. In the Indian tradition, a pinnacle on a house will generate good fortune. Most hipknobs had a symbolism related to the 'tree of life', and sometimes, as in Frisia (northern Holland and northwest Germany), the Odil-rune. The Frisian name for this - Eeyen-eerde - means 'own earth' and 'family', being a sign of ownership and belonging to the land. Local lore asserts that these symbols were erected to draw in good luck from the air into the roof of the house, not to ward off harmful forces.

Although of a relatively late origin, chimneys have often borne protective patterning. The chimneys on large house of the Tudor period have intricate brickwork patterning, and similar patterns were used on mass-produced chimneypots in the Victorian period. In southern England, the plant known as Houseleek or Syngreen was grown on the roof as a prophylactic against lightning and as a general protection of the house against fire. It is possible, though no-one has done any experiments to check the hypothesis, that such ornament alters the electrostatic field of the house, changes its internal charge, and actually reduces the possibility of lightning strikes. Bargeboards beneath the gable often bear the tangled thread pattern in the form of a vine scroll, dragons or just a wavy edge. This protective pattern is still a living

Protective dragons on a building in Hitchin, Hertfordshire, England

tradition used every day on shop awnings and summer parasols over outdoor restaurant tables. Until the rise of the modern movement in architecture, numerous other fitments ornamented the average building These include metal pinnacles in symbolic protective forms: the cross, Man rune, sunwheel, church tower- and weather-cocks, louvres and cupolas.

Weathercocks, more common on church towers and spires, have an origin in Pagan Imperial Rome, where they adorned tombs and other buildings on active sites. The cock is a protective emblem, being used also on door hinges and as doorpost protection. As the highest object in the area, the gilded cock on the tower-top was the first part of the town to receive the rays of the sun in the morning, heralding the day. Weathercocks, that is ones which swivel in the wind, as opposed to fixed tower cocks, indicate wind direction, and the prevailing conditions of the day, as well as heralding the rising of the sun. They are therefore useful indicators of weather and the more subtle attributes of the wind.

Chapter 13
The Ancient Craft of Timber-Framed Building

To harmonise human products with the natural world is the goal of Earth Harmony, and to understand this better, we can look at examples of this from the past. Things made by craftsmen from natural materials are intended to be harmonious, and craftsman-made buildings harmonise with their surroundings. The wooden framed buildings which were the vernacular architecture of northern Europe are examples of the true qualities of this craft.

These buildings were made by people who had served long apprenticeships to acquire the ancient skills of their trade. This ability was more than just handiwork, the technical manipulation of tools; it was an intimate knowledge of materials and technique on an inner, non-intellectual, level. If it is possible to teach the intuitive faculty, then traditional craft did it. In wooden building, the craft tradition involved all aspects of construction, from materials to erection. It knew the qualities of its material, wood; the correct and most appropriate ways to cut up timber to gain the maximum strength and the most usable material from any one tree; it used the appropriate sequence to erect a building from its component timbers; and it had the inner knowledge of orientation, both of the whole building and the timbers within it.

The earliest wooden buildings were erected directly on the ground, and the posts inserted in post-holes. These post-holes are a familiar feature of archaeological excavations, where they inform us of the ground-plans of old buildings which once occupied the site. The timber-framed buildings of which we are all familiar, however, were essentially movable, erected upon a sill beam into which the main posts were inserted. The sill beam rests upon a stone or brick plinth, and it is in this that the foundation offerings were made. Only after the foundations, of brick or stone, had been laid, could the wood frame be erected upon it. In the construction of a wood-frame building, the erection of the first frame is an important act, but not to be confused with the foundation event. Appropriately, a timber-framed building has four distinct constructional elements. Unlike a brick or stone building where the walls must be erected before the roof, the timber-frame building is integral, being composed of four types of self-supporting frame. These are the wall frames, which make the long walls; the cross frames making the dividing walls and gables; the roof frame and the floor frames. These four types of frame are jointed together to create the entire house frame, which is then infilled and roofed to complete the structure. The frames were always pre-fabricated and transported to the site for erection, but this does not mean that the buildings were not tailored precisely to the sites upon which they were to stand. Pre-fabrication does not mean standardisation, necessarily, and in any case, to the craft tradition, standardisation is anathema, for everything is custom-made as appropriate.

The old craftsmen took great care over things which to-day would be ignored, such as making carpentry joints with hidden features, or symbolic patterns of beam fixings. Frames which were to stand up were first assembled flat on the ground. The face which did not touch against the ground is called the upper face, and this is the side which faces outwards in the completed building, or when part of an inside cross wall, towards an important feature of the building. For example, in barns, the upper faces of trusses faced onto the middlestead, the place where the threshing was done. When timber buildings were erected, they were prefabricated at the sawpit, and then dismantled for transport to the place where they were to be re-erected. Because of this, each timber was given an identifying number and mark to show where it was in the frame and to which frame it belonged.

Because of the traditional nature of the craft, these symbols are derived from Roman numerals, modified in the same manner as those found on ancient wooden calendars in northern Europe. It is rare to find modern 'Arabic' numerals, although the roof beams of King's College Chapel, Cambridge (c.1515), bear them. Although nowadays carpentry is considered unimportant, the Kings of medieval Europe retained carpenters amongst their retinue. Just as a King would employ a Master Mason to design and oversee the construction of his churches, castles and city walls, so too would he have a Royal Carpenter. The roofs, spires, wooden halls, and even furniture like King Arthur's symbolic Round Table, were the work of Royal Carpenters, skilled in all aspects of the craft. One masterful example of

The runes of the Elder Futhark as used in Northern Tradition house location, construction and protection.

Royal carpentry exists today in the shape of the octagonal wooden lantern tower at Ely Cathedral. Built around 1340, this spectacular masterpiece is the work of Royal Carpenter William Hurley.

There are many intricate technicalities hidden within the carpentry of even the simplest timber framed building, varying from locality to locality and period to period. However, the basic techniques of timber frame building harmonise at all levels in terms of siting, materials and construction methods. Very subtle differences in technique in lowland and highland frames, for instance, show a craftsman's awareness of locally-appropriate methods. In England, there are three recognisable 'schools' of timber frame construction: firstly, the 'Eastern School', which used closely spaced vertical timbers known as 'close studding', producing tall narrow panels, and with curved braces at the corners between the sill and posts. Secondly there is the 'Western School', which had wider spaced timbers, producing squarer panels, often with decorative patterns made from timber around the corners, and thirdly, the 'Northern School', which dispensed with a continuous sill at ground level, having the main posts inserted in the foundations.

In any wooden framed building, an infill between the beams is required to make a serviceable wall. This was most commonly 'wattle and daub'. In close studded buildings, oak laths were wedged horizontally between grooves cut in the sides of the uprights. In buildings with larger spaces between uprights, holes were drilled in the underside of the upper timber of a panel, and a groove in the top of the lower member. Into these apertures, oak staves, pointed at the top end, and with a chisel-shaped bottom end were inserted vertically. Around these uprights, a weft of pliable wattles of hazel or cleft oak was woven in a basket-weave pattern. In East Anglia, staves were arranged horizontally with ash or hazel wattles tied to them. However the wattle was constructed, it was then covered in a mixture of materials that varied from location to location, usually including clay, dung, chopped straw, horsehair and other, more magical, ingredients. When this was thoroughly dry, it was limewashed, or alternatively a coating of plaster was used to make the daub weatherproof.

Although most surviving timber-framed buildings are painted black and white, it is likely that this was not their original appearance. Black and white is probably a nineteenth-century fashion. In earlier times, most timbers remained unpainted, weathering to 'oak grey', though tarring was sometimes carried out to protect the more exposed timbers. Infill panels would have been a natural lime colour, a rather ochre tint, or may have had a pink tinge from the sand used in the plastering. In Germany, France and Scandinavia today, brown or other coloured timbers are common, and panels are often lined-out with a thin painted line of various colour. Although uncommon now in England, painted symbols were formerly widespread, as can be seen in old engravings. Similar protective or symbolic painting can be seen today on old buildings in many continental towns and cities. In addition to painted symbols, plaster lends itself to taking protective symbols, incised with a stamp or done freehand by the plasterer. An important development or variation of this is the technique of plaster and pargetting, which reached its greatest development in the eastern counties of England. A covering of split timber laths was nailed to the wooden frame, and on top of this, two coats of lime plaster were applied. A similar, separate, cladding was applied inside, creating an early version of the cavity wall, in which various magical and protective objects could be deposited.

The timber framed buildings of the 'Eastern School' allowed this technique better than the others because of the closeness of the vertical members. This type of cladding allowed overall pargetting of a building without the hindrance of the structural timbers, as in 'half timbering'. Pargetted patterns range from geometric forms to full representational modelling. For repetitive patterns, plasterers have wooden stamps; often special combs are used to make wavy lines (a protection against lightning), and other plaster-modelling tools can be used to create more complex patterns. A popular division of the wall surface is a panelled arrangement, mimicking half-timbering, inside which various patterns have been applied. Full representational modelling combines an artistic interpretation of a legendary or sacred theme with a protective function. The famous pargetted gable of the Sun Inn in Saffron Walden, Essex, which faces north, is a good example. The figures of the legendary East Anglian hero Tom Hickathrift and the Wisbech Giant stand on either side of a large circle - the sun disc. Here, the eternal combat between darkness and light, good and evil, in the shape of fearsome warriors, guards a northerly entrance.

From China to Europe, it is customary to use representations of demons and warriors to protect against hostile forces, and English pargetting also has this function. If we examine a pargetted building, we will often find that a certain prominent symbol or representation faces towards a harmful direction like north-west, or towards another street or entrance, protecting the building from the ingress of evil spirits or harmful forces. In addition to

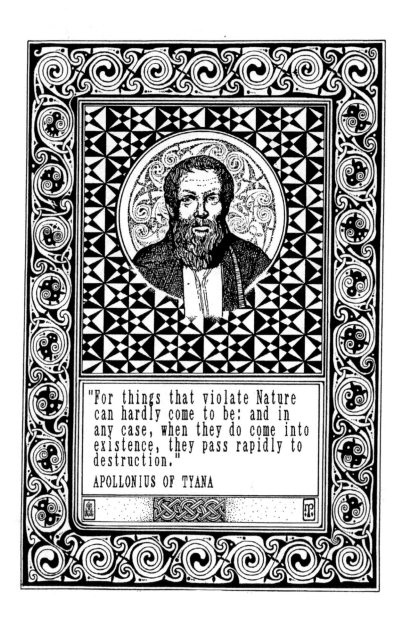

"For things that violate Nature
can hardly come to be: and in
any case, when they do come into
existence, they pass rapidly to
destruction."

APOLLONIUS OF TYANA

*Apollonius of Tyana, the Pagan teacher of 2000 years ago whose words
about the balance of Nature are so relevant to-day,*

wattle and daub or plaster and pargetting, half timbering also allowed other forms of infill. The most common of these is 'brick nogging', an infill of bricks, either laid in conventional courses, or in a herringbone pattern. Alternatives to normal brick courses are initials and dates, or, especially in Germany, protective symbols like the Donnerbeson (thunderbroom) or various Runic forms. Brick nogging is best when done in square panels, which was the common form of German Fachwerk (timber framing). The modern timber-framed buildings constructed according to the principles of Baubiologie (bio-logical architecture) by the German architects Karl-Hermann Schwabe and Guntram Rother use brick nogging and stone infill between the timbers. Their practical and harmonious contemporary timber-framed buildings in use in Germany to-day show that this method of construction not only has a past but also a future. Traditional timber-framed construction also continues in Alsace, South Germany and the South Tyrol, where the guild system of training craftsmen is maintained. And recently, the first timber-framed building to be erected in London for several centuries, the Globe Theatre, was opened.

In England, a great change in building came about in towns after a series of disastrous 'Great Fires', which consumed the larger parts of several important towns. The most significant 'Great Fires' were at Nantwich, 1583; Dorchester, 1613; London, 1666; Northampton, 1675 and Warwick, 1694. These fires led to the passing of new regulations which prohibited the erection of new wooden buildings, and prescribed new construction with designated materials and methods. The new buildings were built in stone or brick by 'architects' whose traditions were derived from Renaissance methods of proportion and aesthetics, largely ignoring the traditional techniques of foundation, orientation, and protection. At Warwick, for instance, wooden frame building construction was prohibited, and a set of rigid rules was enforced on the new structures which replaced those burnt in 1694. The Warwick regulations were very precise. They specified that the ground floor should be 14" above street level, reached by steps. The rooms had to measure ten feet from floor to ceilings, and walls had to be 18 inches thick at ground floor, 13 inches at first floor, and 8 inches at the garret. Such regulations allowed no room for special cases tailored to variant conditions of the location. Because of the enforced changes in towns, the character of building there altered, and, because towns set the fashion for the country, the erection of wooden-framed buildings there ceased, too.

By examining ancient timber-frame buildings in situ we can learn how harmony was achieved in the past, and gain an insight into how we can achieve it now. One of the best illustrations of harmonious principles in traditional wooden-frame buildings is the medieval open hall. The design of these halls incorporates a series of features in a formal layout where all the elements have a precise significance. Basically, the open hall is a large, timber-framed building whose main space, two stories high, was open to the rafters. At either end of this main hall were end bays or sometimes transverse wings, which were used for storage and living accommodation. Sometimes the hall was entered directly through a side door, but access was usually from a passage running across the width of the building between two cross-frames.

The correct orientation of this passage is east-west, giving a southern entrance from it to the main hall. To the south of the passage were two service rooms, the pantry for bread and the buttery, for beer. Entering the hall through the south door, one was facing the Presence, the dais or platform upon which the lord or king sat at the High Table. This layout can be seen today still in colleges at Oxford and Cambridge. Between the door and the Presence in the 'upper end' of the hall in early times was an open fireplace at the centre of the hall. Across the hall, which was open to the roof beams, was the so-called central open truss. This structural roof support was never actually at the centre of the hall, being a few feet to one side or the other of the centre line. This meant that the truss itself avoided the central fireplace, and did not have more subtle effects upon the central nave of the building. In the medieval hall, the upper face of this central truss faced northwards, towards the Presence. This is the face which had not touched the ground during pre-fabrication.

In the Northern Tradition, the north is the direction of the Gods, and so the north-south axis of the medieval hall mirrored this hierarchical view of society and the cosmos. At the southern end were the services and the servants, in the centre, the fire, and at the upper, northern, end, the Lord. Beyond the upper end of the hall were the private apartments of the Lord and his immediate family. The orientation of the hall meant that there was no north door, but that the hall was entered from east or west. The orientation of halls does not follow this pattern invariably, for within the practice of Earth Harmony, all of the local factors must be considered. In a village or town, the overall street plan, where the whole town is seen as a unit in the countryside, reduces the orientational rigour required for an isolated building. When we are examining an area to discover the factors acting upon it, we must take these variations into account.

A few ancient records give us information on the layout orientation and protection of buildings. The Icelandic *Grettis Saga* tells us that the old Norse halls were built on an east-west axis, but with the Lord's seat again in the northern side. Here, the seat was flanked by two consecrated wooden posts, the High Seat Pillars. These bore the image of a deity, usually Thor, and God's Nail, a symbol composed of the Ing-rune containing the eight-petalled flower, symbolising the sun due north at midsummer. This protective pattern of God's Nail has been used ever since as a protective device on buildings. Timber is carved readily, and lends itself to integral ornamentation with a symbolic content. Of all of the timbers in a wood-frame building, the member known as the Bressummer, forming the sill of a projecting wall, is the constructional element most likely to be carved with protecting ornamental designs. As a projecting element, it is the 'leading edge' of the building with regard to the street, and requires additional protection.

In many English, French and German examples, the 'tangled thread' pattern was used on the Bressummer. Sometimes this took the form of a vine scroll complete with grapes, or it was pods overflowing with seeds, which were painted in protective colours. Buildings with a hipped roof need what is called a Dragon Beam, a supporting timber running diagonal to the plan of the floor. These are required also in the construction of buildings where the jetty (overhang) goes round a corner. The Dragon Beam is supported by the Dragon Post, which is a corner post with an upper part overhanging in both directions, formed from an inverted tree. This is an inversion of normal practice in wooden building, where the posts are used in the same direction that they grew on the tree. But it is identical with the method of making staves for travelling and personal protection. Usually, the Dragon Posts are carved, sometimes with a dragon, but often with guardian human or demonic figures. Notable protective carvings include the 'chained devil' in Stonegate, York; the 'bearded man' on a farmhouse at Terling, Essex; the 'hag' on George Boote's house at Felsted in Essex; and the phallic figures in Bridge Street, Cambridge. These carvings have a connection with ships' figureheads, which were often referred to as the 'luck' of the ship, intended to ward off the spirits of the sea. Sometimes, wooden carvings on buildings use the same iconography as figureheads, such as the crowned lion on the 'Red Lion' at Martlesham in Suffolk. The forms made by the exposed beams

190

on the outside of a timber-framed building have been recognised as having significance as runic characters. The form known in German Allamannic tradition Fachwerk as Man is known to be a runic character of protection, whilst the addition of basal braces makes it a Wild Man. Timber framing for gable ends makes the Tree of life pattern, and is said to bring fertility and prosperity to the inhabitants. This pattern was being used still in the suburban houses of the 1930s.

It is often said that old timber framed houses were built of ships' timbers, but there is no evidence for this. Good strong timbers from demolished houses were used in new buildings sometimes, unlike today, when they are almost always burnt. They are encountered frequently as roof timbers in brick-built houses, but timbers from ships were not suitable for construction work after years of immersion in sea water. Very occasionally, super-annuated maypoles were used as house or barn beams, or as ladder compo-nents. As it was customary to renew a maypole every three years, and it was considered sacrilege to burn the wood, acceptable uses had to be found for it. One old maypole, bearing the character 'M', was discovered in 1883 in use as a rafter in a barn at Chalgrove in Oxfordshire. Clearly, the qualities of the maypole were being turned to the protection of the barn. Examination of any ancient timber-frame building will reveal many such marks and carvings, which, when taken into account with the surroundings, orientation, etc., will give indications of the good and bad places in and around the structure.

Protective Signs and Sigils

There are several signs or charms which are useful for protecting a house or room in any circumstances. Like much of our modern culture, these are derived from many sources, but they share the common function of warding off harm. Among those in use today are the Aegishjalmur, the Mitsu Domo, the labyrinth, Yang and Yin, the shield-knot, runes and religious images. The Aegishjalmur is the Icelandic symbol for irresistability, the western equivalent of the eight trigrams. Traditionally, it was carved on doors or painted on walls to ensure security and good fortune. It is available as modern silverware or as wall plaques. An oriental equivalent, also in use in Europe and north America is the Japanese Mitsu Domo which is hung onto a wall as amulet against fire, flood and theft. The Chinese Yang and Yin, symbolising the law of the unity of opposites, is a common amulet in places where there is a Chinese community, but as early as the beginning of this

The round tower of Copenhagen Cathedral, built according to Qabalistic principles, and immortalised in literature by Hans Christian Andersen in his fairy-tale The Tinder Box.

century, it was being used in English house building of the Arts and Crafts tradition. One can be seen on a house of the period at Church Rate Walk, Cambridge, where the symbol adorns a rain collector at the top of a drainpipe. The shield-knot is a pattern which goes back to Classical times, when it was common in pavement mosaics in Roman villas and public buildings. On a wall, it is a protector against harm coming from the north-west, which in all traditions is the direction of ill-fortune and death. A notable example of the shield-knot is carved in stone over the side door of the synagogue at Trieste in Italy, evidence of a practical tradition of its use for door protection. This sign has a subtle geometrical relationship with the Classical labyrinth, also used for door protection.

Many of the traditional signs for house protection in Europe and north America are derived from the runic script. The runes are the ancient magical alphabet of northern Europe, traditionally given to mankind by the god Odin. Historically, the runes are an amalgamation of the characters of old North Italic, used by the Etruscans, with the ancient Hallristningär of prehistoric northern Europe. In creating the runes, the phonetic use of the Etruscan script was allied to the ideographic symbols - a form of picture-writing - of the north. Each rune was ingrained with a meaning on more than one level, interpretable by different parts of the brain, bringing psychic integration to the user. The phonetic aspect is processed by the left-hand, analytical, side of the brain, whilst the ideographic aspect is processed by the right, the intuitive area. In addition to being a character in a phonetic alphabet, then, each rune has a precise meaning, being connected with a god or power. Carving or painting such a sign, with full consciousness of its meaning and a belief in its efficacy, will give this emblem, in the mind of its user at least, a protective function. In a society where the meaning, or at least function, of each sign is recognised, then everyone using the building will feel protected by it. If, as is believed by the practitioners of such protection, that the signs have an intrinsic power to draw in good energies and expel bad, then they are operating also on the transhuman level.

The earliest full runic alphabet had twenty-four characters, which developed over the centuries as language and society changed, until in late Anglo-Saxon times, there were thirty-three characters. In Scandinavia, the runic row contracted to sixteen characters, and finally a few remained in use in calendars, heraldry and house protection. It is with house protection that we are concerned here. There are only a few runes used in house protection, but these are ubiquitous. They are those runes concerned with possession, enclosure and the invocation of the defensive qualities of the Gods. These are the runes *Gyfu, Eolx, Ing, Odil* and *Dag*. The last three runes are consecutive at the end of the early 24-rune row.

Gyfu is the rune shaped like the 'X' of the Roman alphabet. It is the Pagan symbol of consecration, literally, a gift to or from the gods, and is found on doorframes, wood- and brickwork. This symbol was taken over as the general sign of consecration, although technically the Christian cross should be vertical with one arm longer than the other three. There are cases of Christian priests marking buildings with such crosses during ceremonies of purification or exorcism.

Eolx is a defensive rune. Literally 'elk', it invokes the power of the animal. It is found in brickwork patterns and in the design of timber framing. In Germany, this rune is known as man, but has similar defensive properties. It is an interesting coincidence that this protective sign is the preferred form for lightning conductors.

Ing is the most commonly found protective pattern. This rune is the symbol of the God Ing, personification of the generative principle and limitless extension. The sign has three forms. The first is the diamond pattern, which is the enclosed form of the rune, often seen in brickwork, or as cutouts on barge-boards, doors or shutters. The second form is the classic Ing-rune, which is restricted to brickwork or wood framing, and finally, the third is an extension of this, often called diaper-work, which may extend across a whole wall. The main entrance to St John's College in Cambridge has a fine example of this. As a symbol of generation, the Ing sign produces well-being and prosperity for the inhabitants.

Odil has a complex of meanings centering on 'homestead', 'possession' and 'family'. Often, the symbol is used as a protector at the end of a roof-ridge, especially in north Holland and Germany. Sometimes, Odil is seen in brickwork as a variation of Ing.

Dag is the rune meaning day or light, and, by association, the sun. It is used as a protective sign on door frames and so-called 'witch posts'. The sign may be painted or carved on doorframes, window-shutters and sometimes doors. When painted on doorframes, it should be in blue and white or green and white. There is a variation from Saxony in green, blue and white. The *Dag* is a common sight in Germany and Holland, where enormous barn doors are

194

often painted in this way, and visible for miles. It is the traditional protection on the shutters of windmill windows in Holland, too.

Connected with the *Yang and Yin* and indirectly with the shield-knot, the *Chinese Pak Kwa*, an octagon containing the eight *trigrams* of the *Book of Changes*, the *I Ching*, and sometimes with a Yang-and-Yin symbol at the centre, is a protective device widely used in chinese geomancy. Its form is very similar to the protective device known in the west as the *Maltese Cross*, and has some connection with painted *Dags*. This Pak Kwa symbol is sometimes deployed as a flag or cloth, usually red in colour, or may be a wooden or plastic plaque screwed to the wall, painted on the inside of a shop or restaurant window, or sometimes a larger structure in stone or concrete at the entrance to a temple or shrine.

One of the most popular means of remedying a harmful influence is the use of a mirror. The deflection of harmful energies by means of mirrors is customary in many cultures. The ceremonial fans, essential parts of the regalia of shamans, magicians and Chiefs of various West African tribes, contain small mirrors embedded as part of the overall symbolic pattern. These are said to repel demons, as are the jewellery containing mirrors, and various articles of clothing into which mirrors have been sewn which are common in the Indian subcontinent and other parts of Asia. The reflective powers of polished precious metals in jewellery, and even the reflectiveness of cut gems themselves, have the effect of reflecting harm back towards its origin. It is probable that this function is the origin of reflective metallic and jewel-encrusted regalia for monarchs and aristocracy. The carrying of reflective objects for protection occurs in many ancient myths. The most striking of these is the ancient Greek legend of Perseus, where he carries a polished metal shield which he uses as a mirror to prevent him looking directly at the petrifying demon Medusa. In Earth Harmony, mirrors are used to protect buildings rather than individuals. A sophisticated example of this is in the mosaic on the pillars and ceiling of the Shwe Dagon Pagoda in Rangoon, Burma, which contains thousands of mirrors for their protective value.

In Europe, *"witch balls"*, were hung in windows to ward off harm, and the best known and now most widespread protective mirror is the Chinese geomantic mirror. This is a circular mirror surrounded by the eight *trigrams* of the *Former Heaven Sequence* of the *Chinese Book of Changes*, the *I Ching*, set in an octagonal frame. There are also Europeanised examples in

195

use with the eight festival/direction symbols of the Elder Faith in place of the trigrams. Among other things, these eight patterns.symbolise the eight directions, a powerful charm against all kinds of harm. These mirrors are placed at points where harmful forces are deemed to be threatening a building and causing illness or discord. Chinese geomancy tells us that harmful energies - *Sha ki* - travels in straight lines, along roof-ridges, fence-lines and especially straight roads aligned upon buildings. Placing the Pak Kwa on the centreline of such a flow will disrupt it and prevent it having any effect upon the building and its occupants. These mirrors can be seen anywhere there is a Chinese community or even just a Chinese restaurant, showing a continuation of geomancy in everyday use, and giving a good indication of where to look for harmful influences.

In my own practice of Earth Harmony, I sometimes make use of geomantic mirrors. A few years ago, a friend of mine moved into a new flat on Castle Street in Cambridge, which faced directly along a straight road, Gloucester Street. Traditionally, this is a bad position, which in this case was made worse by a tall church spire directly in line at the other end. Among other things, my remedy for this imbalance was to install a geomantic mirror facing the centreline of the street. A few weeks after this was done, the street was blocked by a fence, and demolition work began. A new building complex was erected on the site of the street, and a new street built on a different alignment out of line with the flat being protected. The new building blocks all view of the church spire, and the road has been moved.

The conventional western viewpoint of these events would assert that there was no connection between them, and that the plans had been drawn up and authorised before the mirror went up. The mirror's presence would be seen as a coincidence with the unrelated planners' decision. According to Chinese geomantic theory, the mirror's presence would have helped the work to go ahead to restore balance to the protected place. Clearly, these views of the workings of the world are incompatible as they stand. An alternative viewpoint is that as everything in the Universe is linked in many ways, any action taken at a place has an effect there, possibly far-reaching. Traditional remedies and protections of places, used for centuries and found to be successful, may operate outside the commonly-understood direct causal workings. Whatever the underlying cause of the Gloucester Street diversion, the mirror achieved its intended effect, and the harmful influence was removed.

196

Runic Correspondences

Rune Name	tree(s	herb	colour	polarity	element	deity	symbolic meaning
Feoh	elder	nettle	red	f	fire earth	Frey/Freyja	the primal cow, Audhumla
Ur	birch	Iceland	moss green	m	earth	Thor/Urd	horns of the ox
Thorn	oak/thorn	houseleek	red	m	fire	Thor	the thorn, hammer of Thor
As	ash	fly agaric	dark blue	m	air	Odin/Eostre	the ash Yggdrassil
Rad	oak	mugwort	red	m	air	Ing/Nerthu	wheel under cart
Ken	pine	cowslip	fire red	f	fire	Heimdall	fire of the torch
Gyfu	ash/elm	pansy	royal blue	m/f	air	Gefn	sacred mark
Wyn	ash	flax	yellow	m	earth	Odin/Frigg	wind vane
Hagal	ash/yew	bryony	blue	f	ice	Urd/ Heimdall	structural beams, hailstone.
Nyd	beech/rowan	snakeroot	black	f	fire	Skuld	fire-bow and block
Is	alder	henbane	black	f	ice	Verdandi	icicle
Jera	oak	rosemary	blue	m/f	earth	Frey/Freyja	sacred marriage of heaven/earth
Eoh	yew/poplar	bryony	dark blue	m	all	Ullr	vertical column of the Yew tree
Peorth	beech/aspen	aconite	black	f	water	Frigg	the womb, a dice cup
Elhaz	yew/service	sedge	gold	m/f	air	Heimdall	the elk, the flying swan, open hand
Sigel	juniper/bay	mistletoe	white	m	air	Balder	the holy solar wheel
Tyr	oak	purple sage	fire red	m	air	Tyr	the vault of the heavens above the cosmic pillar
Beorc	birch	lady's mantle	green	f	earth	Nerthus Holda	breasts of the Earth Mother Goddess
Ehwaz	oak/ash	ragwort	white	m/f	earth	Frey/Freyja	two poles bound
Man	holly	madder	tiver red	m/f	air	Heimdall/ Odin/Frigg	human being
Lagu	osier	leek	green	f	water	Njord/ Nerthus	sea wave, waterfall.
Ing	apple	selfheal	yellow	m/f	water/earth	Ing (Frey)	the genitals
Odal	hawthorn	clover	ochre	m	earth	Odin	land, property
Dag	spruce	sage	blue	m	fire/air	Heimdall	balance, (night, day
Ac	oak	hemp	green	m	fire	Thor	mark tree
Os	ash	'magic mushroom'	dark blue	m	air	Odin	mouth, speech
Yr	yew	bryony/ mandrake	gold	m/f	all	Odin/Frigg	yew tree, bow
Ior	linden/ivy	kelp	black	f	water	Njord	Jörmungand, the world serpent.
Ea	yew	hemlock	brown	f	e arth	Hela	earth-grave
Cweorth	bay/beech	rue	tawny	f	fire	Loge	funeral pyre
Calc	maple/rowan	yarrow	white	f	earth	Norns	grail-cup
Stan	witch hazel/ blackthorn	Iceland moss	grey	m	earth	Nerthus	sacred stone
Gar	ash/spindle	garlic	dark blue	m	all	Odin	spear of Odin

Wolfs-angel	Yew	wolfsbane	blood red	f	earth	Vidar	wolf-hook.
Ziu	oak	aconite	orange-red	m	air/fire	Tyr	lightning-bolt.
Erda	elder/birch	mint	brown	f	earth	Erda	Mother Earth
Ul	buckthorn	thistle	orange	m	air	Waldh	turning-point
Sol	juniper	sunflower	sunlight	f	fire	Söl	the sun's disc

Ogham Correspondences

Letter	Name	Tree	Colour	Bird equivalent
S	Saille	willow	fine	hawk
N	Nuin	ash	clear	snipe
H	Huath	hawthorn	purple	crow
D	Duir	oak	black	wren
T	Tinne	holly	dark grey	starling
C	Coll	hazel	brown	crane/heron
Q	Quert	apple	green	hen
M	Muin	vine	variegated	titmouse
G	Gort	ivy	blue	mute swan
Ng	Ngetal	reed	green	goose
St/Z	Straif	blackthorn	bright	thrush
R	Ruis	elder	blood-red	rook
A	Ailm	elm	blue/piebald	lapwing
O	On	gorse	yellow	cormorant
U	Ur	heather	purple	skylark
E	Eadha	aspen	red	swan
I	Ioh	yew	dark green	eaglet
Ea	a/Koad	aspen	green	
Oi	Oi	gooseberry, spindle	white	-----
Ui	Ui	beech, honeysuckle	tawny	-----
Ia	Io/Pe	guelder rose	white	crane
Ae	Ao/Xi	pine, witch hazel	multicoloured	starling

Traditional buildings, made from local materials, often harmonise better with the surroundings than those made from metal and concrete, Little Moreton Hall, Staffordshire.

Gaelic Alphabet Correspondences

Letter	Name	Meaning	Numerical equivalent
A	Fhalm	Elm tree	1
B	Beath	Birch tree	2
C	Calltuinn	Hazel tree	3
D	Doir	Oak tree	4
E	Eubh	Aspen tree	5
F	Fearn	Alder tree	6
G	Gart	Garden, Vineyard	7
I	Iubhar	Yew tree	8
L	Luis	Rowan tree	9
M	Muin	Vine	10
N	Nuin	Ash tree	11
O	Oir	Furze	12
P	Beith-bhog	Poplar	13
R	Ruis	Alder tree	14
S	Suil	Willow tree	15
T	Teine	Fire	16
U	Uhr	Yew tree	17

Chapter 14
Modern Architecture and Earth Harmony

At the present time, the modern world has a sense of staggering from crisis to crisis, with imminent collapse into disorder and dissolution. Apart from the arms race, the continuing destruction of the natural world has reached critical proportions and the resultant famines and catastrophes are everyday news. The state of the world today is the result of historical processes deriving from the present dominance of the scientific industrial culture and its implicit relationship with the world. This state has come about as the inevitable consequence of industrialisation, for there is a radical difference between traditional ways of life and industrial civilisation. Traditional ways are part of the natural cycles of the world, causing minimal disruption, whilst industrial civilisation has caused an irreversible alteration of the world, largely through the vast quantities of material produced and transported.

The massive increase in the quality of production, use of materials and energy consumption was the most destructive feature of the expansive phase of the Industrial Revolution, which both caused and depended upon the creation and deployment of novel forms of transportation- the turnpike roads, canals, railways and, finally self-propelled road vehicles. The alterations brought about by transportation are all around us: it is scarcely possible for us to conceive of a village, let alone a town or city, without mechanical transport systems. The enormous quantity of energy spent in transportation of material and people oliterated local self-sufficiency and disrupted the delicate ecological balance of which we, as human beings, are part. The vast expansion of cities, which still continues in the 'Third World', has led to the depopulation of the countryside, necessitating the mechanisation of agriculture, whilst cities have become overpopulated, creating new physical and social problems.

The invention of mechanised transport was the major factor in the separation of human experience from the natural world. The operating constraints of railways meant that no longer was it possible for each station in each town to tell the time by the sun -local time- but that a centralised time reckoning, 'railway time', was necessary. 'Railway time' destroyed local observation and placed a necessary reliance on the clock, kept in order by synchronisation with the guard's watch on the first train of the morning from Euston, Paddington, or wherever the railway company had its master clock. Railways, too, removed a perception of place from the passengers and blurred local boundaries by allowing the use of non-local materials in building. This process continued with the imposition of state education and the invention of mass communications.

The flight to cities caused by industrialisation had the more subtle effect of making urban life and values the dominant cultural power in any nation. During any industrialisation, rural things rapidly assume an association with backwardness and even stupidity, and much traditional knowledge, necessary for survival in the physical, social and psychic realms, became fragmented, misunderstood or survived devoid of context as little more than superstitious observance. The oral transmission of knowledge and technique, the rural way of preserving skills and wisdom, was discounted. It was thought to be unreliable and of questionable accuracy, dependent upon the skills and abilities of the communicator which, being rural in origin, were considered to be inferior and of less authority than the printed word. The knowledge of 'old wives' medicine', rural building methods, traditional geomancy and survivals of the Elder Faith were shunned or even actively persecuted by people in authority who had been educated in the urban manner. Local traditions, customs, dialect and even languages were actively or accidentally discouraged and, finally, abandoned. Along with this went local awareness and knowledge of the qualities and character of various places. The gradual attrition of indigenous local culture thus came about as a result of the dominance of industrial urban mass culture and the assumption that it was modern and, therefore, superior in traditional ways.

This separation from the environment has been a long process, but it was only in the twentieth century that it was elevated to a creed. Totalitarian ideas and politics have always wished to erase the past so that their vision of the future would not be 'tainted' by remnants of a former age. But, in the early years of this century, worship of the machine and technology was formulated by the Italian Futurists into the new totalitarian principle. They idolised the 'new beauty', the beauty of speed', exemplified by the racing car and mechanised warfare, recognising the break with the past that this represented. A leading theorist of this new creed, Antonio Sant'Elia, preached that the new architecture must be defined as 'the architecture of cold calculation...(rejecting)...all that is heavy, grotesque and unsympathetic to us - tradition, aesthetics and proportion'. Marinetti, the leader of futurism, hoped that the world's cities would soon be razed to the ground and rebuilt without any trace of the past. In the same vein, Le Corbusier, whilst not rejecting proportion, dreamed of the day when Paris would be a massive collection of glass and concrete tower blocks standing in open grassland with trees, punctuated by transport highways.

Modern science, which Futurism romanticised, became successful by ignoring the interrelationship between things, isolating objects and phenomena for analysis before generalising the results and drawing conclusions. A deliberate dehumanisation, or at least a wish to make things beyond the human frame of reference, is part of this process. One senses an almost gleeful delight in this process in the pronouncement by Sir James Jeans, the physicist: *'The history of physical science in the twentieth century is one of progressive <u>emancipation</u> from the <u>purely human</u> angle of vision'* (author's emphasis). Sciences (and architecture) which ignore the human deliberately also have no requirement to be pursued for the good of the human race. Traditional views of the universe studied the parts within the context of the whole and with the requirement that knowledge should have human relevance. The understanding of the interdependence of interrelationship of all things within the universe stands in stark contrast to the break in equilibrium caused by modern civilisation. The maintenance of harmony has been the aim of many traditional faiths, the study of the natural world being a means of understanding and celebrating this harmony. Traditional science sought to understand the place of the human race in the cosmic order, whereas modern science has a tendency to discount the human as an irrelevant accident. Because of this, the modern study of science is the first in history which has led to the destruction of the subject under investigation.

The Futurists claimed that it was man's destiny to defy and deny nature. By technology, they claimed, he would overcome the seasons, day and night, and the nuisances of topography. Nature was seen merely as a repository of materials for human exploitation - a resource with no worth beyond the material. This view of the human race and the future, a woeful ignorance of human ecology which ought to have been deposited in the science fantasy file, was taken up by those who ought to have known better. Totalitarianism, whether the old-style Fascism which sprang out of Futurism, or the technocratic modernism of today, has brought the simplicity of the Futurist image without understanding its implications. This vision, 'Pitiless' but magnificent', as Le Corbusier put it, has gone through several stages in being translated into the squalid realities of our time. The wars wrought this century by the practical application of this ethos have brought about the dreams of Marinetti and Le Corbusier in many cities of the world.

The underlying ethos of some elements of the modern movement has been the conscious rejection of the natural, stemming from a seeming fear of nature and a predilection for the outer forms of scientific and technological equipment. Following the 'ornament is a crime' school of thought, artists and architects of the Dutch De Stijl school, for example, dreamed of the day when there would be no plants and every city would be gleaming, rectilinear and painted in primary colours. This ethos was a conscious realisation of the war against nature which had been pursued throughout the industrial era; the forms and fashions which developed as the result of investigations of the technology in architecture almost invariably ignored place. Le Corbusier's celebrated dictum, '*A house is a machine to live in*,' unconsciously echoed the frame of reference of modern architecture: the mobile vehicle. This is partly due to the 'portable person' concept I outlined in Chapter 1, the belief implicit in modern life that people are the same no matter where they are-on earth, in a building or in a moving vehicle. This fallacy of interchangeability has led to what I call 'oppressive architecture'.

Oppressive architecture is building which seems out of place in its location, producing feelings of anxiety or oppression in users. Most commonly, this is caused by the lack of harmony or even any sort of relationship of the building or 'development' with its situation. Oppressive architecture is characterised by massive scale: tower blocks dozens of storeys high, or perhaps half a mile long, with endless repetition of identical elements, or enormous featureless slabs of artificial material. Such places actually the very site upon which they are located, not only the archaeological underlay (giving the effect of construction on virgin soil), but also the patterns of the landscape itself. This has the effect of obliterating the distinction between one place and another. Uniformity of design not only exists within the area of such a development, but also with similar developments in other cities or even other continents, where only the language on the signs and graffiti is different.

The uniformity between one part of a building and another can lead to disorientation, only signs indicating where one is; this denies human

204

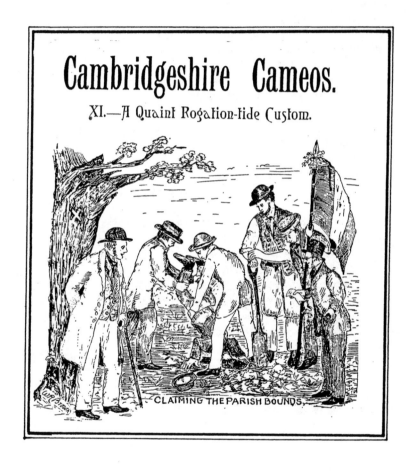

Beating the Parish Bounds in Cambridgeshire in 1895. Drawing by 'Urbs Camboritum (W.R. Brown).

qualities in favour of supposed scientific methods. This is exacerbated by the excessive plainness of modern buildings and the slavish following of Adolf Loos's dictum that 'ornament is a crime'. Such early twentieth century polemicists of architecture had no concept that what they called ornament might have psychological, psychic or even a physical function. The subtle currents of the micro-climate and the psychic needs of humans which might be affected by seemingly ornamental structures were swept away in a materialistic reaction against historical eclecticism and the mystic view of the building. Although the founders of the modern movement in architecture were attempting to liberate people, and some of their best buildings succeeded, seemingly the greater part of their following has constructed oppressive architecture which has contributed in some measure to the social problems of larger cities.

Almost invariably, the questions appraised by architects have been those of form and function, not place. Only when the oil crisis of the early 1970's focused attention on the energy-inefficiency of most houses was it realised by the architectural profession that orientation had some meaning beyond the mystic. In another of his house-object analogies, Le Corbusier compared the house with a tool: 'We throw the out-of-date tool on the scrap-heap,' he said, and exhorted architects to do likewise to the house. But now, the time has come when the Futurists' architecture of this era is bound likewise for the scrap-heap and architecture, paradoxically named 'post-modern', is superseding it. It is the inevitable fate of all things that they have their day and then pass, but it is to be hoped that, in our age of ever-expanding knowledge and information, the best of all ages and cultures can be synthesised. Within the rural tradition were certain attitudes, albeit forced upon people by necessity but no less valid and eternal, that life is the continuous recycling of materials and energy through the cycles of seasons, years and lives.

This realistic understanding is in stark contrast with the industrial view where materials and energy exist as part of a one-way system, beginning with extraction, passing through the production line to obsolescence and the rubbish dump. The traditional, rural view of this unidirectional squandering would see this waste as contrary to nature or as blasphemy against the Creator, but, even from a materialist viewpoint, squandering and wasting the world are obviously doomed to disaster.

The unique and special nature and combination of conditions whose study is the preserve of earth harmony must be appraised and understood if we are to reclaim the intimate knowledge and unity with nature which existed in pre-industrial times. To live in equilibrium with our environment by working within the universal laws by which everything is governed will bring peace and harmony on a human level, reflecting the equilibrium of the cosmic order. Our scientific knowledge and technical expertise should be used to enhance our methods of reinstating harmony. The experiments have been conducted: some have succeeded and some have failed. Both mystical and scientific traditions have reasserted our oneness with the earth and the knowledge that our joint desires are linked inextricably. The earth harmony way is one of striving to regain that unity of life and of using all the means at our disposal to achieve it.

Chapter 15
Practising Earth Harmony

"The sun's going to shine in my back door some day,
And the wind's going to come and blow all my cares away" -
Traditional American blues song.

Everyone wishes to live comfortably and so since the earliest times, people have tried to create dwellings to achieve this. However basic, every dwelling is an attempt to exclude external conditions so that those living there have some protection from the weather and intruders. This protection can take a multiplicity of forms, but their underlying principle is that within a dwelling, comfortable living conditions can be achieved only by some modification of the climate, both outside and inside. The most important factor which determines the inner climate is the relationship of the dwelling to external factors, most importantly, the location of the house itself. A house can be built in a sheltered locality, or conversely in a place where it may suffer various effects from wind, rain and snow, depending on the degree of shelter. The conditions inside similar houses in different locations, then, may be very different from one another. Whatever the overall causes, these problems can be modified by harmonising with or subtly altering the microclimate in the immediate surroundings of the building.

Whether we are building a new house, or living in an existing structure, we can discover the factors affecting it, and do something about them. What can be done depends to a great extent upon the actual design of the building itself, its location and orientation, the material and form of the walls, the roof and the degree of insulation these provide. These factors are subtle and require much study before appropriate action can be taken, so most commonly the 'technological fix' is used in the form of control of the internal conditions by means of air conditioning and heating. This moves the problem elsewhere, with an increased imbalance at another point caused by air pollution from the power generation and heat pollution from air conditioning units.

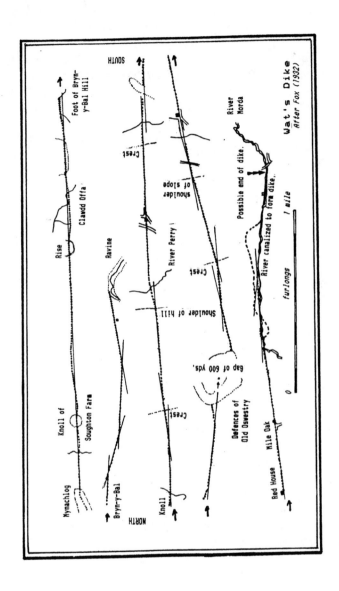

Wat's Dike, a rectilinear boundary-ditch between England and Wales, evidence of the highly-sophisticated abilities of the 8th century Anglian surveyors and locators linking earlier landscape features including the Iron Age hill-fort of Old Oswestry.

One of the most vital factors in harmonising a dwelling with the environment is orientation. There are a number of elements affecting the most appropriate orientation of a building, of which the local effects of the sun and the winds are major factors. Appropriate orientation takes account of measurable physical factors, and arranges them to accommodate for the more subtle energies which require management. In a climate with cold winters, heating is a primary concern, and in a hot climate, cooling may be necessary. Wherever we are on earth, all heat which is not generated artificially in a house comes from the sun. The orientation of the room or house towards the sun is thus a basic way of energy-saving in colder climates. Orientation to the south of rooms which are used most frequently maximises any heating effect that the sun may produce, and makes the best use of sunlight through much of the day. An eastward orientation of rooms is second best, making use of the morning sun only, helping to warm them up after the coldness of the night. South of the Arctic Circle, northern exposures receive no sunlight at all, necessitating more heating and lighting than southern exposures. Practically, the northern aspect should be used for rooms which are used sporadically, and which require less heating than those used continuously. It is not surprising that these key orientations, rediscovered in the twentieth century by 'solar architects' are precisely those prescribed by traditional geomancy. Like the buildings sited by the locators of old, modern energy-saving houses tend towards harmony with natural forces.

The general effects of orientation remain the same wherever they are carried out (substituting south for north and vice versa in the southern hemisphere, of course). However, the location of a dwelling has considerable effects upon this general rule, for the other major factor, the wind, must be taken into account also. The wind has a cooling effect - the stronger the wind, the greater degree of cooling. It deprives a place of heat during cool periods, but also removes heat during hot summers. Hilltops, ridges and high points in general have a greater exposure to the wind than flatter, lowland, locations, and generally a lower average temperature. They are colder both in winter and summer than comparable unexposed areas.

Examination of vegetation, especially trees, can give a rule-of-thumb indication of the degree of cooling on a high point, as it will be sparser and stunted by comparison with that growing in less exposed areas. Slopes facing towards the prevailing winds are relatively cooler, while slopes that face away from the wind are sheltered from it, and have a more advantageous microclimate. The direction and pattern of the winds are affected by geographical features from a global to a local level.

Major mountain ranges and hill ridges affect and modify the prevailing wind direction; sites on large flat areas are subject to the wind as much as an exposed high point, and locations close to large bodies of water, such as lakes or the sea will be tempered by the wind. An area between hills is sheltered from cold winds, but equally in summer may not receive beneficial cooling breezes. Irregular or broken terrain will tend to dissipate the prevailing wind force, and a combination of these patterns will have a combined effect. Just as each piece of terrain has its unique character, so does the pattern of the wind crossing it. The force and direction of the wind at any individual place therefore is dependent on a hierarchy of factors from the local to the global level, demonstrating the essential interconnectedness of everything on Earth. When we harmonise a structure with local conditions, we are harmonising also with the entire planet.

The actual directions of prevailing winds at a site need to be taken into account when calculating the optimal orientation of a dwelling. Buildings orientated 45 to 90 degrees away from the direction of the prevailing wind, present the least wind attack on the surface and a minimal heat loss. Ventilation openings work best when at right angles to the direction of the wind. These factors must be taken into consideration along with solar illumination and the traditional elements of Earth Harmony when making a final decision on orientation. Strong prevailing winds can be deflected or minimised by the planting of shelter belts of trees or the construction of earthworks. Shelter belts are mass plantings of fast-growing trees upwind of the dwelling to create a windbreak at right angles to the direction of the prevailing winds. Shelter against strong winds is gained by planting closely-spaced broad tree belts on the windward side of a structure, but they must be large enough to prevent the strong wind from affecting any part of the building. In Britain, protection against cold winds can be obtained by planting to the north and east. The presence of shelter belts in the landscape is in itself an indication of wind problems, and their traditional use can be seen at various places. In eastern England, rectangles or parts of rectangles of tree plantings shelter the homesteads commonly called Valance Farm. Shelter belts are very valuable in windy places, but such a plantation of trees also has the effect of deadening smaller air movements, producing stagnation, and so should not be put too close to buildings.

The kinds of trees used for shelter depend upon the requirements of the site. Deciduous trees shed their leaves in the autumn, and are leafless in winter. These allow light to penetrate in winter, and provide shade in summer, but they give limited protection against the wind in winter, when it is most needed. Evergreen species retain their foliage at all times of the year, so their function as windbreaker is as good in winter as in summer. However, with global warming taking place, certain popular evergreens used to-day will not live to their full potential lifespan. So it is necessary to plant species that will cope with rising temperatures, and still be flourishing centuries from now. In creating shelter belts, it is probably best to incorporate plantings with some form of earthwork, to ensure that a complete barrier is formed. Earthworks by themselves are not quite as effective, but can be harmonised readily with the terrain. Although shelter belts are usually planted to break strong winds, slow air movements caused by the cascading of cold air downwards to accumulate in valleys and hollows, can also be deflected by planting at an appropriate area at the upper levels of such vulnerable depressions.

Where shelter belts are non-existent or impossible to plant, the full force of winds can be reduced by creating protection for certain parts of a building. Wind velocity increases at the corners of buildings. Wind effects can be reduced by the design of corners, as in much traditional architecture, or by the erection of barriers. In windy areas, modern houses often lose roof tiles from wind action. Traditional house construction in such areas had chimneys at each end of the house, or gable ends which prevented the wind from lifting ridge tiles. Even 'ornamental' dragons' heads and hipknobs served this useful function. To prevent wind effects at ground level, the creation of 'dead air spaces' next to doors or windows can be accomplished by planting trees, so long as they are species which will not undermine the foundations of the house. The traditional protective trees like Rowan and Elder are ideal. Ivy or vines growing on a wall will have an effect on the microclimate of the wall, providing 'dead air space'. This will have a slight warming effect in winter and a shading effect in hot summers.

The most obvious danger is the damage caused by high winds and traditional house design can mitigate this. In the modern urban environment, the reverse has occurred and artificially-created winds are a major problem. In some modern developments, the wind is deflected and channelled by the injudicious placement of large tower blocks. In some cases these buildings have been so badly designed and sited that their interaction with the winds has caused windows to be sucked out and shower plate glass on passers-by in the streets below, requiring remedial reconstruction. On a smaller scale, the eddy currents of wind blowing the litter around in "dead corners" of shopping precincts is a common site. These problems stem from an incomplete understanding of the relationship of building to the natural environment. The forms of buildings must relate to the overall climatic area in which they are built, for each area has a physical structure which ought to be accommodated. In a temperate climate, for instance, the position of a dwelling in a conurbation affects its local climate. In temperate urban areas, air temperature increases from the outskirts towards the middle of the city. Within this overall temperature gradient, buildings on south facing slopes will have a higher average temperature than those elsewhere. Also the type of cover present affects the local climate.

In the urban mass, there are 'heat islands', with a higher average temperature caused by various factors. The temperature over paved areas is always greater than over grassed areas or parks. In temperate climates, the response to changes in weather is slower in built-up areas than in the country. Urban areas have a higher minimum temperature than the surrounding countryside, and response to weather, time of day and seasonal changes is correspondingly slower, and there is a greater independence from them. The surfaces surrounding a dwelling can have a major effect on the environment within. In temperate climates with hot summers, the reflected glare and heat from a gravel, asphalt or concrete surface, such as a back yard, can be intolerable. A grassed surface is better, and ground cover of small shrubs is probably the best, creating a more hospitable microclimate.

Variations in average temperature are subject to complex cycles, which accentuate the local differences in average temperature. The maximum difference is at dusk, with the onset of night-time cooling of grassed areas. In rural areas, at the onset of night-time, the temperature begins to fall, but in urban environments it remains relatively static because of heat stored in the urban fabric - buildings, roads etc. - and by increased use of heating and lighting. The relative composition of building mass to parkland in a city, and their geographical relationship to one another, can create distinct air flows at certain times of day, with consequent effects upon the inhabitants.The effects on the inhabitants or users of a building of increased (or diminished) air pressure over long periods of time are little-studied. However, certain winds such as the Mistral, the Föhn and the Sirocco are

According to traditional perceptions, proper measure must reflect the general dimensions of the human frame, which, as the microcosm, reflects the dimensions of the world.

known to have effects upon human behaviour. When they blow, a greater amount of human unease, manifested as violence and an increase in crimes, occurs.

Earth Harmony and the Urban Environment

The urban environment is composed of many elements which make harmonious living extremely difficult. Cities are by their nature overcrowded, not only with people, but with their mechanised transport, and it is this which has caused the most changes in that environment. The wholesale demolition of parts of cities for enlarged roads, and the design of buildings to accommodate vehicles radically altered the architect's perception of space and scale and altered planning regulations. The modern city is characterised by mass flows of transport, whether by private vehicles or public transport of various kinds on and below the surface, and this has repercussions in every aspect of urban life. Whatever their propulsion method, and wherever these vehicles operate, they are the cause of forms of intrusion into the environment, physical, psychological and psychical.

Of all of the urban transport modes, and these include passenger conveyors, cars, taxis, buses, trolleybuses, duobuses, trams, light rail, monorails, underground and elevated railways, the most intrusive is the private motor car. The significance of their everyday dominance of the traffic scene has been discussed and argued over for years, but an important factor which is usually overlooked is the effect of parked cars. Any modern settlement is characterised by a large number of stationary vehicles left unattended for long periods. Typically, cars are used for transporting workers to their place of employment, are left there all day, and then are used to take them back home in the evening. This means that there are two distinct phases of occupation: the area full of vehicles, and the area empty of vehicles. The difference in character between a car park when it is full and when it is empty is quite marked. Apart from the physical intrusion of the vehicles, the visual effect, the difficulty of seeing across the area, there are other, less apparent, differences. Cars are driven by heat engines which burn fuel at high temperatures in order to extract energy. In so doing, they produce considerable amounts of waste heat which has to go somewhere. That somewhere is the atmosphere, and when parked, a vehicle remains for several hours at a higher temperature than the surroundings. So one effect of car parking is to alter the microclimate. The quality of the air is altered by exhaust gases emitted by cars, and when parked, oil and other waste materials from cars accumulate on the car park surfaces. Cars are mostly metal, and so have an effect upon the Earth's magnetic field wherever they are. Large numbers of cars parked together disrupt the natural field of the Earth, with unknown effects on human beings.

Cars can be treated as mobile buildings, with all of the effects that buildings have on the character of a site. This way of looking at vehicles is not new and revolutionary, for in the East Anglian 'nameless art' and certain non-European systems, there is a tradition of treating boats and ships in this way. The modern car, which is an implicit denial of place, has been designed to be unchanging regardless of location. As a piece of modern urbanism, therefore, it is fitting that the car should be treated as a mobile building. The implications for Earth Harmony of this view are considerable. The effect that parked cars can have upon any nearby habitation can be marked. Unlike permanent buildings, which do not go away, the effect of parked cars is sporadic or cyclic at best. Given that according to traditional systems of geomancy, certain geometric arrangements such as the 'secret arrow' can lead to problems, similar arrangements of cars in car parks can lead to similar results.

Apart from the effects generated by the presence of cars in streets or car parks, we have the problem of what happens when the car parks are empty. Usually, car parks are empty at night and at times when the facilities they serve are closed, such as at weekends, public holidays and strikes. Empty car parks are large barren areas of tarmac, concrete or other paving material, interspersed by fences or vehicle barriers, bollards, signs and occasionally trees. These large surfaces are 'dead areas' with no function when empty, and create similar bad energies to those empty expanses beloved of modern town planners. Large empty areas around tall buildings became popular in the 1930s-50s as a reaction against the overcrowded slum tenements of many nineteenth century cities. This reaction led to the idea of the tower block standing in acres of featureless space as a means of getting air to the inhabitants, and hence promoting health and (contradictorily) aiding the circulation of motor vehicles. Of course, we all know now that things did not work out like that, but the legacy of this kind of thinking exists in town-planning regulations which lead to large empty spaces in cities. Featureless expanses of concrete, or even ingenious juxtapositions of bollards, textured paving and carefully chosen 'street furniture' are still empty spaces if natural human activity is forbidden there. If such places cannot develop into meeting-places and markets, they are destined to be generators of anxiety and alienation, empty places blasted by swirling winds and terrorised by marauding gangs.

The most characteristic effect of motor transport in cities is air pollution. Cars and buses spill their exhaust gases directly into the air behind them, and where there are large concentrations of motor vehicles, there are large concentrations of atmospheric pollutants. The location of a city with relation to the surrounding hills and winds, the type, of buildings and their layout all contribute to our experience of this pollution. Such cases are well-known in Los Angeles and Athens, where their location is such that motor exhausts are trapped in a layer of air over the city and chemically altered by sunlight to create a more-or-less permanent smog. The concentration of such a petrochemical smog is not constant throughout a city, as it depends on the local topography. Local air currents created by tall buildings, or urban hills will cause a lessening of the concentration, whilst enclosed areas will trap and might tend to accumulate poisonous exhaust fumes. Someone having to live in such an environment would do well to investigate these factors.

The effect of sources of pollution on a dwelling and its inhabitants depends a lot on the prevailing winds. This was demonstrated tragically in one of the worst outbreaks of Legionnaires' Disease ever to occur in Great Britain. In 1984, thirty-three people in Glasgow died in the epidemic. General practitioners in the city were asked to send samples from patients suffering respiratory complaints to a medical laboratory for tests. The consultant bacteriologist studying the samples, Dr Ronald Fallon, noticed that patients suffering from Legionnaires' Disease came from addresses with the same postal code. The area where most of the victims came from was Dennistoun. Analysis of wind direction and speed showed that the bacteria were being carried downwind of a brewery cooling tower, where the organisms were growing. People living or working within a certain distance of this tower were being exposed to a disease-causing agent.

This outbreak is a good example of those factors which must be taken into account when studying an area. In this case, there was a tragic outcome for those unfortunate enough to live downwind of the cooling tower. Their chances of catching the disease were related to the location of their dwellings or workplaces, and the likelihood of bacteria-carrying air from the cooling tower entering those buildings. Thus the orientation of windows and doors, and even the location of furniture within the building, affected the

The Way is the End.

likelihood of a person inhaling the contaminated air. Whilst it is not possible to protect against unforeseen events like Legionnaires' Disease, this outbreak shows how that these seemingly insignificant factors can be literally a matter of life and death. Another serious intrusion into the urban environment is sound. Technically, sound is described as a physical vibration perceived by the ears. Unwanted sound is often described as noise pollution, which can have a detrimental psychological effect upon those exposed continuously to it. The physical effects of sound on the human body have been known and used for thousands of years. Detrimentally, the European martial arts use the war cry, a blood-curdling yell, such as "Hallelujah!", "Thor's Aid!" or "St George!", which momentarily lowers the blood-pressure of the opponents giving a split-second advantage for the assailant. On the positive side, pure sounds and music have been used since antiquity to create psychic calm, states of heightened consciousness and healing atmospheres.

On another level, noise pollution can cause physical damage. The destructive power of sound is told in the legendary destruction of Jericho by the Israelites, and French experiments in the 1960s with infrasound demonstrated the awesome power of directed low-frequency vibrations. In the urban environment, sources of noise include most forms of mechanised transport, building construction, road works, and industry. This takes two related forms: noise and vibration. Vibration causes physical damage, by shaking buildings to pieces, causing cracking and finally failure of their structural materials. Heavy road transport is the worst and most common cause of vibration damage, although underground railways are a secondary factor in cities. Large old buildings are especially vulnerable to vibration damage. This problem dates from one of the earliest applications of electric traction to underground railways, in London in 1900. Even though the trains ran over 60 feet below street level, serious vibration caused structural damage to buildings above the Central London Railway. This problem was mitigated only by a complete re-equipping of the line with new trains only three years after opening.

Even more modern systems have caused problems, and Milano cathedral has suffered damage from vibration created by the nearby underground railway. In Paris, from 1951, rubber tyred trains, running on concrete rails, were introduced in order to reduce vibration and noise, and this idea has been adopted subsequently in France at Lille, Lyon and Marseilles, and outside France in Montréal (Canada), Mexico City and Sapporo (Japan). But as developments in technology have a way of superseding parallel developments, the noise- and vibration-deadening advantage of rubber tyres on underground trains has now been wiped out by the new technology used in equally silent modern steel wheeled trains. With the invention and deployment of new-technology-based transit systems, doubtless equally novel problems will arise. The psychological effects on people of travelling on silent driverless trains is the latest problem to be overcome by urban dwellers. External noise can be screened to some extent by the erection of a physical barrier between the noise and the habitation. Roads are placed in cuttings, but this has other effects in the environment, such as bringing chaotic airflows, and accumulation-points for airborne pollutants. Embankments or mounds are used as screens; sometimes trees are added or are used independently of earthworks. Walls are not uncommon along motorways in urban areas, especially on the European continent. To reduce noise intrusion, buildings have been sited at right angles to roads, with no windows facing them. Sometimes double glazing is installed, which requires artificial ventilation systems which often draw in polluted air anyway. Or non-residential constructions, such as storage or garages, are placed in front of the main building to act as a screen.

Chapter 16
Geomantic Considerations

It is apparent that there are many complex factors acting upon the places in which we live. If we are to do something to improve our own living environments, however, first we must obtain as much information as possible about the prevailing conditions. It is possible to look at these systematically, for in any town or city, there are eight classes or elements of relevance to earth harmony and the character of the place being considered. They are:

1. The legends and history of the foundation of the town or city, and its original layout.
2. Places of power within the town or city:
> Churches, chapels and temples.
> Crosses and mark stones.
> Commemorative or legendary trees.
> Cemeteries.
> Proclamation stones, traditional meeting-places, assembly halls, sports stadia.
> City-, Town- and Guildhalls.
> Marketplaces.
> Traditional sites of fairs.
> Execution places.
3. Watercourses.
4. Underground structures:
> Geological structures and fault lines.
> Landfill and made ground.
> Ancient tunnels and cellars.
> Modern subterranea: underground railways, roads, car parks.
> Sewers and water supply.
> Electrical cables and telecommunications.
5. Ancient boundaries, road and street layout.
6. Haunted sites, poltergeist activity, sites of unexplained phenomena.
7. Traditional and reputed good and bad places, sites of notable events, e.g. murders, accidents.
8. Sites of above average occurrence of illness, suicide, stress, conflict

1. Legends and History

Legends concerning the foundation of a city or town give valuable information on the perceived purpose and character of the place, its geolocation and its function. Places are often named after a prominent geographical feature, which gave the original town its character. Examples of this are Dublin (Dark Pool), in the Irish Republic and Brownhills in Staffordshire, England. Places are named after their historical founders, like the Saxon King Edwin at Edinburgh, Scotland, or posthumously after famous individuals like Llanbabo in Anglesey, which is named after the honoured British King Pabo Post Prydain (Pabo, the Pillar of Britain). Sometimes a place was dedicated to a principle personified as a goddess or god, bearing the deity's name, such as Athens, Greece (the goddess Athena); Wednesbury, England (Woden); Oesterholz, Germany (the spring goddess Ostara), and Heliopolis, Egypt (Helios). Christian saints and other divine beings are commemorated at many places including Los Angeles (Nuestra Señora de los Angeles), San Diego, Santa Barbara and San Francisco in the United States, two St Iveses and St Neot's in Britain, Santiago in Spain, Saint-Omer in France, etc. The principle behind the deity or sacred being is the power still ruling the place today, in customary observances, such as fairs, pardons, carnivals and civic ceremonies; in the unconscious of the inhabitants, and in its feel as a site.

If a city was planned or arose at a central point in the landscape - the district's navel or omphalos - this may be reflected in its name. Names which have a sound like meridian or median were central points of this type. The most important of these is Milano in Italy, originally called Mediolanum, the central place. In England, Meriden in the West Midlands, marks the site of a central assembly-place of the woodsmen of the Forest of Arden. Such centres can be expected to have special properties in relation to the surrounding landscape, expressing both the character of a centre and of its whole surrounding area.

Investigation of a town's history may show it to have been a "plantation" of the middle ages, or, in former colonial territories, to be laid out on "plantation" principles. In Europe, such places were founded as replacements for old towns no longer inhabitable, or as new cities free of Imperial or royal rule. Sometimes, the town's name reflects this: Fribourg in Switzerland, and Freiburg-im-Breisgau in Germany were founded as alternative settlements. Likewise the several Newcastles and Newports in Britain. Towns such as these are laid out according to recognisable principles, using a gridded street layout itself related to the features of the landscape. The many towns known as Bastides founded by French and English kings during the thirteenth and fourteenth centuries conform to these principles. Bern and Salisbury, important examples of these principles, have been dealt with above. Such places were founded to reflect the cosmic order, and continue to do so, even though the customs observed to maintain the order may have lapsed. However, Londonderry, the last city in the British Isles laid out according to this idea, has other qualities. It is necessary to examine local conditions first-hand to discover the inner spirit of any place.

In order to find out as much as possible about any settled place, we must look first at the foundation legends. Although these may be elaborate and fanciful by modern standards of story-telling, they often contain many features relevant to the landscape as it exists today. Nowadays, foundation legends are usually dismissed as fanciful explanations of how the town came to be where it is. However, it is worth probing deeper into the meaning of such legends. In many European city foundation stories, divination seems to have played a major part. Often, the foundation has come about through an extraordinary encounter between the founder and an animal. At Bern, Switzerland, the founder was out hunting when he noticed a bear: the monks who founded Durham looked for a dun cow; whilst at Delphi, in Greece, eagles were used in divining the omphalos that was held to be the middle of the world. Such places divined by animals or by human interpretation of animal behaviour, are often commemorated geomythically in coats of arms or sculpture that present the myth in pictorial form. At Durham, for instance, a carving of the Dun Cow can be seen on the Cathedral, and at Bern, the city's coat of arms is a brown bear. Even at this very superficial level, the mythical attributes of the foundation are still very much a living part of everyday consciousness.

At a deeper level, the legends tell that somewhere in the present city is a special place whose Anima Loci first caused the founder to create a settlement there. Important places within the town will related to this original, divined, place of power, drawing their own strength from it. Dwellings close to or between such places may be stressed and suffer imbalance. One such complex legend, which has all the typical elements of geomythology, accounts for the foundation of a major English cathedral. The cathedral city of Ely surmounts a small rise in the once-impassable fenlands still called the Isle of Ely. The city, in reality a small market town, was once a mighty and important monastic settlement, but is now frequented more by tourists than by devout worshippers. The building that the tourists come to see - Ely Cathedral - dominates the flat fen landscape for many miles around. Thirteen hundred years ago, Aethelthryth (otherwise called Audrey or Etheldreda), daughter of King Anna of East Anglia, founded the monastery on an uninhabited site. Although married twice, to the annoyance of her husbands, she had sworn a vow of virginity, and kept it. In the twelfth year of her second marriage, she became a nun in the monastery of Coldingham in Berwickshire. When her husband attacked the monastery with the intention of reclaiming her, she fled to Ely by a road which she punctuated by several miracles. On the journey, at Altham, she thrust her ashwood staff into the ground. In the morning, it was discovered that the staff had put forth leaves. It grew and, in later years, was the greatest ash tree in the district. The place was re-named Etheldredestow in recollection of this typical miracle, which can be seen as a geomantic act, restoring balance and fertility to the landscape.

Arriving at Ely, Aethelthryth fixed the location of her new monastery at Cradendune, about a mile south of the present cathedral, on the site of a Roman church. Evidently, this was an incorrect decision, for the monastery was soon moved northwards to its present location. In the year 673, the monastery began to function. Six years later, when Aethelthryth died, the brethren of the monastery (both monks and nuns) went by boat to the ruins of Cambridge, where, in the defensive earthwork known as the Armeswerk, they found, by divination, a magnificent marble sarcophagus of Roman workmanship. In this splendid tomb, the nun was buried, and around her, the usual cult of miracles and cures grew up, leading to her canonisation as Saint Etheldreda. In connection with her saint's day, October 17, a fair was granted, and at this the many shoddy trinkets sold there to visitors became known as St. Audrey's jewellery, rapidly corrupted to Tawdry jewellery.

Without the intervention of religious belief, reputed miracles and monastic organisation, the city of Ely as it exists today would not have come into being. Whether we accept these miraculous acts at face value, interpret them as the manipulation of subtle energies by occult means, or dismiss them as the delusions of fanatics, we cannot deny that without a belief in them in the past, today's world would not exist as it does. Thus the study of these legendary foundations is more than an interesting pastime, it is an investigation of the fundamental basis of many places, giving us information about the nature of various places of power. The legends are a description of the experiences of people at that place, interpreted in the way of the times. As at Ely, their actions, based upon their experience of and belief in the non-material world may create sumptuous buildings, change the names of places and add new words to the language.

2. Places of Power

These appear to-day as centres of spiritual power and the seats of secular administration. The former category includes chapels, churches, minsters, monasteries, temples, hofs, war memorials, gurdwaras, mosques, and synagogues. The latter category includes town halls, castles, palaces, and parliament houses. There are many traditions of the complex tasks undertaken to find the correct sites for churches, crosses and markstones, and in former times their role in the life of a town or city was paramount. In traditional terms, major sacred buildings are sited on places of great concentration of önd, and are continually charged up by ceremonial rituals, prayer and devotional thoughts. The internal layout of such places, and the building's relationship to surrounding structures, give many clues to the varying character of each part. Important places in a church, such as altars, shrines, tombs of kings and saints, fonts, labyrinth pavements, towers and spires, mark places where people have perceived concentrations of önd in its many forms. The character of a sacred building often sets the tone for a whole town or village, not only because it is the most prominent structure in the place, but because everything else in that settlement refers to it. When towns were founded, the holy places of the Anima Loci were the first to be set aside and consecrated as special. As the reference point of the town, the sacred site enshrined the principles and aspirations of the founders. As such, its continued existence is a witness to the continuity of these principles to-day.

In many modern cities, wars, redevelopment and the decline of religion have led to the obliteration of many ancient holy and sacred places. The active sites of the Anima Loci formerly marked by the cross, chapel or church, however, have been left, and, if the redevelopment has not entirely destroyed the character of the site, then some of the spiritual energies or subtle qualities once controlled by the building may be acting still. In the modern urban environment, however, this uncontrolled önd may be causing damage to those who live over them or nearby. When analysing an area, it is very important to rediscover the site of lost or destroyed sacred buildings as well as those still in existence, for the overall structure once took all into account. Places of power are not good places to live. They are places where humans can gain contact with the Anima Loci, other states of consciousness or being through ritual, prayer or meditation. To live at such a place is to receive an excess of spiritual power, radiation or önd, which will lead to illness. Only those who were divinely mad, like hermits and oracles, occupy such places in traditional societies. In large complexes, such as palaces, the places of power are not the places where people live, but the chapels and throne rooms, where ceremonies and decisions are enacted.

The secondary sacred sites, the chapels, wayside shrines and crosses, as well as central markstones or the consecrated milestones at the beginning of ancient sacred roads, play a lesser role in the management of this ki. These are the ceremonially-charged objects and places which interact locally with human and non-human energies, modify harmful influences and act as distribution-points to the immediate locality. It is a belief of certain people, including both 'energy dowsers' and churchmen, that churches and other sacred sites where religious services are still celebrated are in some way continually recharging the locality with spiritual power which then is channelled along watercourses, roadways and similar conductors to other places. On the other hand, unlike places where religious services are held, crosses and mark-stones, may never receive direct spiritual attention. In many places in former times, the traditional ceremony of 'Beating the Bounds' would have the function of recharging these places with spiritual energy, but in most places, this custom has lapsed. Where it continues to be performed, the boundaries are maintained spiritually as they have always been.

These minor monuments of the landscape, especially central-point markers like London's Charing Cross, are nevertheless conceptual centres which still hold some symbolic power over the human mind, for they mark sites of great, if largely unrecognised, importance to the city. The recent restoration of some important geomantic landmarks in various places attests to this. Destruction of such landmarks, rendering he place alfreka, is much more likely to happen by accident or default than the demolition of a church or other major sacred place. Destabilisation of a city's harmony may thus occur by accident, unless steps are taken to preserve ancient monuments for both their historic and locational functions. Historical research can indicate whether the town being studied once had a mark-stone, cross or mark-tree at the centre. Old maps may show the precise position of such a central marker, for in many places the passage of time, wars, the erosion of cities by motor traffic and redevelopment have caused the removal of such markers.

To live on the site of such a marker is considered very unfortunate. But it is always possible, if the will is present, to restore lost holy places. The recent restoration of the London Stone in London and the Pagan holy stone at the centre of Vilnius in Lithuania are fine examples of the reconstitution of tradition.

Sometimes, the destruction of earlier street layouts by war or redevelopment has left to incongruous remains. Sadly, places like this can be seen in many cities, where a medieval building or fragment of former street stands isolated amid a sea of concrete paving, or in the centre of a road complex. Occasionally, the ruins have been left as a memorial, such as the famous church in the centre of Berlin, or the skeletal remains of the Hall of Industry in Hiroshima. But most relics are not as evocative as these carefully-preserved ruins. The process which has led to the isolation of fragments of earlier layouts is exemplified by the Bargate in Southampton, once the main gateway of the town. At the end of the last century, electric trams were introduced as modern transportation. They had to go through the Bargate on a single track, and special vehicles with domed roofs were used. Soon, this was found inadequate, so demolition slewed the tramlines round the outside of the gate, where former walls and buildings had stood. Later still, the trams were removed completely, and so were the buildings around the Bargate. Now it stands alone, nothing but a spectacle or 'focal point' surrounded by roads and buildings whose arrangement is determined by the road pattern, not the former street alignments which had been laid out in Saxon times. The function of the gate, as a marker of the boundary, is totally subverted, as stubby fragments of walls stand now on either side as buttresses between the gate and the traffic. In an age when such symbols have tended to be discarded, these old buildings, listed by the government as historic relics, have been reduced to outdoor curios which have lost their context, and any ceremonies connected with them are long since discontinued.

Redevelopment has left another legacy - the loss of recognition of sanctity. The nature of sacred places has been discussed above, and evidence presented that they are indeed something special. This, however, is no longer recognised in the modern urban environment. Secularisation, and the destruction of sacred places in this century's wars has led to a desacral-isation of many places of power. This does not mean that these places have lost their innate power, just that human recognition of the fact is blunted or lost. In many places, the sites where churches once stood have been converted into gardens. Here, in the summertime, office workers eat their lunchtime sandwiches, so the site's power is still imparting peace and tranquillity, unrecognised. However, in many places, the boundaries between sacred and secular which are so important have been broken down or become diffuse.

The incorporation of churchyards, which in reality are consecrated, sacred, ground, into larger parkland or pedestrianised zones, often blurs this distinction. In Thetford, Norfolk, for example, a pedestrianisation project removed the walls of St Cuthbert's church and 'integrated' it into a paved area. The word 'integration' was used by those who described the project when it was carried out. The same thing has happened since at the church of St Andrew's the Great in Cambridge, and in other places. The idea of 'integrating' a sacred site, which by its very innate nature is special and separate, into a secular, urban setting, is to misunderstand the nature of the sacred. In too many places, the ancient spiritual centres of localities, the churches that stand on former Pagan places of sanctity, are passed by and no longer recognised as of importance to the whole community. Redevelopment has tended to place these buildings as elements in a visual composition. Instead of having a multiplicity of human uses, as in the past, they have been transformed into objects to be viewed from focal points, standing amid undulating seas of brick or at the centre of a circular 'theme' in the paving, and so on. In these areas, the position of things, such as trees, which have an effect, are done without regard to the Anima Loci, thereby altering randomly the character of the site itself. In general, theoretical considerations, derived from a desacralised view of the world, have taken over, downgrading places of the otherworld into mere spectacle.

Cemeteries are important places in the character of towns. Consecrated places for the burial of the departed, cemeteries are rarely built upon. Many small parks in inner cities are former cemeteries and yards of churches long since demolished. These green spaces have not been built upon, owing to the tradition that one risks disharmony by building over the resting-places of the dead, and the consecrated nature of the ground. Traditionally, the consecration of the cemetery serves the function of containing the spirits of the dead, and preventing them from "wandering abroad". Consecrated boundary walls and symbolic entrances such as lychgates or cemetery lodges were made specifically to reinforce the separation from the world of the living, and to keep the spirits in. As repositories of human remains, such places are very charged, and in traditions all over the world, living close to or overlooking a cemetery is avoided if at all possible. The market-place, the Forum of the Roman tradition, is a significant feature in most towns. Markets are centres of great human activity, and in the older towns they were centred upon places divined to be appropriate for commercial transactions. The traditional layout of a market is with reference to a central point, a stone, cross or fountain, upon which the emblems of secular authority were displayed. Marketplaces serve also for proclamations, assemblies, processions , mystery plays, street theatre and fairs. The central stone was often the Afroup or proclamation stone upon which only the Lord's or King's herald was permitted to set foot when making an official proclamation to the assembled townsfolk.

The town hall or guildhall, seat of municipal power, is the development of the moot-place, and overlaps the site-function of the castle, that relic of feudal authority whose geolocation was always carefully considered so as to be a place of both strategic and spiritual importance. In cities like Bern, the castle was located on the head of the dragon-landform. Psychically, the centre of any city is its administrative headquarters, in whatever form it may take: castle, military fortress, Bishop's Palace-Cathedral, royal palace, town hall or Party Headquarters. This centre is a generator of energies which may be beneficial or harmful: their effect depends upon the nature and intent of the power exercised by the administration. This was recognised in the Bishop of Exeter's report titled *Exorcism*, which was published in 1972. It warned that the office of an organisation devoted to greed or domination can often generate psychic trouble or act as a dispersal centre for harmful forces and demonic interference. It is clear that a centre of political power or the worship of Mammon, situated on a place of power, will affect a large area for good or ill. Even on the purely physical level, living near a political headquarters will involve disruption for the resident when VIPs come and go, with their associated bodyguards, street closures, closed circuit television, identity checks and personal searches.

3. Watercourses

The supply and flow of water is fundamental to life itself, and so in the location of human habitation water supply has been always one of the major considerations. In the principle of balance in the middle way, too much water is as undesirable as too little, and the practical considerations of waterlogged ground, destruction and illnesses associated with dampness, the insecurity of waterside dwellings, and on the other side the defensive and protective aspects, must be considered. The disposition of watercourses is fundamental in European techniques of location. If it is not prone to flooding, a dwelling by a river will bring benefit to its inhabitants, so long as the river is not flowing directly away from the building. Traditionally, evil is excluded by flowing water, and beneficial states of ionisation are created by running water, producing harmonious feelings in people. Formerly, it was customary to place synagogues by rivers, and the spiritual qualities of holy rivers, such as the Ganges, are used by the adherents of many faiths. According to geomantic tradition, the direction of the flow of önd is like running water. Consequently, when the locator examines the flow patterns of water in the landscape, he or she will be able to detect the flow of önd, thereby determining one aspect of the character of a place. Towns located within the loop of a meandering river, like Durham and Bern, are well-situated both strategically and with regard to more subtle factors, and enclosing watercourses like moats are held to be almost as effective. The form of the watercourses and the direction of flow will enhance or reduce the benefits, depending on the overall conditions of the site.

The siting of traditional holy springs, or sacred fountains is important, for these places are sources of önd. Artificial wells, when sunk at the right place, create energies. Because of this, many ancient wells have been incorporated into sacred buildings, such as those beneath the cathedrals at Chartres and Nîmes in France, Peterborough and Winchester in England, and Glasgow in Scotland. Wells are the prime connections between the underworld and the middle world, the forces that lie beneath the earth's surface and that which is above it. Wells are channels for these forces. Digging a well, or even just thrusting a pipe into the ground at an appropriate place, will enable the locator to bring this power to a place which needs it. The connection between wells and dowsing does not need elaborating here.

4. Underground Structures

Everything built on Earth has an underlying geology which affects the structure in some way. The type of clay, gravel or rock; the forms and patterns of rock strata, fault lines and other geological discontinuities affect the overlying buildings. Natural radiation from rocks such as granite may increase the radiation exposure of residents, and more physical problems, such as the danger of earthquakes, attend faulted areas. Geopathic zones are also associated with faults, which either generate their own radiation or permit higher levels of radiation originating deep in the earth to reach the surface. Landfill areas, too, where housing is built directly upon a pit filled to the brim with rubbish, may cause problems. If toxic waste has been buried, then almost imperceptible traces of solvents may be present in the microclimate of the area. Increased concentrations of the radioactive gas Radon may be associated with landfill.

By their very nature, artificial underground structures are out of sight and out of mind to the average person, yet their presence has an important effect upon any place. Large structures, such as the subways for underground transport systems, footways, sewers, water mains, power and telecommunications tunnels, create underground space analogous to a new artificial surface. This is most apparent in big cities, where underground shopping malls connected to transport systems are commonplace. Subterranean flows of önd and watercourses are disrupted, diverted or blocked by these structures, whose steel reinforcement or cast-iron lining diverts, obliterates or magnifies the magnetic fields present in the ground. Electrical cables, the rails or overhead wires carrying power to subterranean transport, and the large magnetic fluxes created by traction motors create new electrical and magnetic currents inside the tunnels and the surrounding ground which may affect the inhabitants of nearby buildings by interacting with natural terrestrial energies and the body fields of micro-organisms, plants, animals and human beings.

Sewers lie beneath the streets and buildings of every civilised town, and these carry large water flows, and so must be treated as watercourses equivalent to natural underground streams. Sometimes, the larger sewers in major cities have been created by placing natural surface streams underground. The physical effects of urban underground water, long ignored, have recently become noticed again. With the decline of manufacturing industry, and a consequent reduction in water use, the water tables in large cities are rising. In Birmingham, this has caused problems with the foundations of old highrise buildings, and in Liverpool, the underground railway system is now prone to flooding. Cellars and crypts are subterranean spaces which cut through lines of magnetism and other energy in the ground, but, like natural caves, act as accumulators for the energies being channelled into them. Underground structures cut out all influences from above, whether solar radiation or manmade radio transmissions. If these radiations have an effect on the human organism, then people in subterranea are removed from these influences, and will experience a

231

different state of being. The use of subterranean structures for initiation into various mystery schools was commonplace in ancient times, and even as late as the eighteenth century, the Hell Fire Caves at West Wycombe and the Chaldon Stone Mines in Surrey were used in this way. Obviously, the qualities of natural and artificial subterranea vary, and local investigation will reveal any influence they may have on the locality, and the quality of life at any specific place.

5. Ancient Boundaries, Road and Street Layouts

According to custom, folklore and documented evidence, the original boundaries in old settlements were laid down according to well-established principles of location related to subtle qualities of the Anima Loci. Although many ancient boundaries have been obliterated or altered over the years,there are a number of simple things we can do to find their courses. We can begin by examining the earliest maps or plans of the town, which can be found at the local reference library, or in municipal record offices. Although very early maps are schematic, they often show the parish boundaries, which are the divisions in a quartered town. Parish boundaries as they exist today have often been altered to 'iron out' the strange kinks and convolutions which once existed. The organisationally-efficient planners of the last and this century did not and do not like boundaries that are not 'rational', that is as straight as possible, or following major boundaries such as roads and rivers. Seeing things through the map, they ignore the subtle differences of terrain which is the reality that guided the locators of old.

Those who laid out towns in the Middle Ages or earlier were not concerned with the administrative convenience of office workers, but rather with the character of the ground upon which the town was being built. The Locator Civitatis was not concerned with the artificialities of maps, but the physical reality of the earth at the place where he was present. Thus, the old boundaries, because of rather than in spite of, their seeming idiosyncrasies, retain indications of the original character of the place, the manifestation of the Anima Loci and the flow of önd. From this original layout we can begin to build up a picture of good and bad places in the town, and what was done to remedy any problems encountered. Apart from the evidence of old maps, it is possible to find out more about the character of boundaries from the customs associated with them. Although most places have done away with any boundary ceremonies, there can be few places which did not have them

232

once, and there are often records of their routes and idiosyncrasies. In a few places, the old custom of 'Beating the Bounds' is observed still, and if this is the case, it is worthwhile taking part in the ceremony to gain the feel of the place and a first-hand knowledge of the boundary marks.

'Beating the Bounds' is an ancient tradition where the people of a village or town would walk around the boundary together on a certain day, visiting all of the markers and making sure that they were still in the right places. If they were not, then they were moved back to the correct position. The boundaries marked in this way were usually the local parish boundary, but sometimes the boundary of a city or municipality. Usually, the people would walk around with the priest, who would stop at the markers, say a prayer and read the gospel. Places called 'Gospel Oak' are a reminder of this practice, and if the tree exists, or its site can be found, then we have located an important mark point in the landscape. Where 'Beating the Bounds' is still practised (and it is possible to reinstate the practice, too), it is customary for each participant to cut a wand of willow or hazel, about a yard long, with which to strike each boundary marker in turn. In former times, the wands were used to whip children in the party at important landmarks. The poor children were also bumped against stones, or thrown into ditches and ponds where the boundary intersected them. This was supposed to imprint the knowledge of the location of the boundary markers into the children. Fortunately, this brutal element of the tradition has been discontinued in surviving bounds beatings. At certain places known only by custom, cross-shaped trenches were dug in the ground and boys stood on their heads in them. This was done also at major mark-stones, possibly the last truncated remains of human sacrificial rites conducted to sanctify the boundaries when they were first laid out. Whatever their origin, they certainly had the function of imprinting the place in the memory, which, in times when oral transmission was the only means of retaining information, was essential.

Special places on boundaries are indicated by the idiosyncratic routes that the boundary line takes there. Unfortunately, these places are dwindling in number as the process of 'ironing out' boundaries continues, and the fascinating character of such places is wiped out. Buildings constructed at boundaries have a special character, and they are often public houses. But when the boundaries create interesting anomalies, as at the Tydd Gote public house near Wisbech in the Fens of the Cambridgeshire border, where the bars are in different counties, and used to have different closing times.

However, such instances are on the decline, for they eventually succumb to the bureaucratic wish for uniformity. The old areas known as 'No Man's Land' which once existed at some junctions of three counties have all been 'normalised'. The owner of the celebrated 'Republic Cottage' which once stood quite near to where this is being written, but which was in no county was in the fortunate position of remaining untaxed, so perhaps that was one reason why these places were suppressed. However, as artificial creations, 'No Man's Lands' existed for a reason, even if the modern mind cannot fathom what that reason was. They were the vague terrain between boundaries, the places of access to the otherworld, resorted to at festivals of the dead like Walpurgis Night and Hallowe'en. It is appropriate that the name 'No Man's Land' was applied to the area between the opposing trenches on the Western Front in the First World War - an area entangled with barbed wire and strafed with gunfire - truly a place of death and the dead.

The 'normalisation' of boundaries has led to the demise of many colourful 'Beating the Bounds' ceremonies, which were as much part of the local character as any listed building or 'World Heritage Site'. For example, an old house called Hornshayne at Farway in Devon, stood at the junction of three parishes. When 'Beating the Bounds' took place, the participants made a small boy crawl along a beam in the roof, so that the boundary would be followed in its entirety. Recorded instances like this are more than just quaint anomalies of Old England. They give information to the investigator of the locality about the character of a place, and in the example of Hornshayne, the important fact that boundaries are not just lines on the ground, but can have a three-dimensional aspect within buildings.

The ritual observance of these perambulation ceremonies had several functions. Socially, they were gatherings at which all of the villagers or townspeople could get together and define their own territory. In religious terms, it enabled the priest to re-sanctify each point with prayer and ritual. Magically, the perambulation renewed the psychic barrier which every community needs to shelter it from supernatural dangers, and finally it was believed that it promoted the fertility of the area. The columnist 'Urbs Camboritum' (W.R. Brown) of the *Cambridge Daily News*, writing in 1895, noted "*In some country places the rustics believe there is some magic in this business, and that the crops show up better for this periodical farce, fondly fancying that the Goddess of Nature rewards the observance of the custom*". These boundary markers take several forms: sometimes they are unmarked stones, whilst in other places one finds markers like small tombstones with letters or even full inscriptions. Most boundary trees were cut down long ago, and the custom of planting a new tree to replace the old one has lapsed. Occasionally, a line will be marked in the pavement by a brass strip, but in the urban environment, with its reliance upon recorded documentation, most visible signs of boundaries and their markers will have been obliterated. The most we can hope to find in many places is a change in the style of lamp posts from municipality to municipality in a large conurbation. Despite this, there is often a surprising continuity in the layout of towns: expansion which has taken place along ancient roads, themselves former prehistoric trackways, retain their alignment. There are a number of recognisable street patterns which can be found in every country. In a town where various systems or none have been used over the years, then direct analysis of the streets' relationships to the site being examined is needed, using basic principles, such as the height of the site, road orientations and watercourse disposition.

Historical research using old maps and deeds is the only way of tracing this development. It must be borne in mind that it was rare until this century to obliterate completely the old layout of the land when building anew. In some places, new developments were laid out on former estates, preserving alignments which may have been laid out according to mystical principles. For example, in Birmingham, the Colmore family developed the Newhall Estate in the 1740s on the site of a country estate. This was laid out in a grid of streets, with the main axis, Newhall Street, following the former alignment of a tree-lined avenue. If these original avenues were laid out according to certain principles, then the present street will embody these principles still, preserving dimensions and orientations which can be recovered and analysed.

6. Haunted Sites, Poltergeists etc.

In any area which has been inhabited for any length of time, psychical phenomena will have been experienced by some of the population. These phenomena take many forms, including the apparition of ghosts, lights, phantom animals, poltergeists, and spontaneous human combustion. These phenomena tend to have local recurrences, and every town has its local lore of haunted houses. Places where there is an above-average tendency for road accidents to occur - the so-called 'accident black spots' - may be included here. Although many theories have been forwarded to account for such phenomena, it appears that these sites are places which are not in harmony with the surroundings. This imbalance may be intrinsic to the location itself, or may be the local result of a wide-scale imbalance, the disruption of önd flows, on-lays and alfreka sites. The traditional solution to such problems is the erection of a small shrine, which is empowered by the regular performance of ceremonies that support the Anima Loci, thereby rebalancing the place. Alternatively, this may be achieved by blanking-off of the harmful forces by interrupters and deflectors. This is a more mechanistic solution that minimises human participation.With the first solution, the necessary modification of the surroundings caused by the construction of a shrine limits the need to modify anything else. In a land where disbelief or planning laws prevent the construction of a shrine, the removal or neutralisation of such places by other means is a major function of the locator under contemporary conditions.

7. Traditional Good and Bad Places

Every area of any size has places which have a bad 'feel' or ill repute. Sometimes this is because some crime or atrocity was enacted there in the past, creating 'place memories', because of underground water or energies creating an 'accident black spot', or just through general rumours and local lore about the place. Often, these bad places are houses, or the sites of houses, which seem to reject their occupants. The houses of the Hertfordshire dragonslayer Piers Shonkes, near Anstey, and that of the famous witch known as Old Mother Redcap on Wallasea Island, Essex, are two powerful examples of this. In these cases, it appears that the önd of the houses was imprinted with energies generated by the magic performed there - on-lays that made it impossible for anyone else to live in them.

Houses or apartment blocks built on the site of battlefields, cemeteries, slaughterhouses, concentration camps, prisons or plague pits can be considered to be bad places because the ground there is alfreka. The harmful effects on the tenants comes primarily through the psychic on-lays that exist at such locations, and secondarily through the psychological stress that people feel when they know that the place was the scene of suffering and death. Notable happenings, such as murders, atrocities and suicides may imprint a place with harmful on-lays, or conversely may be the product of intrinsically bad locations that formerly were alfreka and subject to demonic interference. Lesser sites than these may also generate bad effects through debility and depression, confused emotions, ideas and images. But knowledge that one lives at such a place can be used to remedy any problems arising. Place memories are dealt with customarily with redecoration of a house, reconstruction or exorcism, where harmful on-lays are overlain by beneficial pones, whilst 'accident black spots' can be remedied by classic geomantic methods including staking the ground to deflect the harmful energies or 'black streams' believed to cause the problems. In Germany 'interference transceivers' were installed at 'accident black spots' on certain Federal Highways, apparently with success. These commercially-manufactured transceivers are arranged on posts above the ground to emit horizontal waves which intercept and neutralise the vertical radiations that dowsers find emanating from the earth at these places.

8. Sites of Illness

Since the 1920s, most notably in Germany, much study has been made on Geopathic Zones, namely those places where a greater than average incidence of illness has been noted. Unfortunately, it is not uncommon to find houses, shops or offices where successive tenants succumb to identical illnesses from no apparent cause. When examining a locality, the locator should strive to discover such places, and use an effective method to nullify the effect. The case of 'cancer beds' is well known, and dowsers trace the cause of such place-induced illness to bands or streams of water or radiation running beneath the place where the victim spends most of his or her time, such as bed. In addition to illness,certain houses have a disproportionate occurrence of marital breakdowns, family strife and interpersonal conflict, which is another indicator of imbalance at a location ascribed to geopathic stress.

Although, since time immemorial, traditional wisdom has told of such places, geopathic zones were first described as such only in the 1920s. During the twenties, the Stuttgart radiesthesists W. Melzer and H. Winzer analysed the incidence of cancer in the city on a geographical basis. They collected data which had no apparent connecting features, until dowsers suggested to them that they should check the location of geological fault lines under the city. On doing so, they found that the districts suffering the highest incidents of cancer were those overlying the five major geological faults of the district.

In January 1929, Freiherr Gustav von Pohl investigated the small town of Vilsbiburg in Lower Bavaria in south Germany, looking for underground forces detectable with the dowsing rod. The Baron drew up a map of the area, marking upon it houses where his dowsing indicated that there were geopathic tendencies. Independently of von Pohl, the local Medical Officer of Health, Herr Bernhuber, marked an identical map with the houses in which inhabitants had perished from cancer within the previous ten years. On comparison, the Medical Officer of Health noted that he had been in 54 houses, and in each one, the beds had stood on the lines von Pohl had drawn on his map. Subsequent work by dowsers, mainly in Germany, has refined and expanded upon von Pohl's work. In recent years, Köthe Bachler, Herbert König, Ernst Hartmann and Jörg Purner have continued in the tradition, bringing further insights.

Usually, such geopathic zones are noticed only when someone falls ill, for no apparent reason, and then their condition improves drastically when they are removed from the place in which they were ill. The notorious 'cancer beds', for which many German dowsers routinely check, are found to overly veins of underground water, usually coinciding with other 'energy lines' which various dowsers ascribe to one or other of the systems of lines claimed to exist which are known as the Curry Grid and the Hartmann Grid. These German energy lines have the same affect as and are probably identical with the 'black streams' found by British dowsers, who have a parallel but different tradition .

Many fieldworkers in dowsing claim to have found grids of energy lines: probably the earliest was the French dowser François Peyre in the late 1930s, and one of the most recent is the American Zaboj Harvalik. What these grids are has been the subject of much speculation and argument among dowsers, for some are incompatible with others, which must shed doubt upon the objective reality of some if not all of them. Nevertheless, it is established that local centres of some sort of energy of the önd variety can be found in stagnant concentrations at places detrimental to human well-being. The proven successes of many dowsers show that, even if their descriptive systems are only symbolic and not physically real in a scientific sense, their techniques are of benefit, and should be employed.

Harmonisation
Once all of the factors have been investigated as well as time and resources allow, they should be documented in some form, such as on an annotated map, which will give an overall picture of the area. If it is found that one lives on a geopathic zone or a place of power, then remedial action should be taken at once. The worst cases may quite possibly be so bad that no action can be sufficient to remedy the problems. Then the only solution is to

look elsewhere, or if already living at the place, to move. The task of the moniser is, however, to restore balance and promote harmony, so only at the last resort should moving out, which is a negative reaction, be preferred to a remedial response, which is positive action.

Chapter 17
Appropriateness

If we are to understand and do something about these problems, we must cultivate the qualities of appropriateness that lie at the heart of Earth Harmony, an understanding of which can be found in the writings of many country authors as well as 'nature mystics'. Their understanding of the relationship of cottages and villages to the landscape is a reflection of a world quite different from the high-tech urbanism which causes so many problems. There are many writers and artists who have sensed the essence of the organic qualities of the setting of traditional buildings, even when they have not recognised that actual practices existed to achieve this harmony. Although they appear to have no spiritual background, te best modelmakers, keen students of subtle character of places, also recognise this organic, harmonious relationship of building to country. In 1950, the pioneer modelmaker John Ahern wrote that he had recognised a deep relationship between a countryside and its buildings, which he found rather difficult to define. He noted that buildings repose in the landscape, and that buildings and their settings are part of each other. Looking at model cottages and villages, it is possible to recognise this intuitively, whether or not the spirit of the place, or the type of place, is captured in the model.

At the full size level, harmoniousness or lack of harmony is recognisable easily, even when detailed analysis has not yet been carried out. If a person to live in a place which he or she recognises as unharmonious, it must have an effect upon the them, even if that effect is only manifest on the psychological level. Even at this basic level, where disharmony has psychological effects, we must consider the possibility of psychosomatic illnesses, the effects of a place upon behaviour and its implications in interpersonal relationships. Constant stress through disharmony, however caused, must lead to a breakdown sooner or later. When multiplied a millionfold in an inappropriate urban environment that exists with no regard for harmony, then it is a recipe for many of the urban ills we know so well. Conversely, to create an appropriately harmonious environment, harmonising and integrating the many influences present, is the first step in reclaiming the harmony of the individual and society.

Although Earth Harmony is concerned with the world as it is now, and what we can do in our dealings with it, we cannot ignore the past. Everything which has taken place in the past, every thought, every action, every accident, has gone to make up that state which is the present. It has been one of the more unfortunate traits of modern thought to imagine that the past can be erased or ignored, and that it has nothing to teach us. Hopefully, that phase of development is now over, and we can analyse past methods with the intention of gaining knowledge and wisdom which will be of use today and in the future. It is this basic knowledge which is at the root of traditional systems of geomancy, such as the Etruscan Discipline, the arts of the medieval Locator Civitatis, the practices of East Anglian cunning men or the dowsing techniques of German architects. Whilst we need not copy the outward forms of these traditions, they contain many valid principles which have much to teach us. Often, the outward form of things are copied whilst the essence is not understood. In the past, this copying has been used sometimes to create inappropriate but fashionable ornaments devoid of function. By working with the essence of any ancient system, we can apply it to the present-day world, even though the outward forms may be totally modern.

In its widest sense, Earth Harmony includes many elements, some of which may appear esoteric, and others which would be considered just "common sense". However, the very concept of common sense has been attacked by those intellectuals who go under the collective term of 'post-moderns'. However, reality has a way of reasserting itself eventually upon even those who attempt to deny it by means of intellectual acrobatics. It is all too obvious from many sources that the concept of common sense has been abandoned by many architects and planners, who have chosen to build according to an ever-changing series of untried theories or as fashionable artistic experiments. The disastrous use of tower blocks for housing, now recognised as dehumanising, came about as a result of the distancing of architects from real human needs, and the abandonment of appropriate traditional principles in the furtherance of socio-political theories. Added to this remnant of one disproved ideology are the 'deconstructionist' and 'anarcho-capitalist' theories that society should not or does not exist, and that only market forces should be followed when doing anything.

Although the vast majority of structures are still made according to such bankrupt ideas, today the activities of bio-logical architects take into account many aspects of house design, materials and environmental siting which have parallels in the customary designs of pre-industrial cultures. Commonsense practices such as using materials which cannot harm the environment or people are recognised widely as important to the well-being of those who have to live in the houses. But still, the application of sound principles is far from universal. Also, because, in the vast majority of cases, it has not been taken into account for more than a century, millions of buildings exist in which it is not possible to live a healthy life. Such dwellings, which pass the conventional tests for fitness for human habitation, have a built in 'illness factor', caused by the siting, materials and designs by which they were constructed. Many people's illnesses may actually be 'house sickness', sub-clinical disabilities caused directly or indirectly by their home environment. Habitation which does not take into account such factors as magnetic, electrostatic and electric fields, radon gas buildup, etc. is at best accidentally correct. The likelihood is, however, that it will be negative in this respect, and disharmonious, leading to unease and disease in the inhabitants.

Ironically, early in the nineteenth century, the Romantic poets recognised the dangers of the then-rampant industrialisation of the world. If their observations had been taken seriously by the politicians, capitalists and engineers of the time, then our present society's dissociation from Nature need not have taken place. The recognition of the Anima Loci in the works and actions of Percy Bysshe Shelley and William Wordsworth was in the mainstream of geomantic recognition, and in 1818, Samuel Taylor Coleridge made a very significant observation when he drew the distinction between mechanic and organic form. Form is mechanic when on any given material we impress a predetermined form, one that does not arise necessarily out of the natural properties of the material: on the other hand, organic form is innate, it develops from within so that the fullness of its development is one and the same with the perfection of its outward form. On the spiritual level, this is analogous with the relationships of önd with the Anima Loci. Sanctification is organic, whilst on-lay is mechanic. Earth Harmony is concerned with the world as it is now, and what we can do in our dealings with it. By analysis of various traditional methods of Earth Harmony and modern techniques,I have arrived at a methodical means of achieving the balance we seek. These are the significant factors affecting the harmonious location of a house, and the appropriateness of its design.

They are:

1. The surrounding atmosphere of the structure, that is the disposition of everything in the immediate locality: hills, prevailing winds, watercourses, other buildings, roads etc.
2. The quality of the soil upon which the building stands.
3. The shape and topography of the site: hills, slope etc.
4. The orientation of the building.
5. The ground plan.
6. The measurements used, the units, geometric forms and how they relate to the site and to the Divine Harmony.
7. The size of the various components of the structure and the relative proportions between them.
8. The position of doors and windows, and their dimensions.
9. The sanitary and drainage arrangements.
10. The material used in the construction.
11. The decorative and symbolic parts.
12. Psychological, ceremonial and ritual elements (electional astrology, founding, naming, etc).

These twelve factors bring into focus all of the characteristics of site and building which must be considered in the harmonisation of that building with the environment. Whilst it is only in exceptional cases that all of the factors can be totally harmonised with one another, the guiding principle is always to bring the elements to the nearest approximation of balance as is possible. To enable us to apply these principles, it is necessary to place our actions into various categories, which are as follows:

1. Primary Harmonisation, which is the location of an optimal site in an untouched natural area, the best possible site with no constraints, the ideal site for the required function, when the structure can symbolise the function in every way.

2. Secondary Harmonisation, which is the location of a reasonable, though imperfect, site, then modifying it to screen out potential harmful influences, and then designing the structure to enhance the beneficial aspects.

3. Tertiary Harmonisation, which is the location of an existing structure for the purpose required. This structure must be as close as possible to the requirement, but requires modification to being it into harmony with the purpose and its surroundings.

4. Remedial Harmonisation, which is looking at what you have already, then undertaking remedial actions to screen out the harmful influences and encourage the beneficial.

Primary harmonisation is rarely possible in the modern world, where almost every piece of land already belongs to a person or organisation. To discover a piece of virgin land suitable for the construction of a house, shrine or tomb is beyond the resources and capability of all but the most wealthy of individuals or state agencies.

Secondary harmonisation is more feasible, though again it is only for those with considerable financial power. It is applicable, however, to state, municipal, community, church and society buildings, and should be a fundamental consideration in such cases.

Tertiary harmonisation is more complex than the foregoing, as it involves considerably more work. It achieves the optimum condition among the multiple possibilities which may present themselves, involving the sometimes lengthy process of finding an appropriate place, and then undertaking the alterations and modifications necessary to harmonise the factors in that location.

Remedial harmonisation is inevitably the most complex, but is also the means accessible to most people to harmonise their lives with the environment. Most people have little choice over where they live and work, so remedial harmonisation is perhaps the most important branch of Earth Harmony applicable to modern society. It is limited in that the larger factors affecting a site, whether it is beneficial or harmful, are unalterable.Harmful factors, such as geopathic zones must be interrupted or deflected by the appropriate means at the disposal of the harmoniser, and other action, such as the appropriate location of furniture, undertaken.

Rules-of-Thumb

As in any craft, earth harmony possesses a number of rules-of-thumb which can be applied to the location, orientation, form and internal layout of dwellings. These rules have been used, generally, in traditional buildings throughout the northern hemisphere from China to Europe, and have served their users well. They can be understood as functioning at several levels: the physical, the strategic, the psychological, the symbolic and in harmonisation with the character of the location. Using these rules-of-thumb, we can look at the location of a building and gauge its likely character and how we relate to it. The position of a building in relation to the landscape or other buildings in a town gives that building a particular character which may produce feelings of happiness or, conversely, unease or illness in those living in it. If we examine these factors, it is possible to prescribe some remedy for those which cause unpleasantness.

The traditional practices of location, wherever they originated, are attempts to harmonise with the various conflicting elements affecting human life at any designated place. In this book, I have examined these principles and, more importantly, how they have been put into practice. The rules-of-thumb given below are derived form this study.

Location

For many reasons, hills and high points are important factors in landscape so in any analysis of the character of a site, they must be examined first. The elevated position of ancient manor houses in northern Europe is an example of their use where the local high point was almost invariably chosen for their location. Such a high point must be high in comparison with the local area but, if there are higher points at some distance, there is no problem. The location of castles in Austria on the second highest point in the district is an example of this. Here, it was believed that the highest points have no water supply and that they are also more prone to lightning strikes but, equally, high points are usually reserved for sacred buildings.

Using a high point has the practical effect of avoidance of flooding; it has a strategic value and gives the inhabitants command over the inherent qualities or energies of the site. Various shaped hills are ascribed certain qualities and often the highest point in a locality will have a dedication to a local god or saint, the personification of the character of that place. Just as people in the past at some time experienced that quality and commemorated it by creating a standing stone, temple or church, so that character still acts upon the human psyche today.

Conversely, it has always been considered bad to live in a dwelling at the foot of a slope or set down beneath street level in any way. A house below street level will have a path or steps going down to the front door which creates bad effects for the inhabitants. An 'area' or basement is particularly bad for psychological, health and geolocational reasons. Remedial work may be done by the creation of a linkage to a higher point, such as erecting a pole with a light on top. On a practical level, such a place may be prone to flooding or the accumulation of dead leaves in the autumn. Strategically, a path running uphill from an entrance is less easy to defend than one running downhill from it. A most advantageous access is relatively indirect and the blocking of direct access from the street or front gate is considered advantageous, for both the strategic reason that it is less easy for assailants to rush a door and the esoteric function of excluding harmful forces on a less tangible level. The path approaching the door should not be U-shaped but then, neither, should it be a straight line, for this is the 'secret arrow' effect also produced by straight roads, roof-ridges, hedges or walls aligned on the entrance

The position of a house in a street can produce effects to the benefit or harm of those living there. Traditional earth harmony rules-of-thumb consider a location to be beneficial if there is a gradual rise along the path from the gate to the entrance door, giving a downview of the path. This is aesthetically pleasing and strategically valuable. Halfway down a slope is not a very good position, as *ki or* 'good luck' tends to flow rapidly through the house and out again. A location at a Y junction of a road, the ancient *trifinium* or meeting of three tracks, is a bad site. Such places are accumulators of energies and tend towards paranormal phenomena. Similarly, such things happen in buildings straddling ancient boundaries. Where buildings have been erected at such sites, they have usually been for transient use and occupation, such as chapels or inns or, in modern times, petrol filling stations. Apart from the modern proneness of motor vehicles to crash into a building at a Y junction, such places have traditional associations with recurrent fires and accidents.

If a building is at the side of a street at the head of a T junction, then it is in the classic 'secret arrow' position, an unfortunate place made worse if there is a large building visible at the other end of the street. The flow of energy towards the dwelling, both in terms of airflows, traffic noise, lights at night and more subtle effects, create a disruptive character to the place at the apex of the junction. Remedial work, such as the alteration of door or window positions, or the erection of mirrors, can mitigate the harmful conditions. Likewise, two streets approaching an oblique junction with a third will create bad effects upon a building at the focus of the junction. Also, if a building is located at the end of a cul-de-sac it is unfortunate, owing to inadequate access and stagnant lack of flow of energies. A building in its own land, with roads on all four sides as in a city block, is prone to malevolent forces as is one with roads running at back and front; this will suffer frequent burglaries and failure in all projects.

Internal Layout

The layout of rooms and the furniture in them have significant effects upon the feelings and relationships of the people who use them. The ceremonial layout of interiors is well known and understood. These formal interiors include courtrooms, schoolrooms, audience halls for monarchs and presidents, theatres and even sacred spaces where ceremonial is uppermost. Such places are arranged according to a pattern which reflects the relationship of the participants in the encounters which take place there. So, in a court of law we have the formal high seat of judge or magistrate, the dock, and accommodation for court officials, jury and members of the public. The formal nature of the proceedings, and the relative status of the participants, is reflected in the structure and layout of the courtroom.

This is partly the result of the form of the legal system, partly customary, partly psychological, and partly with regard to the space available when the court was constructed. All these factors combine to produce the courtroom. In societies more traditional than ours, the courtroom, where it existed, was related also to the site which was considered significant in the carrying-out of justice. Such places therefore reflected not only the standards of society and its relationships, but also the character and structure of the world. It is this element which is lacking from most modern places in the West.

Similar conditions could be described for the other types of interior mentioned above, and factors such as the orientation of the lord's hall have been dealt with in chapter 4. In several of the traditional forms of geomancy which have survived intact into modern times, the rules and forms for the layout of interiors are known. From these, it is possible to determine good and bad room shapes, and the most beneficial layout of furniture inside any room.

In dealing with the layout of rooms, we are concerned with a hierarchy of factors. The primary factor is the location of the building that contains the rooms. Next, comes the orientation of that building and, thirdly, the positioning and uses of the various rooms inside. Of course, the most important factors in any room are the openings by which that room communicates with the rest of the world. The position of the windows and doors has a major effect upon the way the room is used, its lighting and ease or difficulty of access. As we all know through experience, the layout of living quarters can produce stress or restfulness, unease or calm, and any methods which can be applied to improve circumstances should not be ignored.

Circulation of people and subtle energies within rooms are of primary importance. We all know how irritating it is to have to walk around furniture or squeeze through difficult door-ways every time we leave or enter a room. We also know how disruptive it can be if a room doubles as access to another room beyond it, and there are incessant comings and goings through the room. The first instance is an example of the disruptive of flow, the latter an example of excessive flow. In terms of *ki* , the first creates stagnation and an imbalance of excess, whilst the latter allows it to flow away, creating an imbalance of deficiency. Of course, as in all life, the middle way of balances between the extremes is the desirable point.

The relationship between rooms determines the relative amounts of use which each will get and the number of times in the day that their occupants will pass through them on the way to somewhere else. There is also the hygienic question as to the location of kitchens, bathrooms and toilets, relating to the local watercourses. In former times, these were wells and streams but, today, we must consider water pipes and sewers which, if we are to believe the dowsers, have subtle effects upon those living over them.

Most house-building traditions place the main rooms, such as the living and dining rooms, bedrooms and kitchens in the main body of a house, not separate or in wings jutting out beyond the front-door line. Such a lack of balance due to incompleteness is recognised all over the world as harmful. On the psychological level, incompleteness, characterised by unbalanced asymmetry, creates anxiety and stress in the occupants or users of a building with predictable results.

Rooms

The shape of a room largely creates any problems which may be encountered and, in Chinese and Japanese geomancy, there are rules for determining these characteristics. Rectangular, square or even circular rooms are considered good, but those with protrusions hide potential problems. Rooms with irregular multi-angles walls can cause unease, though this problem seems absent in regular multi-angles structures such as the octagonal and deagonal chapter houses of some medieval cathedrals.

Rooms proportioned according to classical geometrical ratios are held to be more harmonious than those which are not.

Many modern buildings in which large concrete or steel beams cut through the space at seemingly irrational angles, or in which upper floors overhang the interior space from above, create feelings of disorientation and unease. This ambiguous space, used now as a display of the architect's technological mastery over materials, was avoided in traditional architecture. In East and West, they are considered to produce an unnerving effect on people directly below them. The European builders of wooden structures arranged beams on symbolic patterns and imbued them with character through protective carvings and paint, plasterwork and pargetting. Chinese geomantics block or disguise such beams and projections with mirrors, colours ribbons or flutes arranged at 45^0 angle to reproduce the octagonal *pak kwa* protective pattern

Entrances

The positioning of doors and windows are important in harmonising the house with the environment. Our entire feelings about a house or business premises may be coloured by the first impression we get at the entrance. Throughout the world, the main doorway and its immediate surroundings are ornamented and protected by magical, religious and symbolic emblems and structures. The protection of the door against harmful influences must be so arranged that it does not exclude the beneficial. A brick-up door may exclude burglars, but one's friends cannot enter either. The lore of the threshold and its protection have been detailed in chapter 4, but it is important to remember that this is not a bygone tradition which has no present-day application. The entrance creates the ambience of the entire house, for everyone who lives there or visits it must pass through that entrance. Great formal entrances, where the visitor is confronted with monumental marble halls, are in instance of this. There, the building has been designed to belittle the visitor confronted with the grandeur and power of the aristocrat or institution he or she is visiting. It is possible to arrange an entrance to do this quite deliberately Albert Speer's *Reich Kanzlerei* built for Adolf Hitler in 1938 was consciously designed to dwarf and belittle the visitor, with massive doorways, overlong corridors and slippery floors. If we are forced to go to such places, we must first fortify ourselves psychically. But when we enter a well orientated, light and airy hall or lobby, we are uplifted and have a feeling of well-being.

It is considered beneficial for doors to enter large, expansive areas, opening into the widest side of a room, giving an overall view. Large, but not overlarge, doors allow the entry of beneficial energy. An entrance which confronts one with an immediate change of direction on entering is disruptive. Such doorways are said to give the occupant the continual feeling of being defeated and, not surprisingly, such entrances have been a major feature of defensive architecture in the castles of old and the concrete bunkers of the present day.

In a house, the position of doors has always had significance. This has varied with time and place but there are certain rules which have universal application. In many cultures, it is considered bad to open a front and a back door simultaneously. On a practical level, this causes the wind to rush through the house, blowing everything around, but also it can destroy a carefully built-up psychical atmosphere. In Ireland, it is believed that to open a back and a front door at the same time is to bring death upon the family in a short while or, or least, that good luck will be blown away. In East Anglia, the front door was opened rarely, except for weddings and funerals. In East Anglican villages today, one often enters cottage by the back door, the front door being overgrown by the garden, often lacking a front path at all.

In rooms, doors are often aligned directly opposite one another; an overlap is bad. Doors slightly out of alignment, the so-called 'bad bite' doors, can lead to disruption, unbalancing the energies in the room by an internal parallel to the 'secret arrow' of room-ridges or fences facing an opening in the house. Different-sized doors on the same axis are likewise liable to cause problems, for large doors ought to give access to important places. Doors which overlap when opened are naturally prone to disaster, such as when door handles or knobs collide or, worse, people walk into one another when coming and going. Physical problems with doors that do not open without much pushing, create an imbalance within the users. Slanted doors, like slanted walls, can cause feelings of disorientation and unease, disrupting the harmonious balance of the household. Techniques for balancing-up shapes, such as a tasselled curtain or screen, can mitigate the bad effects of a slant door.

In any house or room, the place furthest from the entrance is the place with the most energies. We have seen this with the great medieval sanctuary of Beverley Minster where the *frith-stool* of sanctuary was placed as far as possible from the profane world. This principle works in houses, also, and the placement of a bed, desk or favourite chair at the point furthest from the door is beneficial. Functionally, it is bad to have furniture near the entrance of a room as it causes problems with movement. To have one's back to the door when sitting or working is to risk incessant surprise and disruption by people entering unheralded. The ideal place is one where people entering can be seen and the inhabitant's composure is not disrupted by surprise. In turbulent times and places, one's life might depend upon such a viewpoint.

Kitchens

Similar considerations apply with kitchens and other work areas where it is risky to face away from the door. Chinese geomancy places great importance on the position of the cooker in kitchens. If the person who does the cooking habitually faces away from the door, domestic harmony, prosperity and even health may suffer. Cramped conditions or angular objects obstructing easy and relaxed access in the kitchen create disharmony on the physical, aesthetic and psychological planes. If the cooking is done unharmoniously, then the entire household suffers in various ways.

If it is impossible to arrange things so that a chair, desk or work-station is facing the door, then remedial harmonisation is necessary. This may involve the use of a mirror so that the person working or relaxing is not surprised by someone entering, or feels continuous unease that someone might enter at any time. In kitchens, bells or wind chimes can be used near the door so that it is sounded when someone enters.

Beds

One of the places where we spend a lot of our time is in bed. It is said that people spend about one third of their lives sleeping, so the location of the bed cannot be dismissed as having no effect on one's life. In a bedroom, there are three main considerations which, in a house built on harmonisation principles, are reconciled by the geolocation and design of the building. They are the geolocation of the bed itself in terms of its placement over geological features, potential geopathic zones, etc, its orientation and the position of the bed in the room.

The first factor is most important. Many studies conducted over the last sixty years in Germany have shown that many illnesses can be at least partially attributed to the place where that patient slept. The general term

251

'cancer beds' has been given to badly located beds, but this disease is only one of a whole range of diseases and syndromes suffered by people sleeping over active areas. The orientation of beds is a subject which seems to arouse much interest and no less controversy. Bodily orientation in life and death is of great importance, even if we do not recognise that today. In religious usage, orientation varies with religion. The northern European Pagans prayed towards the north, Jews towards Jerusalem, Christians once worshipped eastwards, and Muslims prostrate themselves towards Mecca which sometimes involves intricate calculations to discover its precise direction.

Before the last century, Christian burials were always orientated east-west so that, at the Last Judgement, the resurrected would rise to behold Christ in the East. In some places, this orientation of the dead led to the belief that to sleep this way was bad luck, even courting death. This was not always the case, however. Despite the almost total lack of documentation in most instances, it is recorded that Charles Dickens slept facing east so that he would receive the most positive cosmic flow. Mahatma Kuthumi, Madame Blavatsky's mentor, however, slept north-south.

Bed position and orientation in certain types of traditional building are integral, for such houses are orientated. In Madagascar, the traditional house has a certain form, to which various qualities are attributed by *Vintana*, the traditional system of religious astrological geomancy. Each part of the house is associated with a day of the week. If someone is taken ill, then it is thought that, should that person sleep or lie in the place corresponding with the day of the week on that day, then death will ensue. This is an extreme case of orientation and placement which is in keeping with the rigid interpretation of astrology and divination formerly widespread in Madagascar.

Although the Madagascar example is an extreme, there are several ways of looking at the problem of looking at the problem of bed orientation. Many people seem to believe that there is just one 'correct' orientation which, if they use it, will provide perfect sleep and a harmonious life. A short consideration of the principles of earth harmony will show that it is likely that, in all the myriad possible locations, a single orientation will be the most beneficial. Just as with the orientation of a house there are may other factors which must be considered, so with the orientation of a bed. As each direction possesses a certain quality, so the orientation of a bed to that quarter will tune to harmonise with that quality. If this quality to us, we will suffer some unease or even illness which stems from this quality. Chinese geomancy tells us that a bed facing south brings fame; southwest, a happy marriage; west, fame for one's descendants; northwest, travel; north, good business; northeast, learning; east, domestic harmony; and southeast, wealth. Here, it is apparent that there are no bad directions for a bed.

The other factor is the location of the bed with relation to the room. As with other rooms, it is desirable that a bed should be placed so that it is on the opposite side of a room from the door. If this is not possible, then the remedy is a mirror placed so that the person in bed can see the door and anyone coming through it. Chinese geomancy discourages sleeping with one's feet towards the door because this is the way that corpses are laid out in the morgue. Because we are at our most vulnerable when asleep, there are other sleeping traditions derived from military necessity and the martial arts of east and west.

There are various methods, traditional and modern, of neutralising areas which have a bad influence upon people. Dowsers in various countries have different names and explanations for these places - *geopathic zones*, black streams, 'ley lines', noxious earth rays, etc. - and practising geomants refer to them in other terms, yet the methods used to prevent or neutralise them are similar. 'Cancer beds' can be moved to another location in the room or another room where the character of the place is not harmful to health. Sprung up-holstery is said to channel, magnify or modify the effects of geopathic zones, and removal of such a mattress is recommended sometimes. There is the possibility of using a blanketing layer of insulating material beneath the bed, if it is impossible to move it, and various electronic devices are also on the market to neutralise the energies of such a place.

Other techniques of neutralisation of geopathic zones have been developed. These involve hammering copper or other metal stakes into the ground, iron rods, even nails. These items, known as *interrupters*, are thrust into the ground at places where 'black streams' run or geopathic zones begin. Their effect is to alter the character of the site by means which are still under investigation. There are many different artifacts in use; some people use stakes of specified wood topped off with a twist of copper wire; others use quartz or other natural mineral crystals, or ritually consecrated objects from the religious tradition to which the practitioner belongs. The traditional

West African Ashanti stake is paralleled in ancient Europe by the bronze-wire caducens, such as those found as offerings, in the holy spring at Finthen in Germany, dating from the first century AD. A flagpole, standard, and even a fence post have the effect of altering the character of a site and the building standing upon it. It follows that, if such items are erected without regard to their effects, then they are equally likely to generate harmful effects as good ones.

At the present time, most people do not recognise that they can live more harmoniously, and more healthily, by taking note of where they live and how their houses or flats are arranged. Although earth harmony involves complex factors, even the observance of the simplest rules will bring us nearer to harmony than if we ignore them.

Postscript

Without being present, we perceive the world as a second-hand experience - spectacle. Our personal and collective fictions and fantasies are projected onto outer reality and we experience only a representation of Nature. When we are present, the externality of spectacle is rendered impossible. At the present time, the continuing loss of ancient holy places through on-lay, and alfreka in all its forms is widespread. But this has always happened, and it is only the scale and speed of destruction which has changed. Contemporary times call for contemporary responses - being present, aware to the essential nature of sanctity, what is meaningful, and what is futile. This involves letting-go of the attachment to ancient places which in any case are likely to be alfreka. The continuity which these places once represented is broken. It was broken when traditional society was disrupted by industrialisation, world wars and the development of mass culture. The common land was 'enclosed', and taken forcibly into private ownership, away from the local people. The sacred places went with the land.

Far from being the solution to this disruption, the setting-up of organisations and raising funds to purchase such places when they are put up for sale is part of the problem. To participate in this system of ownership and management is to compound the problem. Such places, when in ownership of anybody other than mindful and reverent local people, suffer at best an on-lay and at worst are reduced to spectacle. Sanctity can be present only when this local 'ownership' is in the form of sacred guardianship. The Celtic concept of the maer or dewar, the generally hereditary, spiritual guardian, is

254

of a totally different order. It is not ownership in the sense of title deeds to real estate, for that in itself is an on-lay stemming from feudalism. Dewarship is the mindful, sensitive communion with the Anima Loci that enables her to express herself however she will.

Finally, Earth Harmony only has practical value if it assists or promotes self-transformation, enlightenment and self-improvement, which in turn will spur the physical action that can bring the landscape into harmonious balance, for example, creating landscapes that are arranged according to appropriate, sustainable husbandry. Such landscapes will not be subject to desertification, or destroyed by flash floods. To bring such a landscape into being is worth more than all the theoretical discussions and arguments in the world, for it promotes life, which is beyond price.

Glossary of Earth Harmony Terms

Aett: Direction or eighth of the horizon in Northern Tradition orientation.

Aegishjalmur: Icelandic symbol of wholeness, and thus irresistability.

Ad Quadratum: Sacred geometry of a building based on squares.

*Ad Triangulum:*Sacred geometry of a building based on equilateral triangles.

Airt: Aett (q.v.).

Alfreka: The condition of having the spirit driven from the land (see Gast).

Anima Loci: The 'place soul' that is the quality of harmony of any location.

Augury: Divinatory system of southern Europe, derived from the Etruscan Discipline (q.v.).

Awen: Bardic sigil for the name of God.

Bellarmine: A brown, salt-glazed witch bottle with a bearded face beneath the spout.

Black Stream: An underground vein or stream of energy/radiation which produces harmful effects in human beings. See Geopathic Zone.

Bressummer: Timber forming the sill of a projecting wall or floor of a timber-framed building, ideally also carved with protective symbols.

Calvary Mountain: Hill modified to be an image of the Stations of the Cross (q.v.).

Centuriation: Ancient Roman practice of laying out the countryside as a grid, incorporating elements of the Etruscan Discipline (q.v.).

Consecration: The charging of an object, person, or place by means of religious or magical ritual.

Dag-Symbol: The runic character for the letter D, used as a protective device on doors and doorframes, mainly in Holland and Germany, but also on English "witch posts" (q.v.).

Dagsmark: Landmark on th horizon over which the sun rises or stands at a division-point of the day when viewed from a certain place such as a doorstone or village centre (also Eyktmark).

Dod: A willow stick, put in the ground as a sight for lining up anything, e.g. a plough furrow or boundary-ditch.

Dragon Post: Corner post of wood-framed buildings, carved with protective images, often dragons.

Druids' Cord: Ceremonial measuring-cord with 12 knots (snotches) dividing it into 13 equal sections.

Eeyen-eerde: Frisian name for Odil (q.v.), signifying ancestral property.

Egg-Stone: A stone marking an omphalos(q.v.).

Electional Astrology: The choice of the most auspicious time to perform a foundation, completion or opening ceremony.

Enhazelled Field: A piece of ground consecrated by hazel staves.

Eolx: Rune of protection, signifying the defensive power of the Elk, otherwise Elhaz.

Etruscan Discipline: The ancient Italian technique of divining holy places in the landscape, using various omens including the compass rose.

Exorcism: The removal of psychic influences from an object, person or place by means of religious or magical ritual.

Eyktmark: Horizon-marker (see Dagsmark, q.v.).

Fachwerk: German word for timber building construction.

Feng-Shui: 'Wind and Water', the contemporary Chinese system of earth harmony.

Fire Festivals: The four cross-quarter-days of the European country calendar, of Pagan origin but celebrated as Candlemas, May Day, Lammas and All Saints' in the Christian tradition.

Foundation-sacrifice: Offering placed in the ground at the commencement of building. Marks the astrological time of birth of the building.

Gar: Rune signifying stability and defence.

Garneting: The use of ironstone in mortar as a protection.

Gast: Barren land, from which the earth spirit has been driven (East Anglian 'nameless art' tradition).

Geis: Sacred prohibition, almost identical with the Polynesian 'taboo'.

Genius Loci: Literally, the Latin for spirit of place describing the subtle qualities of a site, perhaps perceived as a conscious supernatural being.

Geolocation: The placement of a building, etc. in the landscape with regard to the features of that landscape.

Geomancy: The theoretical and practical means of achieving earth harmony. Also a method of divination (see Nigel Pennick's *The Oracle of Geomancy*, Capall Bann, 1995).

Geomantic Act:The fixing of energies in the earth in one place by means of a stake, rod or spike. In mythology, this is symbolised by a hero such as Hercules or St George spiking the dragon to the ground by a sword or lance.

Geopathic Stress: Interference, especially to health, caused by living at a place known to have harmful influences such as underground black streams (q.v.).

Geopathic Zone: An area of harmful influence for humans in which an above-average incidence of non-viral or bacterial disease occurs.

God's Nail: Protective symbol carved traditionally on the pillars beside the King's or Lord's seat.

Gyfu: Rune of consecration, signifying a gift to or from the gods.

Haever: 'Quarter' of the heavens, or compass direction, in the Lancashire geomantic tradition (see Aett).

Hex Symbol: Pennsylvania Dutch protective sign used on farm buildings, derived from German tradition.

Holy City Plan: Square or rectangular plan divided into four quarters by two main streets oriented north-south and east-west.

Hoslur: Sacred enclosure used for judicial combat, literally, 'The Hazelled Field'.

Hytersprite: Benevolent earth spirit in the East Anglian tradition.

Ing sign: .Rune, symbol of the Germanic god Ingve-Frey representing generation and limitless extension, used for protection of doors, window shutters and walls.

Inglenook: Fireplace area in old houses, sacred to and protected by the old god Ingve-Frey.

Interrupter: An object such as a rod or spike used to carry out the Geomantic Act, used specifically to divert or block a Black Stream (q.v.).

Ki: See Ch'i (q.v.).

Ley (Line): Conceptual straight alignment connecting ancient places of power, e.g. churches, holy wells, standing stones, etc.

Locator Civitatis: Title given in medieval Europe to the official who, as a master of the locator's guild, located a site for a new town, laid it out, and recruited citizens to live in it.

Lucky Haever: Auspicious direction in the Lancashire geomantic tradition.

Masking: Blocking or otherwise diminishing 'earth energies' with the use of quartz or other crystals.

Mezuzah: Entrance protection from the Jewish tradition: a symbolically-carved scroll holder containing a Biblical text attached to a door-frame.

No Man's Land: A piece of uncultivated ground at a road junction.
Northern Tradition: The spiritual mystery tradition of Europe north of the Alps, including Celtic, Germanic, Scandinavian and Baltic elements
Nowl: Omphalos (q.v.).
Nwyvre: Ùnd manifesting as 'dragon' energy in the earth at a specific place.

Odal: Rune signifying ownership and dominion.
Odylic Force: Name given by von Reichenbach to the universal energy, Ùnd (q.v.).
Omphalos: Navel of the World, a central point to which the surrounding landscape, city or sacred building is related.
Önd: The 'life breath' or cosmic energy of life and activity, dealt with in earth harmony and the European martial arts.
Orientation: Lining up a person or structure towards the cardinal directions, celestial phenomena or a sacred centre, such as Jerusalem or Stonehenge.

Pak Kwa: Octagonal reflector surrounded by the eight trigrams of the former heaven sequence, of Feng-Shui origin.
Pargeting: Eastern English external plasterwork incorporating protective symbols and designs.

Reflector: A device used to deflect directed energies.
Rig: A straight line on the ground, such as a plough furrow, a line of planted potatoes or a 'ley line'.
Rune: Character from one of the Germanic-Norse families of futharks (alphabets).

Secret Arrow: Harmful energies generated by a road, stream or other straight structure directed towards a door or window.
Shielding: Blocking out energies by means of a wall, earth bank or other substantial construction.
Snor: Druids' Cord (q.v.).
Snotches: knots on the Druids' Cord.
Spirament: önd (q.v.).
Sprite Flail: A magical whip, used in cleansing ares spiritually, made from 9 branches of Bramble (Rubus Fruticosus).

Stations of the Cross: Processional way containing images of the 14 stages of the trial and crucifixion of Jesus Christ.

Tide: One of the 8 divisions of the day.

Tiver: Red ochre used for marking sacred objects. East Anglian traditional word, from Old Norse *taufr*, magic colour.

Transvolution: The process of 'becoming': the underlying mechanism and outcome of 'the way things happen'.

Vastuvidya: The earth harmony tradition of Hindu India.

Vintana: The earth harmony tradition of Madagascar.

Witch Ball: Silvered spherical reflector hung in a window.

Witch Bottle: A magically-prepared bottle, used to ward off harmful influences from a house.

Witch Post: Carved wooden post protecting the hearth area.

Yarthkin: A malevolent earth spirit.

Yattara: Burmese earth harmony.

Bibliography

Alberti, Leon Battista: The Ten Books of Architecture (1452). London, 1986.

Alexander, Christopher: A Pattern Language. New York, 1977.

Alexander, Christopher: The Timeless Way of Building. New York, 1979.

Ayres, James: British Folk-Art. London, 1977.

Bachler, KÛthe: Der gute Platz. Linz, 1984.

Bachler, KÛthe: Earth Radiation. Manchester, 1989.

Baker, Margaret: Folklore and Customs of Rural England. Newton Abbot, 1974.

Banham, Rayner: Well-tempered Environment. London, 1969.

Banti, L: Il mondo degli Etruschi. Rome, 1960.

Bell, A.H. (ed): Practical Dowsing: A Symposium. London, 1965.

Belloc, Alexis: La Télégraphie Historique depuis les temps plus reculés jusqu' á nos jours. Paris, 1888.

Belloc, Hilaire: Stane Street: A Monograph. London, 1904.

Beresford, M.: History on the Ground. London, 1957.

Beresford, M.: New Towns of the Middle Ages. London, 1967.

Bernouilli, Hans: Die Stadt und Ihr Boden. Zürich, 1946.

Bird, Chris: The Divining Hand. London, 1980.

Borst, L.B., and Borst, B.M.: Megalithic Software. Part I, England. Williamsville, 1975.

Bowen, Dewi: Ancient Siluria, its stones and ceremonial sites. Felinfach, 1992.

Bradford, J. Ancient Landscapes. London, 1957.

Brennan, Martin: The Boyne Valley Vision, Portlaoise, 1980.

Broadwood, Lucy E., and Maitland, J.A. Fuller (coll. and ed.): English County Songs. London, 1893.

Brown, R.B. (ed): Rituals and Ceremonies in Popular Culture. Bowling Green, 1980.

Caldwell, J.L.: Notes on the Ceremonial Procedure for Formally Laying a Foundation Stone. RIBA Jorurnal, London, October 1961.

Cameron, Verne L: Aquavideo: Locating Underground Water. Elsinore, California, 1970.

Christensen, Karen; Home Ecology. London, 1989.

d'Apremont, Arnaud: Yggdrasill, l'axe de vie des anciens Nordiques. Combronde, 1995.

Davies, Dewi: Welsh Place-Names and Their Meanings. Aberystwyth, n.d.

de Coulange, F.: The Origin of Property in Land. London, 1891.

de Santillana, G., and von Dechend, H: Hamlet's Mill. Boston, 1969.

Denyer, Susan: Traditional Buildings and Life in the Lake District. London, 1991.

Devereux, Paul: Symbolic Landscapes. Glastonbury, 1992.

Devereux, Paul, and Thomson, Ian: The Ley Hunter's Companion. London, 1979.

de Voto, B.: The Course of Empire. Boston,1952.

Dilke, O.A.W.: The Roman Land Surveyors. London, 1971.

Eliade, Mircea: The Sacred and the Profane. New York, 1959.

Evans, E. Estyn: Irish Folk Ways. London, 1957.

Evans, George Ewart: The Pattern Under the Plough. London, 1971.

Evans-Wentz, W.Y.: The Fairy Faith in Celtic Countries. Oxford, 1911.

Fea, Allan. Nooks and Corners of Old England. London, 1911.

Fidler, J. Havelock: Ley Lines: Their Nature and Properties, Wellingborough,1983.

Fidler, J. Havelock: Earth Energy. A Dowser's investigation of Ley Lines. Wellingborough, 1988.

Fitch, James Marston: American Building - The Environmental Forces that Shape It. New York, 1972.

Flüeler, Marianne and Flüeler, Niklaus (eds): Stadtluft, Hirsebrei und BettelmÖnch. Zırich, 1992.
Gamble, Rev. John: Essay on Different Modes of Communication by Signals. London, 1797.
Graves, Tom: Dowsing. Techniques and Applications. London, 1976.
Graves, Tom: Needles of Stone, London, 1978.
Graves, Tom: Needles of Stone Revisited. Glastonbury, 1986.
Grinsell, Leslie: Folklore of Prehistoric Sites in Britain. Newton Abbot, 1976.
Groves, Derham: Feng-Shui and Western Building Ceremonies. Singapore, 1991.
Hadingham, Evan: Circles and Standing Stones. London, 1975.
Haigh, Diane: Baillie Scott. The Artistic House. London, 1995.
Hammill, John: The Craft. A History of English Freemasonry. London, 1986.
Hancox, Joy: The Byrom Collection. London, 1992.
Harbison, R.: Eccentric Spaces. London, 1989.
Harper, Charles: The Old Portsmouth Road. London, 1895.
Harte, Jeremy: Cuckoo Pounds and Singing Barrows. Dorchester, 1986.
Heimberg, Ursula: Römische Landvermessung. Aalen, 1977.
Heinsch, Josef: Principles of Prehistoric Sacred Geography. London, 1975.
Hersey, J.: The Lost Meaning of Classical Architecture. Cambridge, Massachusetts, 1988.
Heselton, Philip: The Elements of Earth Mysteries. Shaftesbury, 1991.
Hoskins, W.G.: The Making of the English Landscape. London, 1955.
Hutton, Ronald: The Pagan Religions of the Ancient British Isles. Oxford, 1991.
Huxley, F.: The Way of the Sacred. London, 1974.
Jacobs, Herbert, and Jacobs, Katherine: Building with Frank Lloyd Wright. San Francisco, 1978.
Jencks, Charles: Symbolic Architecture. New York, 1985.
Johnson, Hildegard Binder: Order Upon the Land. London, 1976.
Jones, Bernard E.: Freemasons' Guide and Compendium. London, 1950.
Jones, David: Epoch and Artist. London, 1959.
Jones, Prudence: Eight and Nine: Sacred Numbers of Sun and Moon in the Pagan North. Bar Hill, 1982.
Jones, Prudence: Sundial and Compass Rose: Eight-fold Time Division in Northern Europe. Bar Hill, 1982.
Jones, Prudence: Northern Myths of the Constellations. Cambridge, 1991.
Jones, Prudence, and Pennick, Nigel: A History of Pagan Europe. London, 1995.
Jones, Francis: The Holy Wells of Wales. Cardiff, 1954.
Kruft, Hanno-Walter: A History of Architectural Theory from Vitruvius to the Present. London, 1994.
Lawlor, Robert: Sacred Geometry: Philosophy and Practice, London, 1982.
Le Corbusier: The Modulor: A Harmonious Measure to the Human Scale Universally Applicable to Architecture and Mechanics. London, 1954.
Lethaby, W.R.: Architecture, Mysticism and Myth. London, 1892.
Lethbridge, T.C.: Ghost and Ghoul. London, 1961.
Lethbridge, T.C.: Ghost and Divining Rod. London, 1963.
Lockyer, Sir J. Norman: Stonehenge and Other British Stone Monuments Astronomically Considered. London, 1906.
Lofmark, Carl (ed. Wells, G.A.): A History of the Red Dragon. Llanwrst, 1995.
Maas, Michael, and Berger, Klaus W. (eds.): Planstädte der Neuzeit vom 16. bis zum 18. Jahrhundert. Karlsruhe, 1990.
Maby, J. Cecil, and Franklin, T. Bedford: The Physics of the Divining Rod. London, 1939.
Macalister, R.A.S. (trans. and ed.): Lebor Gabála Erinn. Dublin, 1938-41.

MacKenzie, W.M.: The Scottish Burghs. London, 1949.

MacManus, Dermot: The Middle Kingdom. Gerard's Cross, 1973.

Mann, John Edgar; Hampshire Customs, Curiosities and Country Lore. Southampton, 1994.

Mann, Ludovic MacLellan: Archaic Sculpturings. Glasgow, 1915.

Mann, Ludovic MacLellan: Earliest Glasgow. Glasgow, 1935.

Marples, Morris: White Horses and other Hill Figures. London, 1949.

Mermet, Abbé: Principles and Practice of Radiesthesia. London, 1959.

Michell, John: The Old Stones of Land's End. London, 1974.

Michell, John: The Earth Spirit, London, 1975.

Michell, John: Ancient Metrology. Bristol, 1981.

Michell, John: The Dimensions of Paradise. London, 1988.

Michell, John: At the Centre of the World. London, 1994.

Michell, John, and Wagner, Waltraud: Mass systeme der Tempel. Vechelde, 1984.

Michell, John, and Rhone, Christine: Twelve-Tribe Nations and the Science of Enchanting the Landscape. London, 1992.

Mowl, Tim, and Earnshaw, Brian: John Wood. Architect of Obsession. Bath, 1988.

Miller, W.: Die Heilige Stadt. Roma Quadrata, himmlisches Jerusalem und die Mythe vom Weltnabel. Stuttgart, 1961.

Nash, Judy: Thatchers and Thatching. London, 1991.

Nissen, H.: Das Templum. Berlin, 1869.

Ott, Theo (ed): Mensch, Winschelrute, Krankheit. Umwelt-Strahlungen Wie sie auf uns wirken. St Gallen, 1988.

Owen, Trefor M.: Welsh Folk Customs. Llandysul, 1987.

Pálsson, Einar: The Dome of Heaven. Reykjavík, 1992.

Pálsson, Einar: The Sacred Triangle of Pagan Iceland. Reykjavík, 1993.

Pálsson, H, and Edwards, P. (trans): Landnámabók: The Book of Settlements. Winnipeg, 1980.

Pearson, David: The Natural House Book. Creating a healthy, harmonious and ecologically sound home. London, 1989.

Pennick, Nigel: Geomancy. Cambridge, 1973.

Pennick, Nigel: The Mysteries of King's College Chapel. Cambridge, 1974.

Pennick, Nigel: The Ancient Science of Geomancy, London, 1979.

Pennick, Nigel: Das Kleine Handbuch der angewandten Geomantie. Amrichshausen, 1985.

Pennick, Nigel: Skulls, Cats and Witch Bottles. Bar Hill, 1986.

Pennick, Nigel: Einst War Uns die Erde Heilig. Waldeck-Dehringhausen, 1987.

Pennick, Nigel: Mazes and Labyrinths. London, 1990.

Pennick, Nigel: Celtic Art in the Northern Tradition. Bar Hill, 1992.

Pennick, Nigel; Anima Loci. Bar Hill, 1993.

Pennick, Nigel: Practical Magic in the Northern Tradition. Loughborough, 1994.

Pennick, Nigel: Runic Astrology. Chieveley, 1995.

Pennick, Nigel: The Inner Mysteries of the Goths. Chieveley, 1995.

Pennick, Nigel: Sacred Geometry. Chieveley, 1995.

Pennick, Nigel: The Oracle of Geomancy. Chieveley, 1995.

Pennick, Nigel: Secrets of East Anglian Magic. London, 1995.

Pennick, Nigel: Secret Signs, Symbols and Sigils. Chieveley, 1996.

Pennick, Nigel: Celtic Sacred Landscapes. London, 1996.

Pennick, Nigel, and Devereux, Paul: Lines on the Landscape. London, 1989.

Perry, John: Lord of the Four Quarters. New York, 1966.

Petitpierre, Dom Robert (ed): Exorcism: the report of a commission convened by the Bishop of Exeter. London, 1972.

Phillips, Fr. Andrew: The Hallowing of England. Hockwold-cum-Wilton, 1995.

Porter, Enid: Cambridgeshire Customs and Folklore. London, 1969.
Rackham, Oliver: The History of the Countryside. London, 1986.
Rand, Harry: Hundertwasser. Köln, 1991.
Renfrew, Colin: Before Civilisation. London, 1973.
Reuter, Otto Sigfrid: Germanische Himmelskunde. München, 1934.
Reuter, Otto Sigfrid: Skylore of the North. Bar Hill, 1985.
Roberts, Anthony (ed.): Glastonbury, Ancient Avalon, New Jerusalem, London, 1978.
Roberts, Anthony: Sowers of Thunder: Giants in Myth and History. London, 1978.
Roberts, Anthony: Geomancy: a synthonal re-appraisal. London, 1981.
Roob, Alexander: Alchemie und Mystik. Köln, 1996.
Rossi, A.: The Architecture of the City. Cambridge, Massachusetts, 1982.
Schreiber, Hermann: The History of Roads. London, 1961.
Schwabe, Karl-Hermann, and Rother, Guntram: Angewandten Baubiologie: Beispiele aus der Praxis. Waldeck-Dehringhausen, 1985.
Screeton, Paul: Quicksilver Heritage. London, 1974.
Screeton, Paul: The Lambton Worm and Other Northumbrian Dragon Legends. London, 1978.
Scully, Vincent: The Earth, The Temple and the Gods. Yale, 1962.
Shoard, M.: The Theft of the Countryside. Bath, 1980.
Stirling, William: The Canon: An Exposition of the Pagan Mystery perpetuated in the Cabala as the Rule of all Arts. London, 1897.
Sumner, George Heywood: The Besom-Maker and Other Folk-Songs. London, 1888.
Sumner, George Heywood: The Book of Gorley. London, 1910.
Sumner, George Heywood: The Ancient Earthworks of Cranborne Chase. London, 1913.
Tabor, Raymond: Traditional Woodland Crafts. London, 1994.
Taylor, C.: Fields in the English Landscape. London, 1975.
Taylor, C.: Roads and Tracks of Britain. London, 1979.
Taylor, C.: The Archaeology of Gardens. Prince's Risborough, 1983.
Thom, Alexander: Megalithic Sites in Britain. Oxford, 1967.
Thompson, Clive (ed): Site and Survey Dowsing. Wellingborough, 1980.
Trinder, W.H.: Dowsing. London, 1939.
Trubshaw, Bob: The Quest for the Omphalos. Loughborough, 1991.
Tusser, Thomas: Five Hundred Points of Good Husbandrie (1573). London, 1878.
Underwood, Guy: The Pattern of the Past. London, 1969.
Vitruvius: The Ten Books on Architecture. New York, 1960.
von Vacano, O.W.: Die Etrusker: Werden und geistige Welt. Stuttgart, 1955.
von Zaborsky, Oskar: Urväter-Erbe in deutscher Volkskunst. Berlin, 1936.
Wacher, John: The Towns of Roman Britain. London, 1974.
Watkins, Alfred: Early British Trackways, Moats, Mounds, Camps and Sites. Hereford and London, 1922.
Watkins, Alfred: The Old Straight Track. London, 1925.
Watkins, Alfred: The Ley Hunter's Manual. London, 1927.
Watkins, Alfred: Archaic Tracks Round Cambridge. London, 1932.
Williams, Mary (ed): Britain, A Study in Patterns. London, 1971.
Wilson, Geoffrey: The Old Telegraphs. London and Chichester, 1976.
Wheatley, Paul: The Pivot of the Four Quarters. Edinburgh, 1971.
Wood-Martin, W.G.: Traces of the Elder Faiths of Ireland. London, 1902.
Wright, Frank Lloyd: The Living City. New York, 1958.
Zerbst, Rainer. Antoni Gaudí. Köln, 1993.

Index

FREE DETAILED CATALOGUE

A detailed illustrated catalogue is available on request, SAE or International Postal Coupon appreciated. Titles are available direct from Capall Bann, post free in the UK (cheque or PO with order) or from good bookshops and specialist outlets. Titles currently available include:

Animals, Mind Body Spirit & Folklore

Angels and Goddesses - Celtic Christianity & Paganism by Michael Howard
Arthur - The Legend Unveiled by C Johnson & E Lung
Auguries and Omens - The Magical Lore of Birds by Yvonne Aburrow
Book of the Veil The by Peter Paddon
Caer Sidhe - Celtic Astrology and Astronomy by Michael Bayley
Call of the Horned Piper by Nigel Jackson
Cats' Company by Ann Walker
Celtic Lore & Druidic Ritual by Rhiannon Ryall
Compleat Vampyre - The Vampyre Shaman: Werewolves & Witchery by Nigel Jackson
Crystal Clear - A Guide to Quartz Crystal by Jennifer Dent
Earth Dance - A Year of Pagan Rituals by Jan Brodie
Earth Harmony - Places of Power, Holiness and Healing by Nigel Pennick
Earth Magic by Margaret McArthur
Enchanted Forest - The Magical Lore of Trees by Yvonne Aburrow
Familiars - Animal Powers of Britain by Anna Franklin
Healing Homes by Jennifer Dent
Herbcraft - Shamanic & Ritual Use of Herbs by Susan Lavender & Anna Franklin
In Search of Herne the Hunter by Eric Fitch
Inner Space Workbook - Developing Counselling & Magical Skills Through the Tarot
Kecks, Keddles & Kesh by Michael Bayley
Living Tarot by Ann Walker
Magical Incenses and Perfumes by Jan Brodie
Magical Lore of Cats by Marion Davies
Magical Lore of Herbs by Marion Davies
Masks of Misrule - The Horned God & His Cult in Europe by Nigel Jackson
Mysteries of the Runes by Michael Howard
Oracle of Geomancy by Nigel Pennick
Patchwork of Magic by Julia Day
Pathworking - A Practical Book of Guided Meditations by Pete Jennings
Pickingill Papers - The Origins of Gardnerian Wicca by Michael Howard
Psychic Animals by Dennis Bardens
Psychic Self Defence - Real Solutions by Jan Brodie
Runic Astrology by Nigel Pennick
Sacred Animals by Gordon MacLellan
Sacred Grove - The Mysteries of the Forest by Yvonne Aburrow
Sacred Geometry by Nigel Pennick
Sacred Lore of Horses The by Marion Davies
Sacred Ring - Pagan Origins British Folk Festivals & Customs by Michael Howard
Seasonal Magic - Diary of a Village Witch by Paddy Slade
Secret Places of the Goddess by Philip Heselton
Talking to the Earth by Gordon Maclellan
Taming the Wolf - Full Moon Meditations by Steve Hounsome
The Goddess Year by Nigel Pennick & Helen Field
West Country Wicca by Rhiannon Ryall
Witches of Oz The by Matthew & Julia Phillips

Capall Bann is owned and run by people actively involved in many of the areas in which we publish. Our list is expanding rapidly so do contact us for details on the latest releases.

Capall Bann Publishing, Freshfields, Chieveley, Berks, RG20 8TF Tel 01635 46455